Master Alan Goldberg

One must wonder what Master Goldberg, Publisher and Promoter of the event is thinking looking out in this vast sea of martial artists. How did it all start? Over Fifty years ago Alan Goldberg would set 55 in a path in Martial Arts that some of us could only dream of. Master Goldberg's early training was in the art of Shotokan Karate. Having the honor of studying with such Famous master's as Manard Miner and George Cofield. He would later on learn the traditional and non-traditional arts of Five Animal Kung Fu   As the

1970's entered; Master Goldberg would meet a young Master that would take him on the path to where he is at today. That young master's was Jason Lau.

Sifu Lau is the disciple of famed Shaw Bros. stable Master Jiu Wan. Sifu Lau and Master Goldberg would form a student and Master bond that has lasted over thirty years. A friendship so close that they even spent five years living in a Shaolin Wing Chun temple with three other disciples (which he now holds the title of #1 Disciple of the Family.) Master Goldberg jokes of those days as saying, "Sifu Lau would wake up at 2:00 in the morning, telling his disciples it was time to train." For Master Goldberg, it was like a dream. or sometimes woke up the next morning wondering was it or wasn't it. "I would have lived there longer with Sifu Lau, but I was due to get married soon and my wife did not agree with my continued plan of living in a temple." Don't know why not?

When Sifu Lau left New York City in the early 80's, Master Goldberg was left with no one to train with. Sifu Lau suggested he train with the late Sifu Moy Yat of the Yip Man family. This would give Master Goldberg the opportunity to study Wing Chun under two different Sifu's. Allowing him the chance to have a well-rounded education in the art. Known for his longevity in the Art, Master Goldberg is a Pioneer of Wing Chun in the United States.

Master Goldberg is now teaching Wing Chun Kung Fu in the heart of Brooklyn to a small but dedicated group of students. The temple has been active for over 25 years and has had opportunity to expand it as a business. "I have had opportunities to expand, but I am really not interested in having a large school because it loses some of the tradition and close family ties that he has built with his students. The tradition continues as three of his oldest disciples teach in different areas across the U.S.A. Other students include actor Joe Piscopo of Saturday Night Live, Heavy-weight world champion Dimitrius "Oak tree" Edwards, who is notoriously known as the man who broke Mike Tyson's ribs in a sparring match, World renown Orthopaedic surgeon Dr. Richard Pearl. People associated with his Kung Fu Family include Phil Morris from the Seinfeld show and Joe Venerie from the Oldies group the Tokens (The Lion sleeps tonight)

Master Goldberg is the holder of Black Belt Magazines "Kung Fu Instructor of the Year 2004 " and Holder of over 70 other hall of fame awards. He holds positions in many boards in major Martial Arts federations. He is a founding member of Martial Arts Grand Master International Council (MAGIC), a founding member of World Black Belt along with, Chuck Norris and Bob Wall and A board member of the International Sports Hall of Fame with Dr Bob Goldman and Arnold Schwarzenegger

Publisher of Action Martial Arts Magazine, the largest free magazine in the U.S. today, and now also publishes Tao of Wing Chun Magazine. he created one of the nation's hottest martial arts fads such as The Action Martial Arts Magazine Collector Cards. Master Goldberg created Law Enforcement Survival System (LESS), which was the only self-defence course taught to the NYC Emergency Service Unit of the Police Department. Starred in Great Karate Inspirations in which he represented the only person performing Kung Fu. He has an instructional video on Wing Chun produced by Yamazato Productions. , appearing in Rising Suns Production Martial Arts Masters , He has also just taken a position as Vice President of Shaolin Brand Products , .

He was also one of the promoters and Vice President of 21st Century Warriors, which showcased some of the legendary martial artists of our time. This event saw the return of Don "The Dragon" Wilson, Royler Gracie, Orlando "The Warrior" Rivera, Dan "The Beast" Severn and others battling it out on Pay-Per View. Having his own Podcast and now in process of a 24/7 full Martial arts channel on Ruko .

Douglas Wong

Teacher, trainer, and author, Grandmaster Douglas Wong is the founder of the modern-day White Lotus system of Kung Fu. Grandmaster Wong has travelled the world to teach his art through seminars, training camps, movies, videos, and print and electronic media.

Master Wong has trained numerous nationally ranked martial artists, and many of his students can be seen in the film and television industry as actors, stuntmen, and fight choreographers. Others have become bodyguards, expert consultants, and advisors in the entertainment business. A few of the celebrities Master Wong has trained:

David and Keith Carradine (Kung Fu)
Jason Scott Lee (Dragon: The Bruce Lee Story)
Kevin Sorbo ("Hercules: The Legendary Journey")
Lucy Lawless ("Xena: Warrior Princess")
Gina Torres ("Cleopatra 2525")
Ryan Gosling ("Young Hercules")
and many more... More information it need do Google search Douglas Wong Kung Fu.

Cynthia Rothrock

Cynthia Rothrock is a martial arts expert and athlete, who went on to become a film actress, starring in a number of highly successful action movies. She first made a name as an action actress in Hong Kong before going on to wow audiences in her home turf. At the time of her popularity, she was well-known as the "Queen of Martial Arts films."

World Champion

Cynthia Rothrock is the World Champion in martial arts Forms and Weapons (1981-1985). Her goal was to be undefeated and retire after five years. With over 100 competitions, she holds the undefeated worldwide record in martial arts Forms competition. In weapons competition, Cynthia is the first and only woman to win number one in North America against the men—at that time, women had to compete with the men. She holds five Black Belts with a rank of 8th dan Grandmaster.

Acting Career

Upon completing her goal of being undefeated in competition, she began her martial arts acting career starring in movies produced and filmed in Hong Kong. Her first movie, *Yes, Madam* alongside Michelle Yeoh, broke box office records making her a massive star in Hong Kong. After three years of living in Hong Kong, finishing seven films, she returned to the United States to continue her acting career. Today she has starred in over 60 movies and is currently working on upcoming projects.

Celebrated Role Model

Cynthia has been a role model for women in martial arts and film. In 1983, she became the first woman to grace the cover of *Karate Illustrated*. Cynthia is a proud inductee into the prestigious *Black Belt Hall of Fame*, along with Bruce Lee and Chuck Norris. In 2016 she was the first martial artist (male or female) to be inducted into the prestigious *International Sports Hall of Fame* by Arnold Schwarzenegger and Dr. Robert Goldman.

HANK GARRETT

HANK GARRETT -- pro-wrestler, comedian, actor, voice over artist, martial artist, author, teacher

Comedian - Opened as comedian for Tony Bennett for several years at Copa Cabana in New York, Sands Hotel in Las Vegas, London Palladium, etc.

- Listed in "Top 10 Comedians" when appearing in Las Vegas

Voice Overs: Did voices for following cartoons series: GI Joe (Dialtone) / Garfield (Fluffy + Fast Eddy), and others....

- Actor - has appeared in countless movies / TV
- Winner of New York Film Critics Award for "Three Days of the Condor" - played Killer Mailman
- Regular on English BBC-TV Weekly Variety Show starring David Frost - "That Was the Week That Was" (Hank was in London working on this show for 18 months)
- Teacher - Improv and Dialectic Gibberish (accents)
    - Listed in "Wrestling Hall of Fame"
    - Listed in "Karate Hall of Fame" - has Black Belt in 6 forms of Martial Arts
    - Competition Power Lifter and Body Builder (broke New York State Power Lifting record)
    - Raises monies for disabled US veterans (was Front-Line entertainment during Vietnam War). Has raised $53,000 + to date.
    - Speaks to Youth at Juvenile Detention Centers around country
    - Speaks at Adult Prisons
    - Author of bio - "From Harlem Hoodlum to Hollywood Heavyweight" (working on making TV series)
    - Martial Arts
    - Wrestling
    - Acting:
- Three Days of the Condor (movie - played Killer Mailman)
- Car 54 Where Are You (TV series - played Officer Nickelson)

Pauline "Lightning Fast" Seremetis

Introducing Ms. Pauline "Lightning Fast" Seremetis. Pauline is 25 years old and is from Massachusetts. She has been training in the martial arts since 2011. Her journey began at the age of 13. Pauline has experience in Taekwondo, and American Kenpo. She holds a first-degree black belt in Taekwondo from Personal Best Karate under Master Christopher Rappold. She also holds a fourth-degree black belt under Master Jeff Dukes Sr and has the Ed Parker/ Frank Trejo lineage as a 3rd generation Kenpo black belt. She currently is training under Master Steve Arsenault at Steve Arsenault's Kenpo Karate In New Bedford, MA. Pauline is an instructor and tournament coach for his students. She is someone who enjoys learning new techniques and skills as the martial arts is an art where you learn something new every day of your life.

In addition, Pauline competes on the NASKA, Krane, WAKO and WKC circuits. She is a 4X American Kenpo forms Gold Medalist, 3X Sparring Grand Champion, NASKA World Champion, 2X Krane Triple Crown Champion, 1X WKC World Champion and 1X Long Beach Internationals Sparring Grand Champion. Pauline was selected to be on Team NMAC International back in March 2022. She is a member of WKC Team USA. Pauline hopes to model for Century Martial Arts. She is an ambassador for Women's Venum. She was featured in the 3rd edition magazine; Deadly Art of Survival in March 2022. Pauline was also featured in the Point Fighter Live magazine in October 2022. Pauline represented Team USA in Killarney, Ireland at the WKC World Championships in October 2022. She will be starring as a Red Ninja in the movie Warrior Island in August 2023 in Philadelphia. Pauline is an ambassador for future generations to follow the Tiki Code. She also has her own Warrior Island merchandise on the store website.

Pauline has trained with world class champions such as Sifu Kathy Long, Benny the Jet Urquidez, Don the Dragon Wilson, Superfoot Bill Wallace, Sifu Samuel Kwok, Ray Mercer, Dana Abbott, Senior Master Huk Planas, Senior Master Eddie Downey, Senior Master Jeff Dukes, Master Donna Cancila Keating, Master Christopher Rappold, and Master Steve Arsenault.

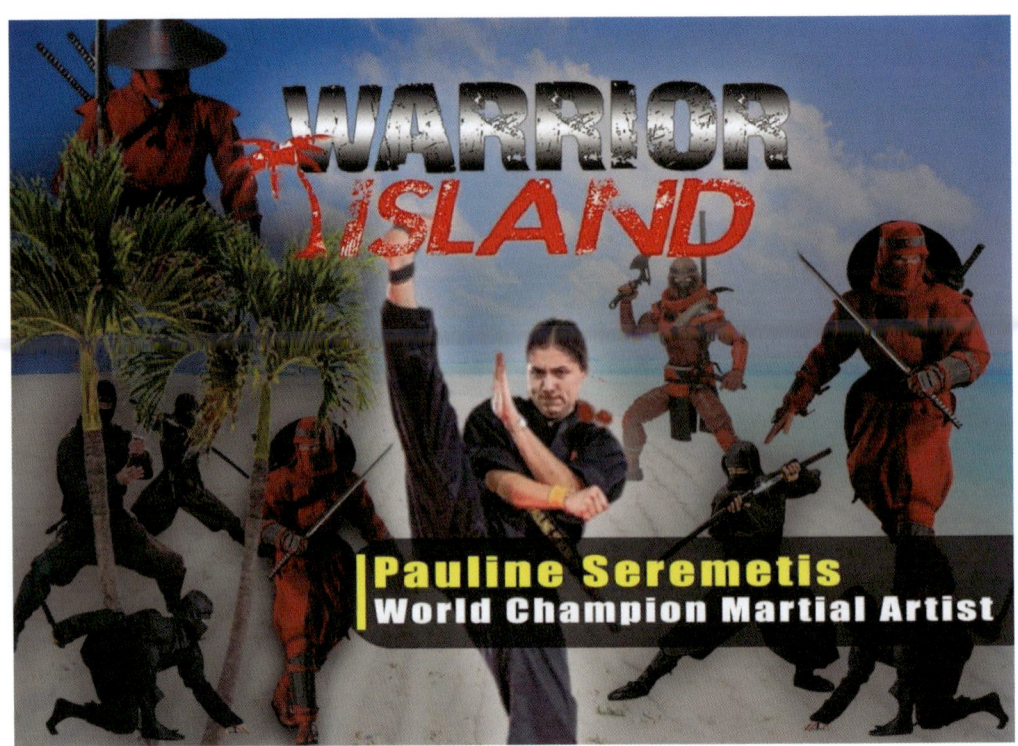

Patrick Strong

Patrick Strong began his study of martial art in 1961 in Seattle, Washington as an original student of the late Bruce Lee. Patrick is Head Instructor of Deep Level Training Systems having trained in a variety of martial arts systems to include Jun Fan/Jeet Kune Do, Hawkins Cheung Wing Chun Gung Fu, Chung Do Kwon Tae Kwon Do, Gracie Jiu Jitsu, Modern Arnis, Balintiwak, Western Boxing,

Kickboxing, and holds the rank of 9th Degree Blackbelt in the Os Hogai Jujitsu System.

Patrick is co-founder and CEO of Deep Level Corp., a California Corporation specializing in accelerated athletic performance and medical therapeutics equipment, as well as methodologies for improving the symptoms of conducting and testing Physiotherapy Interventions for Parkinson's and other neurol-muscular diseases.

He has owned and operated health clubs, designed and developed exercise and physical therapy equipment, and has appeared in Martial Arts magazines, as well as contributing to a number of books, most notably among them "Zen and the Martial Arts," by Joe Hyams.

Eric Lee

Eric Lee was born in Canton, China. His father studied martial arts and Eric would watch him train and this inspired Eric at the early age of three. Eric later began his formal martial arts training under

Chung Ball and ultimately with Grandmaster Al Dacascos. Eric was blessed to study with some of the very best martial artists in the world. These include <u>Grandmaster Al Dacascos</u> – Founder/Grandmaster of Wun Hop Kuen Do
<u>Grandmaster Share K. Lew</u> – Chi Gung
<u>Master Wen Mei Yu</u> – Tai Chi & Chi Gung, Successor of Dr. Hua Huang – Medical Chi Gung
<u>James Lee</u> – Oakland, California
Master Eric Lee trained in both Northern and Southern Shaolin Kungfu. He excelled in the field of martial arts and is credited with winning more national and international awards than any other martial artist in the United States. He has been featured in almost every martial arts magazine in the world. After retiring from competition, Grand Master Lee continues to distinguish himself in the field of martial arts instruction and in the entertainment industry. He also carries on the tradition of his family and his 91-year-old father, by teaching Chinese Health exercises.

Grand Master Lee continues to distinguish himself in the world of martial arts with both his experience and accomplishments. Among his many accomplishments are

Co-Promoter – Coliseum Martial Arts EXPO and World Tournament. 25-time Black Belt & Martial Arts Hall of Fame Honoree. 2-time recipient of the Lifetime Achievement Award.

2 Golden Fist Awards – (Best Weapons Champion, Best Forms Champion) Undisputed "King of Kata" Founding co-member of World Blackbelt, along with notable martial artists such as Chuck Norris and Bob Wall.

Winner of over 100 world titles
Undefeated forms and weapons champion from 1970 to 1974
Recipient of the Armed Forces Appreciation Award
Innovator and Certified Trainer of the flight attendant anti-terrorist training school (America in Defense)
Actor and fight choreographer in over 80 movies and TV productions Las Vegas Legacy Award Winner

Produced a feature motion picture
Taught Movie Action at UCLA

Southern California Motion Picture Council Golden Halo Award Winner
Over 45 years of martial arts experience
Author of many martial arts instructional books and over 40 training videos.

Grandmaster Lee has a wide range of experience, technical expertise, and profound understanding in various martial arts disciplines. Included among those are:

Wun Hop Kuen Do – 7th Degree
Kajukenbo – 9th Degree
Jun Fan Gung Fu – Jeet Kune Do
A.G. Matrix System
Shaolin System
Chi Kung Meditation
Tai Chi
Proficient in over 40 Martial Arts Weapons
Expert in Multiple Martial Arts weapons training
Dao-In
Chin-Na, Grappling, and Judo
Master's Degree in Reiki
Youth and Vitality and other healing arts
Entertainment Industry Background:
Studied with notable acting coaches.
Produced full length feature film Taught Seminars: How to Break into Movies ,Movie Stunt Fighting with Cynthia Rothrock and Art Camacho Studied Film Making and Film Directing Produced 40 videotapes
Writer and Author of 3 books
3 Sectional Staff
The Broadsword
Fight Back – Your Guide to Self-Defense

Travel Host:
Host of the annual Eric Lee China & Hawaii Tour – since 2005

Favorite Training/Hobbies/Interests:

- Acrobatics
- Swimming
- Horseback Riding
- Dancing
- Movies
- Comedy
- Singing
- Hosting Dim Sum lunch parties for friends
- Music of all kinds from rock & roll to country to flamenco
- 1960's – involved in hot rods, attained degree in Automotive Mechanics

Grandmaster Eric Lee is passionate about life and the martial arts. He is always adding to his achievements as he continues to acquire new knowledge and to increase his current knowledge and skill. He goal is to continue to grow as a person, while maintaining a life of balance.

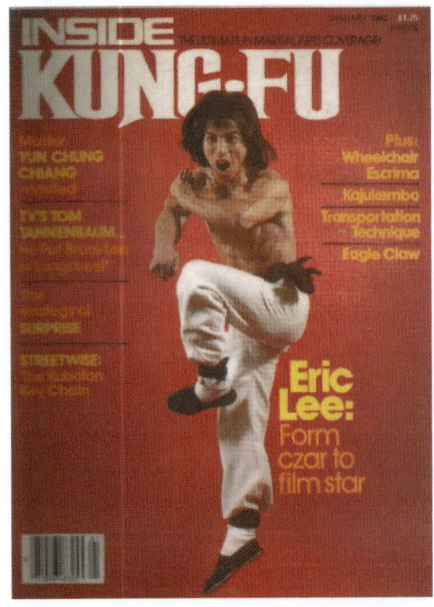

MA TRAINING

01046 JULY 1990
U.S. $2.25
CANADA $3.25

Martial Arts Training

Free Poster Inside!

The 10 WORST Exercises

Strong Wrists/ Strong Fists

Body Shields: Better Than Bags?

Is Your Workout Working?

Save Time! Stretch for Your Kick

Shin Shock: Don't Get Caught

Safer, Faster, More Fun... Trampoline Training!

Q&A WITH JEET KUNE DO EXPERT LARRY HARTSELL

BLACK BELT

World's Leading Magazine of Self-Defense

4 SUBMISSION TECHNIQUES FROM GOKOR CHIVICHYAN

SAVATE FRANCE'S SECRET WEAPON

ISRAEL'S HYBRID SELF-DEFENSE ART

FIGHT LIKE AN ANIMAL!
ERIC LEE'S Kung Fu Strategies

PLUS
- Aikido in America
- Taekwondo Forms Training
- Review of "The Last Samurai"
- Expanded Mixed-Martial Arts Coverage

01043 APRIL 2004
www.blackbeltmag.com
$4.99US $6.99CAN

Ernie Reyes Sr.

Great Grand Master Ernie Reyes Sr. Biography
Great Grand Master Ernie Reyes Sr. of, Ernie Reyes' West Coast World Martial Arts Association, is a 10th degree Great Grand Master Instructor. He was honored as, "One of the Greatest Martial Arts Masters of the 20th Century." Master Reyes has also been inducted into the Black Belt Hall of Fame.

Within his 76 years of life, Master Reyes has received lifetime achievement awards from every national major martial arts association in the United States. He has also been inducted into the ISHF, International Sports Hall of Fame. It's a prestigious award presented to him, by Dr. Bob Goldman, at the Arnold Schwarzenegger Classic to the greatest athletes in the world: Football, Basketball, Olympics, and Martial Arts. The White House had also awarded him with a Lifetime Achievement Award for his dedicated service.

Master Reyes was The National Tae Kwon Do Champion in fighting. In 1977, he represented the USA and was a World-Class winner at the World Championships held in Chicago. He was also rated nationally in forms competition.

Master Ernie Reyes is one of the most versatile martial artists in the world. He is known as the pioneer of creative, marital arts in America. Master Reyes was inducted into the Black Belt Hall of Fame as, Instructor of the year, by producing 9 national champions in one year from one school.

Master Reyes has spearheaded his internationally famous World Martial Arts Action Team for over 45 years. The team is known for performing with a dynamic team of 10 to 50 team members synchronized to powerful and uplifting music. Ernie Reyes' World Action Team is a high-energy performance of drill team precision, acrobatics, unique fight scenes, comical skits, and creative forms, all choreographed to dynamic music and Taiko Drumming. The team is a perfect blending of traditional and modern-day martial arts for your entertainment.

Kick Illustrated Magazine called Master Reyes, "Master of Creative Karate," for his unique martial arts instruction of his students, and creative choreography of martial arts performances.

Budo Martial Arts Magazine in Europe stated that the "Ernie Reyes World Action Demo Team was the #1 martial arts demonstration team in the world." A national karate magazine called the team the Harlem Globe Trotters of karate. The team has been in demand, performed, acted and thrilled audiences of all ages from East Coast to West Coast and has toured worldwide!

The team has been highlighted in every major national karate magazine in America as well as in Europe. The World Action Team has thrilled audiences on ESPN, paid per view cable events, and every major national karate tournament in the USA.

Mainstream publicity from local to national newspapers, San Jose Mercury News, L.A. Times to USA Today, have featured their talents. Local talk shows on network T.V., as well as, CNN News, and People Magazine, have covered their unique and interesting story.

Master Reyes' son, Ernie Reyes Jr., made martial arts history by being the youngest child ever to be rated in the adult's professional forms division at the age of 8 years old.

Ernie Reyes Sr.'s creative martial arts genius led him to Hollywood as a martial arts actor, choreographer, and entertainer. Master Reyes has starred and choreographed for many major films, television projects and movie projects with his son Ernie Reyes Jr.

His son Ernie Reyes Jr. starred in his own television series called Sidekicks, a Motown, Disney, Production, for (ABC Television). Ernie Jr. became a Movie Star. He starred in these films, The Last Dragon, Red Sonja, with Arnold Schwarzenegger, Last Electric Knight, Sidekicks, Ninja Turtles, The Run Down with The Rock, Dwayne Johnson.

Master Reyes also starred in, "Surf Ninjas", with Ernie Reyes Jr. Leslie Nielsen, Rob Schneider, Tone Loc, a New Line Production

WCWMA ASSOCIATION PURPOSE

The goal of Ernie Reyes' West Coast World Martial Arts Association's schools, across the nation, founded by Master Ernie Reyes Sr and Master Tony Thompson, is to create peace, harmony, good health, happiness, and success for massive amounts of people lives. We intend to do it through the way of West Coast World Martial Arts Black Belt and Mastery Success System of Training.

Our Ernie Reyes' West Coast World Martial Arts Association of martial arts schools is to uphold the highest values of traditional martial arts training:

Honour, Loyalty, Family, And Bravery, Built Upon Respect and Discipline!

The founders of the West Coast World Martial Arts Association are Great Grand Master Ernie Reyes and Great Grand Master Tony Thompson.

ERNIE REYES' WEST COAST WORLD ACTION TEAM

SHELDON LETTICH

SHELDON LETTICH is a screenwriter, movie director, producer, and playwright, who written and/or directed a number of classic action films. Prior to his motion picture career he spent nearly four years with the U.S. Marine Corps, serving as a radio operator in Vietnam with 3 rd Battalion, 1 st Marines, and later with the elite 1 st Force Reconnaissance Company at Camp Pendleton, California.

Based partly upon his experiences in Vietnam, he co-authored the renowned Vietnam Veterans play, TRACERS, which was first performed at the Odyssey Theater in Los Angeles. The play then traveled to Joseph Papp's Public Theater in New York City, the Steppenwolf Theater in Chicago (directed by Gary Sinise), and numerous venues worldwide. It received both Drama Desk Awards and L.A. Drama Critics Awards and is still being performed throughout the world.

One of his Vietnam-based screenplays caught the eye of Sylvester Stallone, which resulted in an overall deal with Stallone's White Eagle Productions and led to him co- writing RAMBO III with Stallone. Lettich also wrote the screenplay for the classic martial arts film, BLOODSPORT, which launched the career of Jean-Claude Van Damme. The new action star returned the favor by helping to launch Lettich's directing career with the film, LIONHEART, followed by DOUBLE IMPACT, both of which starred Van Damme. Lettich's next discovery was Mark Dacascos, who debuted in ONLY THE STRONG, a film that introduced the Brazilian martial art of Capoeira to international audiences.

Lettich was also a writer/producer on the historical French Foreign Legion film, LEGIONNAIRE, which starred Van Damme and was shot on location in Morocco. Other foreign countries where he has directed or produced movies include Israel (THE ORDER, THE LAST PATROL), Bulgaria (THE ORDER), Canada & Romania (THE HARD CORPS), Mexico (PERFECT TARGET), and most recently, Russia (BLACK ROSE).

His latest movie is MAX, which he co-wrote with his long-time friend, Boaz Yakin. The film was directed by Boaz and produced by MGM. It was released nationwide in the USA by Warner Brothers in June 2015, and by the end of the summer had grossed $43 million.

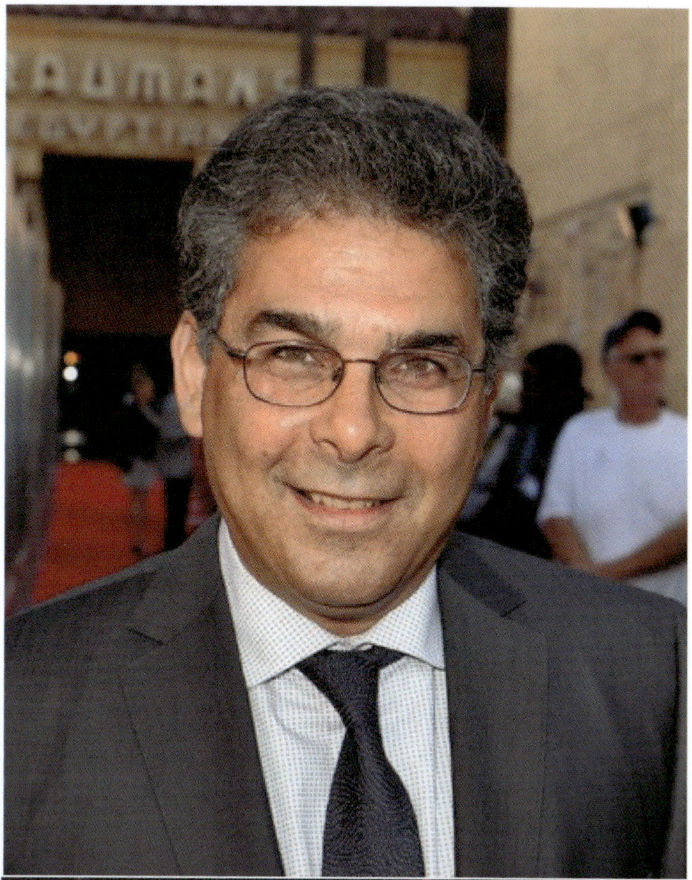

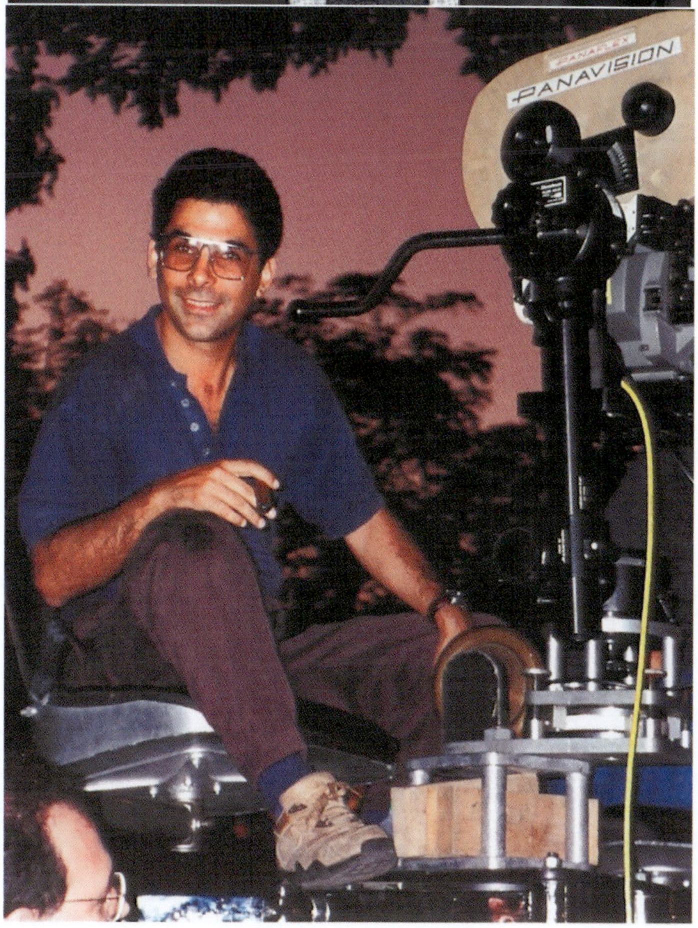
PANAVISION

SHELDON LETTICH
DIRECTOR, LIONHEART

Mario Prado

Mr. Prado is a native of California and calls North Hollywood his home. Unlike most, Mario was born into the film/TV industry, an offspring of artistic production talent. Mario's strength is in lighting and Cinematography. He fits beautifully in the entertainment capital of the World of Hollywood. He was educated at The Art Center College of Design (Lighting) and The Los Angeles Trade Tech (Advertising Graphics) and also studied two years of Architecture at

CSUN. He has also taken numerous extended courses in traditional photography, has given Mr. Prado a broad base of the art of image making.

He is experienced in production logistics and coordinating different departments in stage, TV and feature films. Mario has earned a wealth of experience in problem solving and he is known in the industry as the Go to Guy.

Mario Prado was tapped during the 'Hey-Day' of the Martial Arts Golden Age 70's & 80's. As Photo Editor for Black Belt Magazine – Where he had the pleasure to shoot covers and books of such Stars as Eric Lee, Fumio Demura, Cynthia Rothrock, Stephen Hays, and an impressive list of Grand Masters and a generation of outstanding Marital Artists, teachers and instructors and performers. Add to the list of 30+ international cover magazines for Black Belt Magazine, and series of 12 how to books for the Martial art Industry.

From a host of projects, recently as site manager for a Syfy project Aired - April 2014 Foxy &Company working with Eric Westmore and having worked with People Magazine on special assignment and the pleasure of working with the likes of such notable celebrities as Charlton Heston, Elizabeth Taylor and Funny Man Dorn Deluise. Mr. Prado also played a key role as Lighting Designer for books on celebrities under Robin Leach (Lifestyle of the Rich and Famous series); this grand opportunity has given Mario a solid foundation in the day to day of image making in Hollywood. Mario has covered special events for the G2 Gallery as well as being a key photographer for Celebrities on the Red Carpet at the Oscars.

Mario continued wearing many hats in the production field as a lighting instructor for a Los Angeles base photography school. His mastering from film to digital production has given insight and experience in both these medias. He also has volunteered twice in assisting designing, producing, programming and running a complex lighting system for the Air Force Air Museum in California. Bringing his skills to the Multimedia and Public Affairs office of the 163rd Reconnaissance Wing, setting up programming, a theatrical stage lighting system that was instrumental in the Wings ceremonial process under as a civilian working with Stan Thompson, the creator and director of these Military events. Mario strong design background for printed media kits as well as EPKs (Electronic press kits) and that of film and digital Production including web design for the entertainment industry high end businesses, Mario brings images that speak volumes in all media outlets around the world.

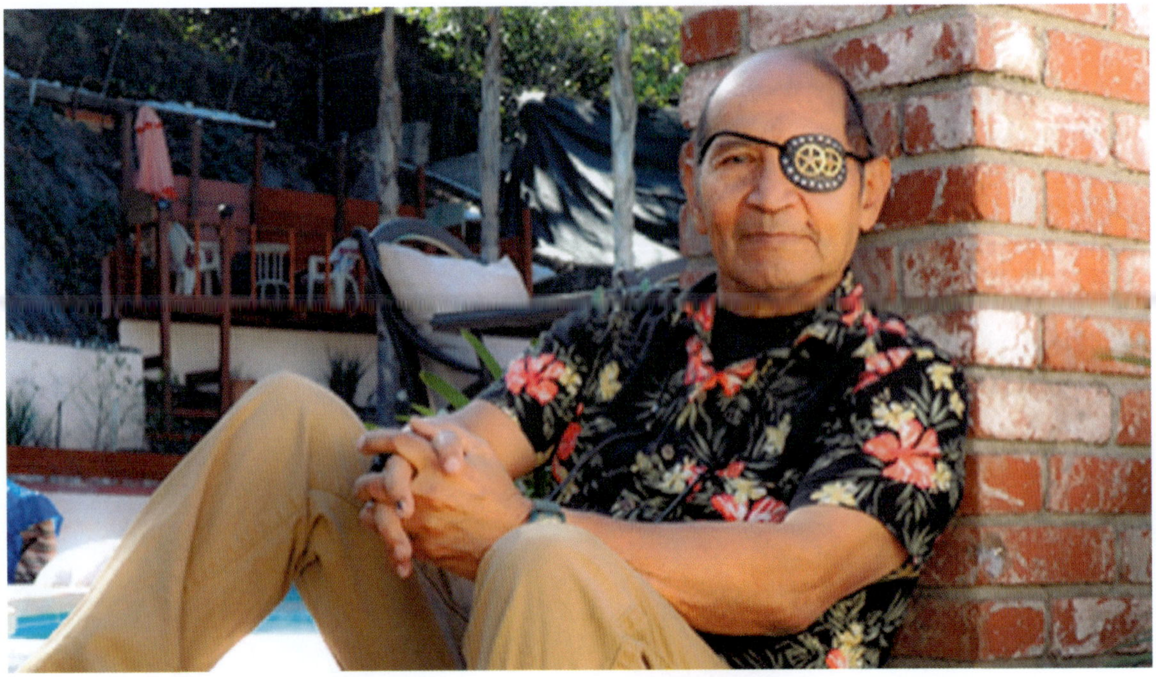

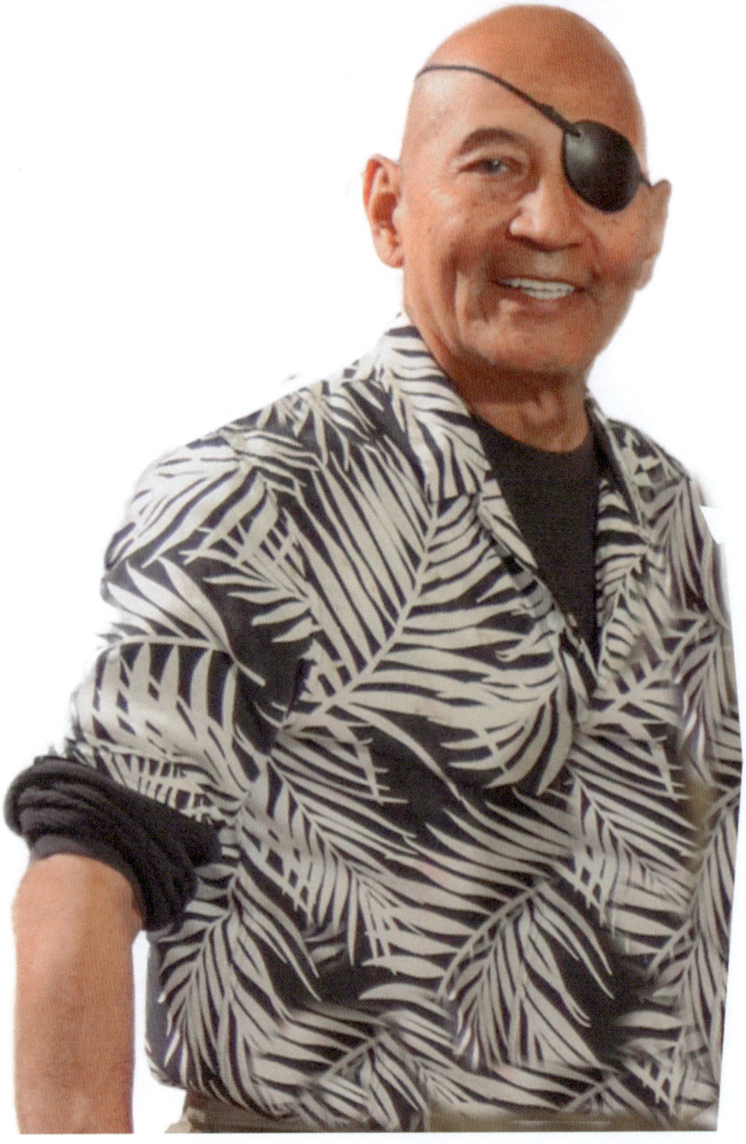

Graciela Casillas

Four-time World Champion Graciela Casillas is a highly acclaimed martial artist and combat sports expert, recognized in 7 National and International Hall of Fames including the International Women's Boxing Hall of Fame and Black Belt Hall of Fame. In 2023, she was named Woman of the Year by California State Senator Monique Limon in District 19. With over 40 years of experience as a student, instructor, and professional competitor, she has gained international recognition as one of the top martial arts and instructor of self-defense in the world.

Casillas made history as the first American woman to simultaneously hold two world titles in both boxing and kickboxing. In addition to her athletic achievements, Casillas pursued her education and received a MA in Education from California Lutheran University and a second MA in Physical Education from Azusa Pacific University. She became a certified Defensive Tactics Trainer and Close Protection Specialist, graduating from Executive Security International and Massad Ayoob Lethal Force Institute.

After retiring from the ring, Casillas turned her attention to teaching martial arts, firearms, tactical training, and writing. She is a WEKAF Stick Fighting World Champion and a GSBA stick fighting world champion, as well as the founder of Shen Chun Do. She retired from Oxnard College as a Professor and Academic Counselor and continues to help provide guidance for undergrads. She was also a columnist for various magazines, including Black Belt Magazine. Casillas authored her first book, The Lioness Within: A Personal Guide to Self-Defense for Women"

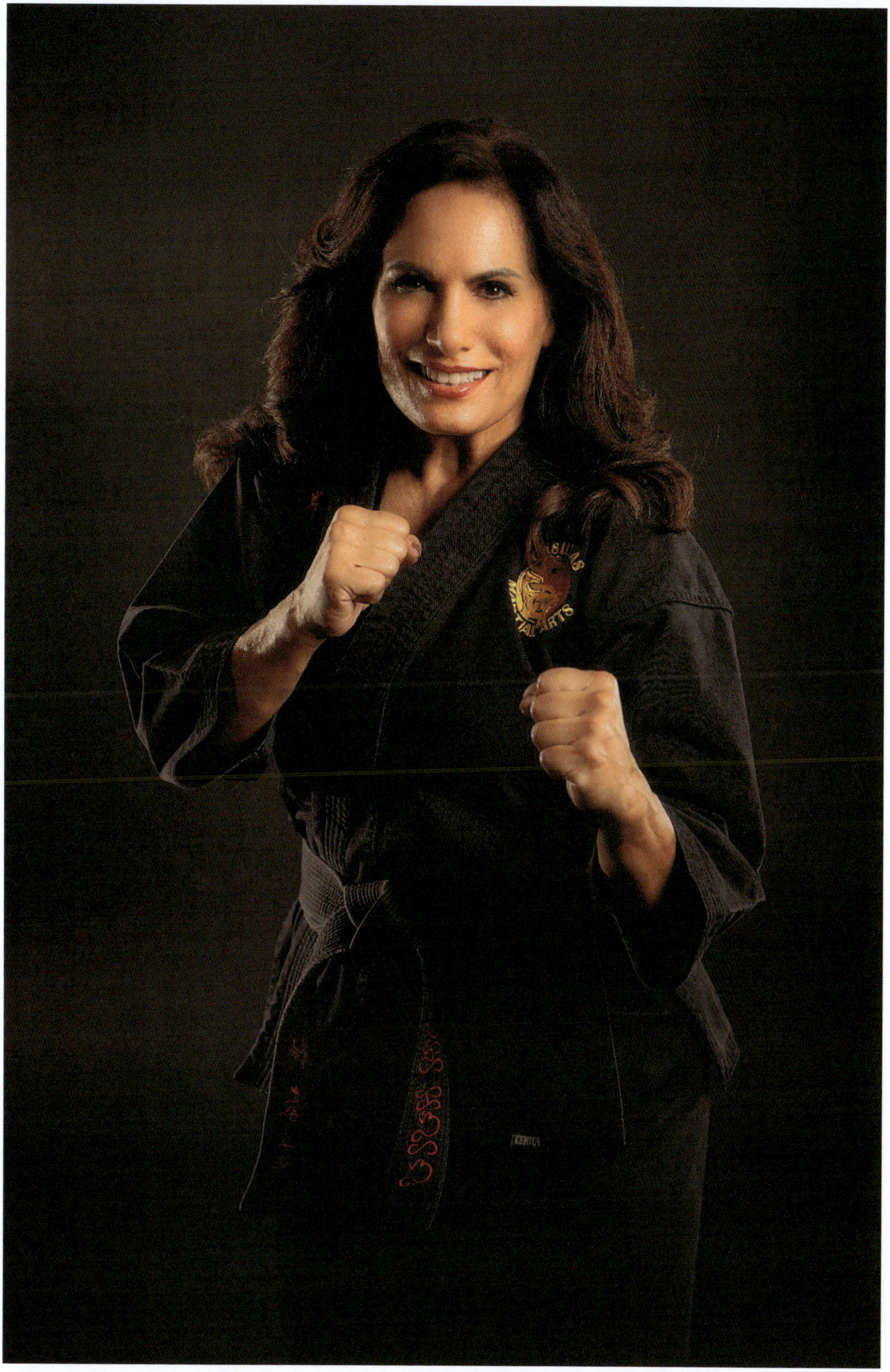

Kathy Long

Kathy long is widely considered to be one of the greatest female fighters of all time. Born on April 21, 1964, in Saint Louis Missouri, Kathy's family moved to California when she was 6 months old.

Long started training in Aikido 1979 . Earning the rank of Shodan, Kathy then branched out and continued her training in Kung Fu San Soo in 1981, eventually earning the rank of 8th Master degree... Always wanting to continue her knowledge she has become proficient in BJJ, Catch wrestling, and Wing Chun, JKD, Kali with Cas

Magda and many other instructors and has taught at the Inosanto Academy for 9 years. Kathy's first kickboxing bout in 1987 happened after accepting a challenge with only 10 days of training to learn how. Kathy was instantly hooked on the sport and began learning everything possible concerning Kickboxing.

Long began her professional kickboxing career in 1989 and quickly established herself as one of the top fighters in the sport. Earning 5 World titles throughout her career in the following organizations; WKA, ISKA, and WMAC and KICK. Long was known for her technical proficiency, speed, and power, as well as her aggressive fighting style.

In addition to kickboxing, Long also competed professionally in MMA, Boxing, and Muay Thai compiling a combined record of 42 wins and only 2 loses. Kathy Long color commentated the First UFC in 1993. Long retired from fighting in 2016 at the age of 52 but has remained involved in the martial arts community as a trainer and coach. Kathy has been traveling and teaching seminars all over the world.

Long is also known for her work as an actress, choreography and as a stuntwoman. The first film Kathy worked on was doubling, choreographing and training Michelle Phiffer in "Batman Returns" she has also appeared in several other films and television shows, including, but not limited to, "Natural Born Killers", "Death Becomes Her" "The Stranger" "Walker, Texas Ranger." "Knights" and others. She has also worked as a stunt coordinator on various productions.

Throughout her career, Long has received numerous awards and honors, and has been on the cover of numerous Martial Arts Magazines including Black Belt Magazine, Inside Kung Fu, Inside Karate to name a few. Long has also been featured in Sports Illustrated magazine and has been inducted into the Black Belt Hall of Fame and numerous others including, Inside Karate and Inside Kung Fu Hall of Fame in 1996 and the World Martial Arts Hall of

Fame and many others. Recently presented with The lifetime achievement award by The Pacific Association of Women Martial Artists, Kathy Long's contributions to the world of martial arts have been significant, and she is widely respected and admired by her peers and fans alike. Her technical proficiency, fighting spirit, and dedication to the sport have inspired countless people to pursue martial arts and to achieve their own goals.

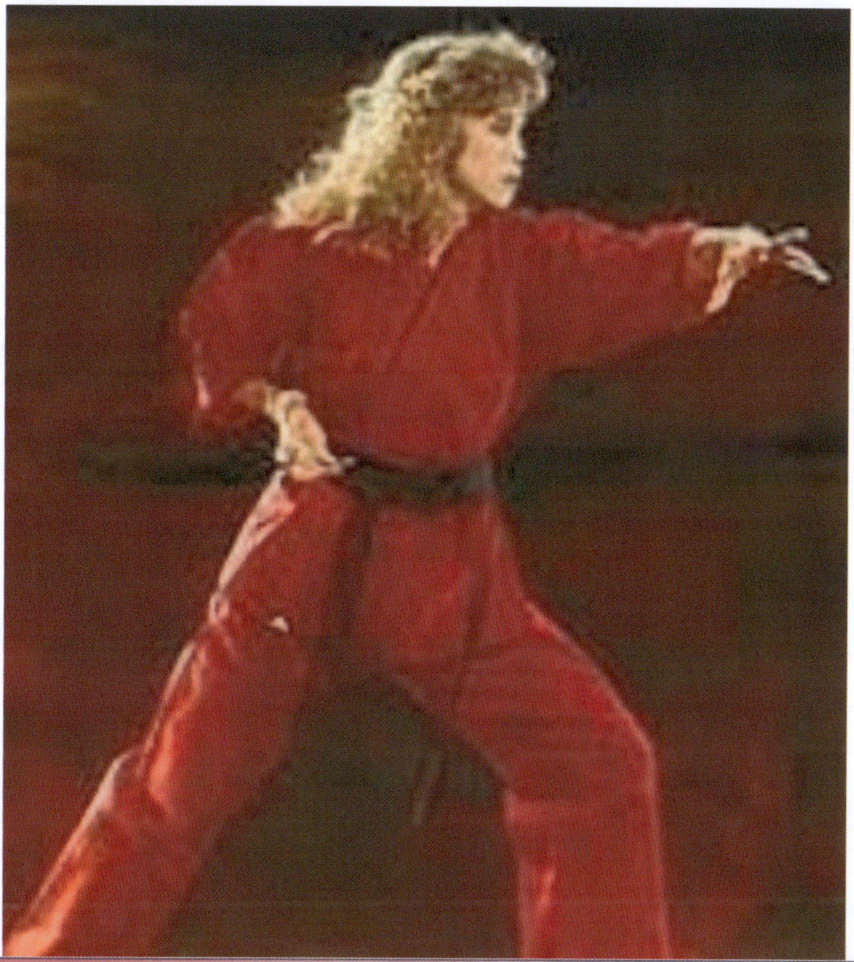

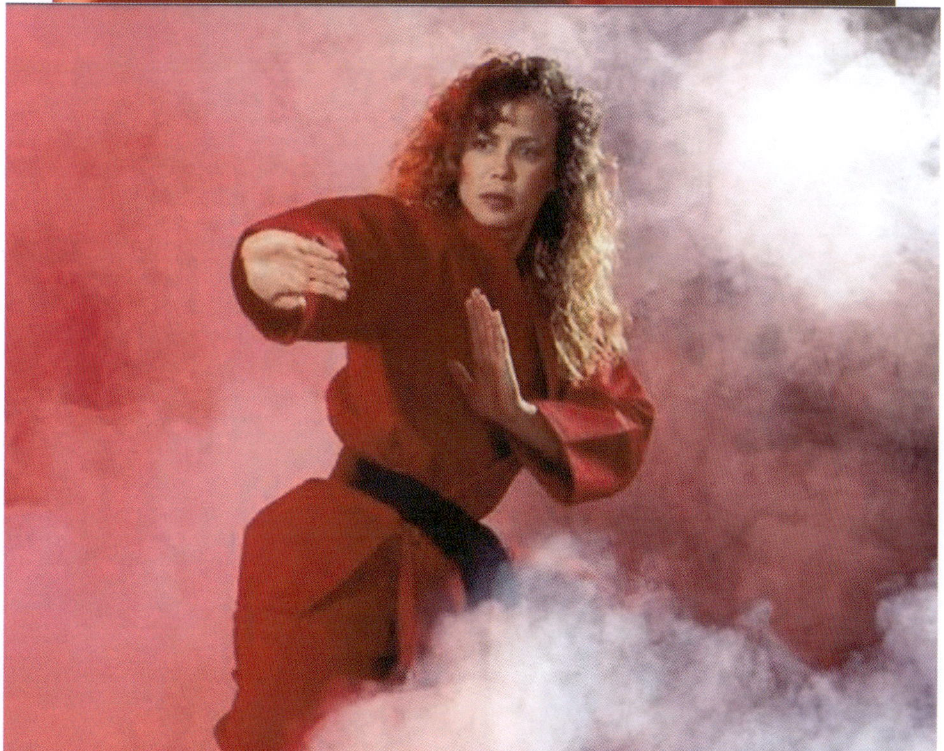

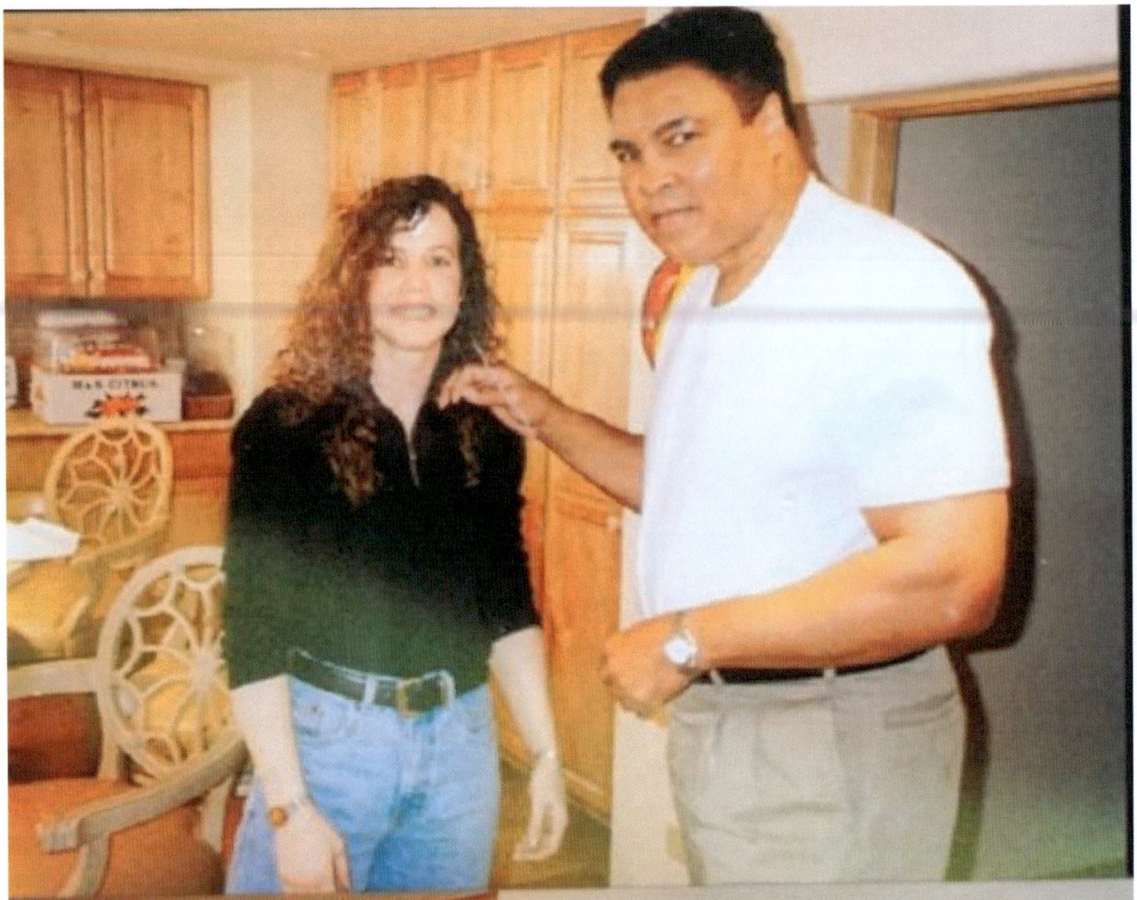

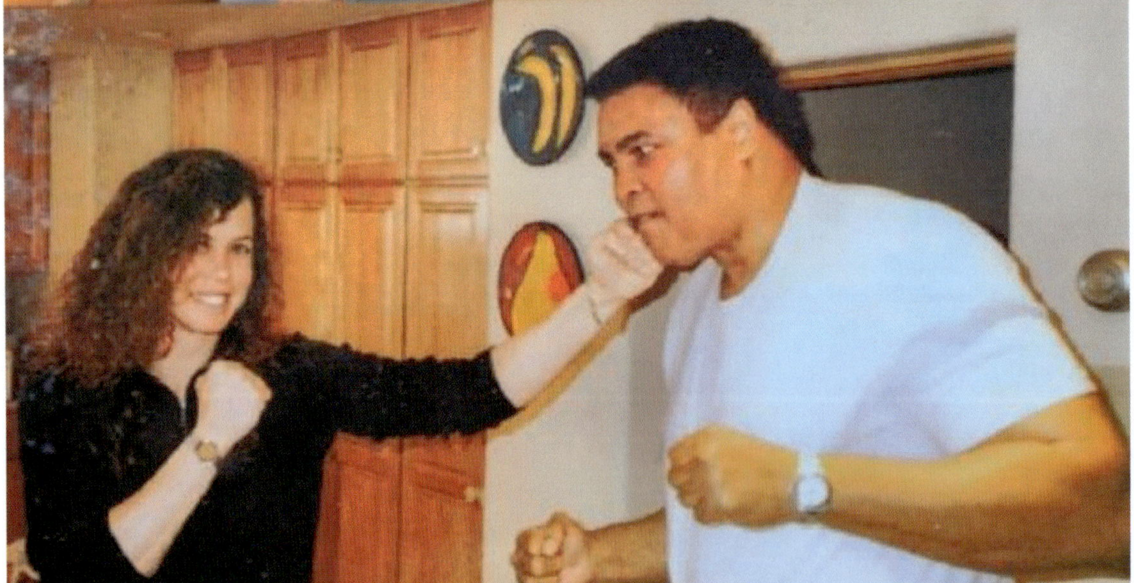

Simon Rhee

Simon Rhee is a 7th Degree Black Belt in Tae Kwon Do and a 4th Degree Black Belt in Hap Ki Do. He is a World-Class Martial Artist known for his beautiful kicks and incredible forms and is a many-time Grand Champion of the tournament circuit. Karate Illustrated noted that, "Simon Rhee has the prettiest kicks, flashiest and most picturesque Martial Arts techniques in the nation". He is world-renowned for his kicking abilities and for his incredible forms. His pictures have graced the covers of many Martial Arts magazines, and he has been involved in the movie industry as a Martial Artist,

Stunt Coordinator, Fight Choreographer, and Instructor to many celebrities. However, it is Master Rhee's charming personality and skill for teaching which has made him loved and respected by all.

Simon Rhee was born in San Jose, California in 1957, but spent much of his childhood in Seoul, Korea, where he began his Martial Arts training. After becoming ill and contracting meningitis as a young child, his parents enrolled him in Tae Kwon Do classes to help strengthen his body. Thus began his lifelong love for the Martial Arts. His intensive training continued in Korea, San Francisco, and then Los Angeles, and he has earned his 7th degree Black Belt in Tae Kwon Do, through Kukkiwon in South Korea and a 4th degree Black Belt in Hap Ki Do, along with extensive training in Wing Chung Kung Fu, Weapons and other Martial Arts. Simon Rhee is well known throughout the martial arts community for his countless victories as Grand Champion in the tournament circuit, in both sparring and in forms. He has been sought out by many major motion picture studios and celebrities because of his talent for instruction, Stunt Coordination and Fight Choreography. Some of his students have included stunt people, fight choreographers and stunt coordinators, professional football players/athletes (Marcus Allen, AC Cowlings, etc.), iconic actors (Faye Dunaway, Heather Locklear, Lorenzo Lamas, Beau Bridges, Eric Roberts, etc.), and comedian Jay Leno. He has doubled Jackie Chan and has worked with some of the best Hollywood actors, musicians and directors including Clint Eastwood, Leonardo DiCaprio, Anthony Hopkins, Jackie Chan, Madonna, Ben Stiller, Ang Lee, Christopher Nolan, John Woo, Brett Ratner, and Tom Cruise.

Simon Rhee has a keen eye for creating the most dynamic fight and action sequences specifically for the motion picture camera, and has available to him an extensive network of the best trained stunt people and equipment to use for specific stunt scenes.

Master Rhee is a member of the International Stunt Association (2012 President), a 2 time winner of the Taurus World Stunt Awards

("Best Fight Scene", 2002; "Best Fire Work", 2007), and numerous Screen Actors Guild awards and nominations, having been involved in the film and television industry for over 30 years as an actor, stunt person, fight choreographer, 2nd unit director and stunt coordinator. He has an extensive body work including motion pictures (The Dark Knight Rises, Inception, Terminator Genysis, Straight Outta Compton, Captain America, The Great Wall, The Lone Ranger, Gangster Squad, Red Dawn, The Muppets, Get Smart, Rush Hour 3, Best of the Best, Memoirs of a Geisha, The Last Samurai, etc.), TV shows (Mistresses, Chuck, Face Off, Fear the Walking Dead, The Last Ship, Jessica Jones, Rush Hour, Heroes, Alias, Supergirl, Grimm, Bones, Sons of Anarchy, etc.), and commercials.

When he is not filming, he continues to enjoy teaching and training at his Woodland Hills TKD Training Center with his panel of Black Belts. Master Rhee has taught thousands of men, women and children the art of Tae Kwon Do for over 30 years. Simon Rhee is a teacher's teacher when it comes to Tae Kwon Do instruction and he has given many dynamic seminars to Martial Artists, Stunt people and, Black Belt Instructors worldwide.

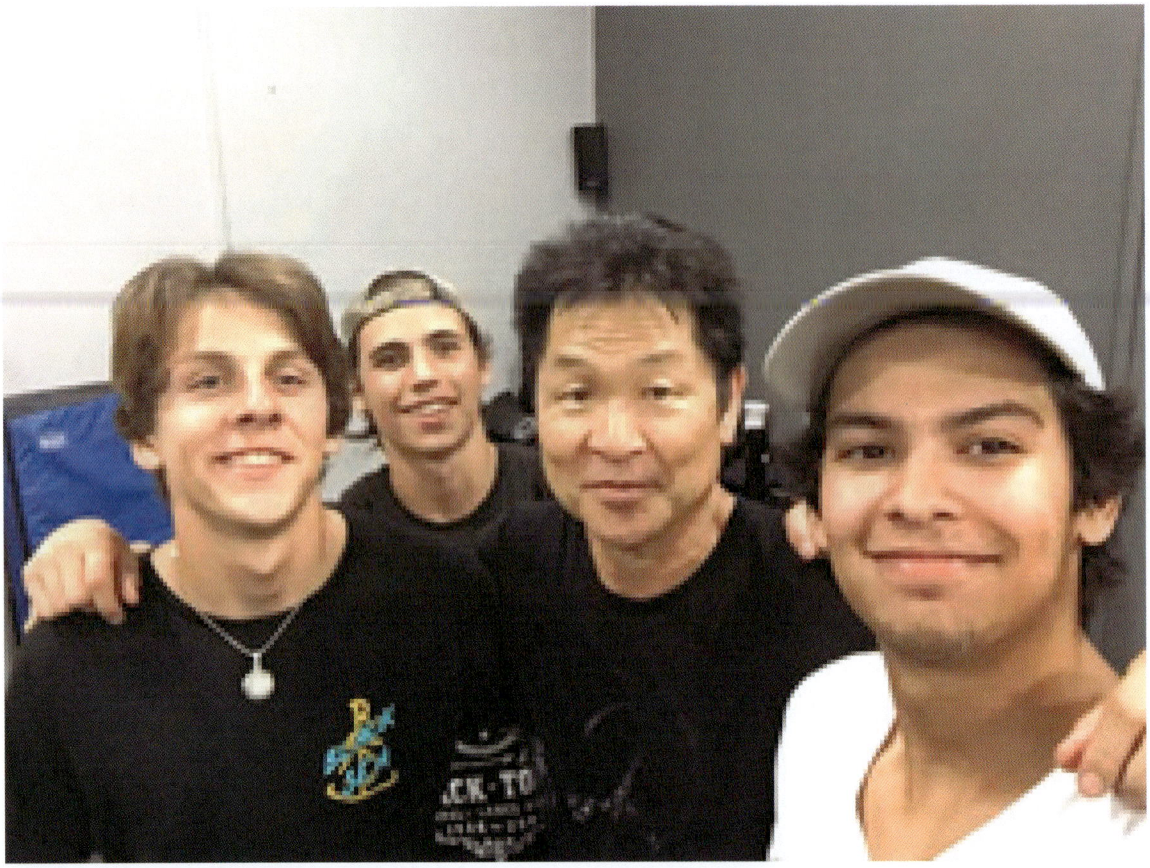

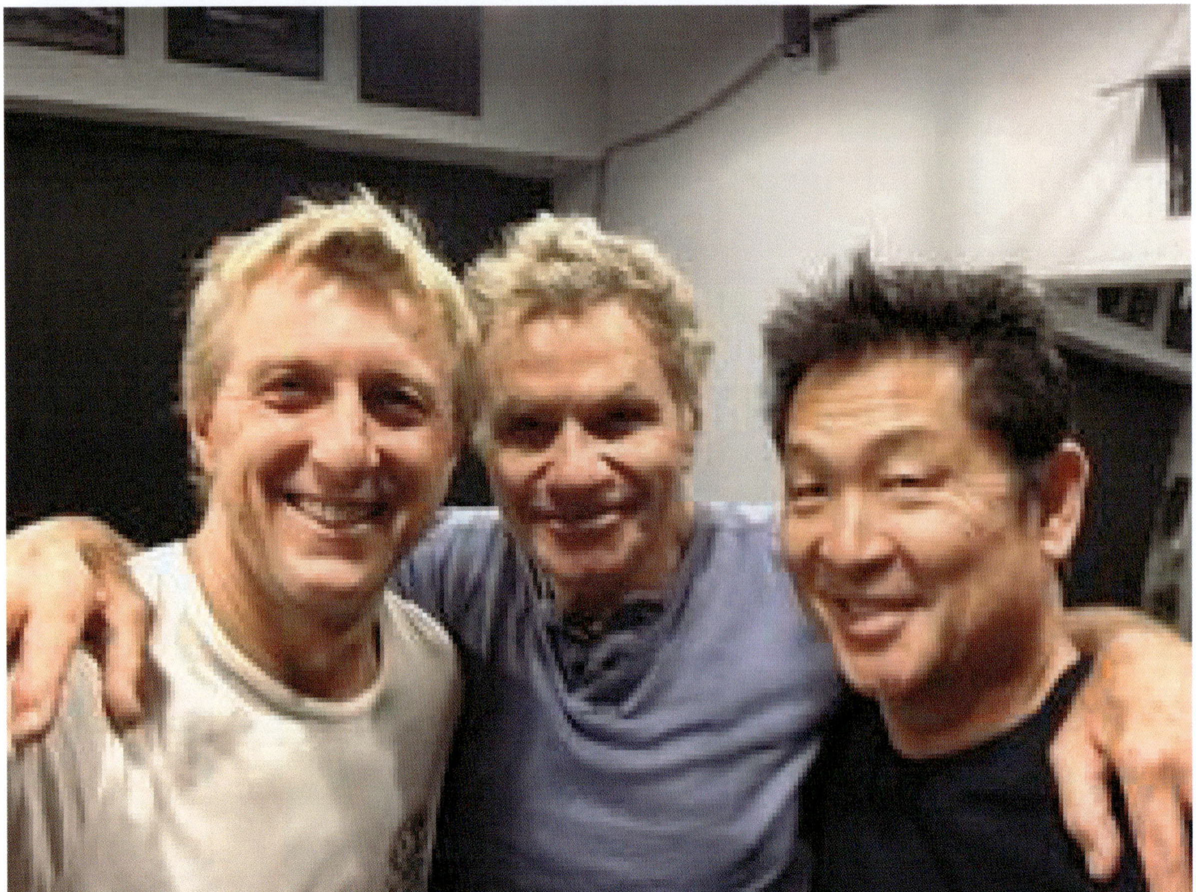

BLACK BELT

MARTIAL ARTS VIDEOS
Are They Worth the Money?

DIARY OF A NINJA
A 1985 Ninjutsu Festival Report

STOP CHILD MOLESTATION:
Simple Self Defense Tips for Kids

FULL-CONTACT TAE KWON DO
Too Rough for Olympics, Too Good for PKA

FIREARMS TRAINING
When Fists and Feet Are Not Enough

THE FIREARM CRISIS
Is It Invading the Arts?

URGENT MESSAGE FOR MARTIAL ARTISTS!
See Page 6

HSING-I KUNG FU
Chinese Wearing Art

SPECIAL SUMMER SWORD SECTION
The Last's Tour Sere Day Be Your Own!

Art Camacho

Art Camacho is considered an accomplished director, fight choreographer and stuntman in independent action films. Dubbed "The Fight Master," by Inside Kung Fu magazine, his directorial work includes Wild League, Assassin X, Recoil, Confessions of a Pit Fighter, Half Past Dead 2, The Power Within, Little Bigfoot, Little Bigfoot 2, The Cutoff, Point Doom, Final Payback, Gangland, Sci-

Fighter, Crooked and more. Camacho went on to write and produce a number of independent films as well as appearing in over 40 movies and television shows.

Camacho has received numerous awards for film direction including awards from Alan Horn (Disney Studios CEO) and Michael Klausman (CBS) and has been featured in several international magazines including Black Belt, Inside Kung Fu, Karate International, Cinturon Negro, Masters and Styles, Secrets of the Masters, Martial Arts Illustrated, the Martial Arts History Museum's Hall of Fame book and most recently, the author of his autobiography, "A Filmmaker's Journey." L.A.'s largest Spanish language newspaper "La Opinion" dubbed him as "One of Latino Hollywood's best action film directors."

He is the host and director of "The Camacho Experiment" on the El Rey Network and is a member of the board for the Martial Arts History Museum. Camacho holds black belts in Wun Hop Kuen Do (6th degree) under Grandmaster Eric Lee, and Hing Ling Do. He also has training in Wing Chun under Grandmaster Samuel Kwok, Jeet Kune do, Kali and Boxing/Kickboxing.

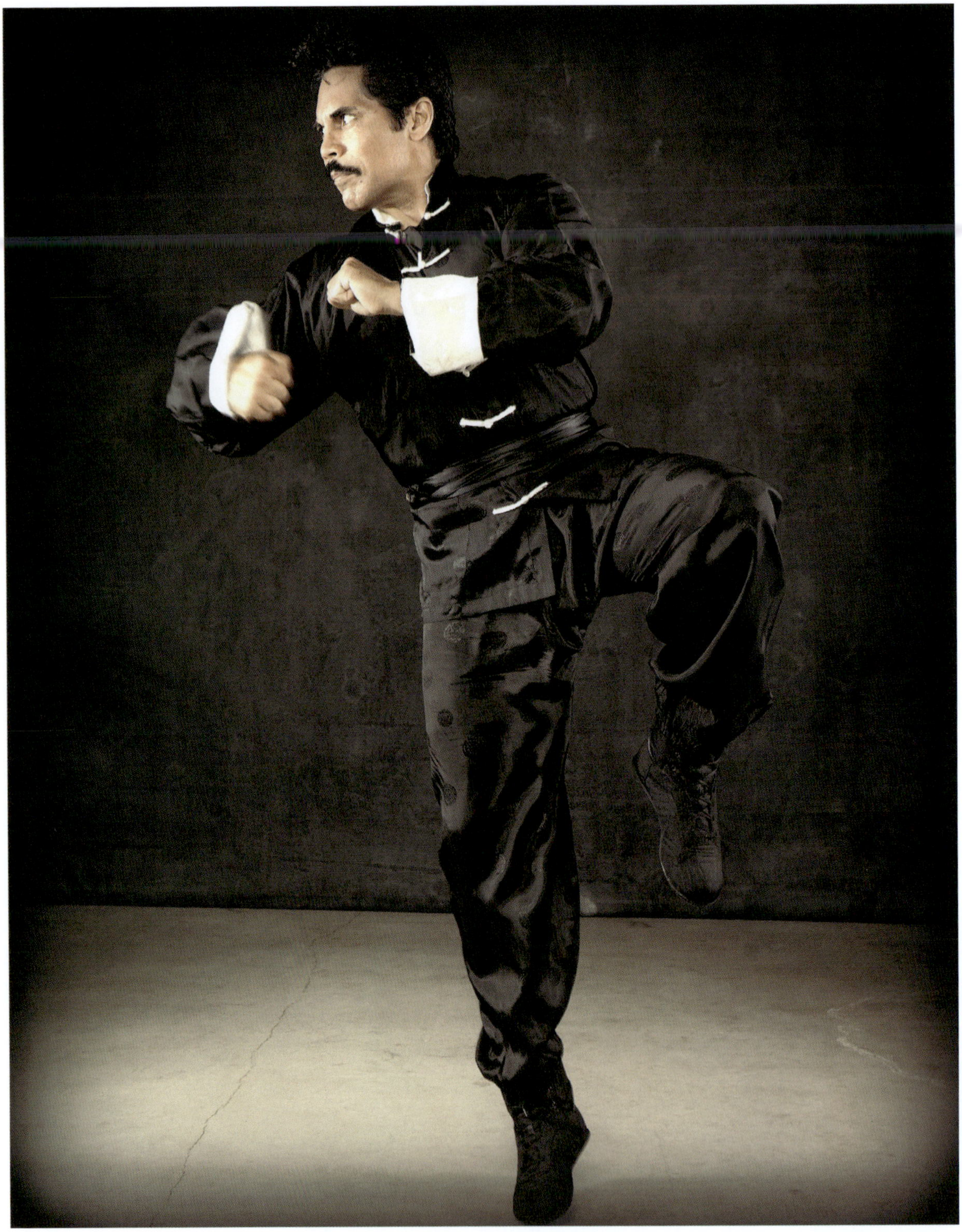

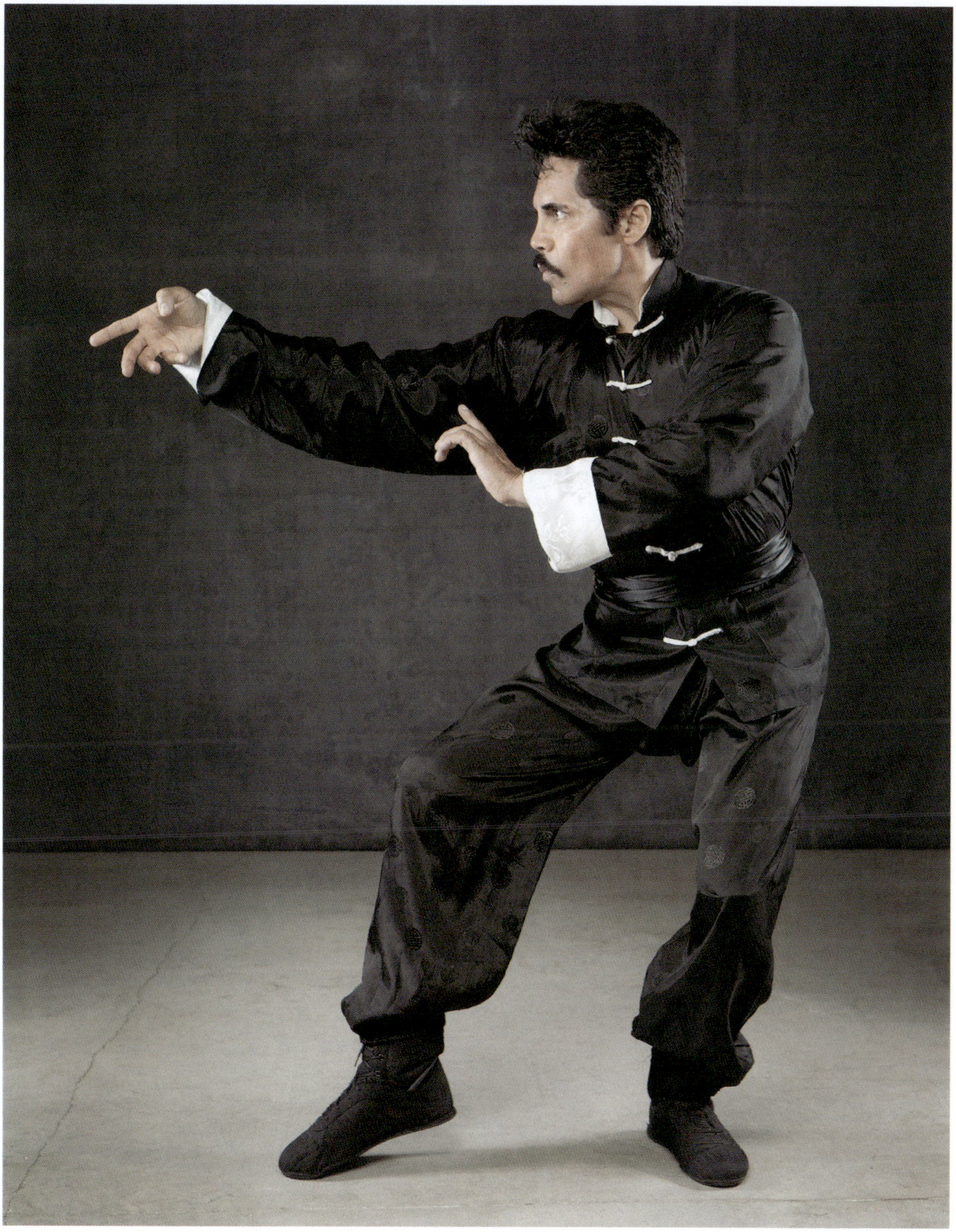

Joycelyne Lew

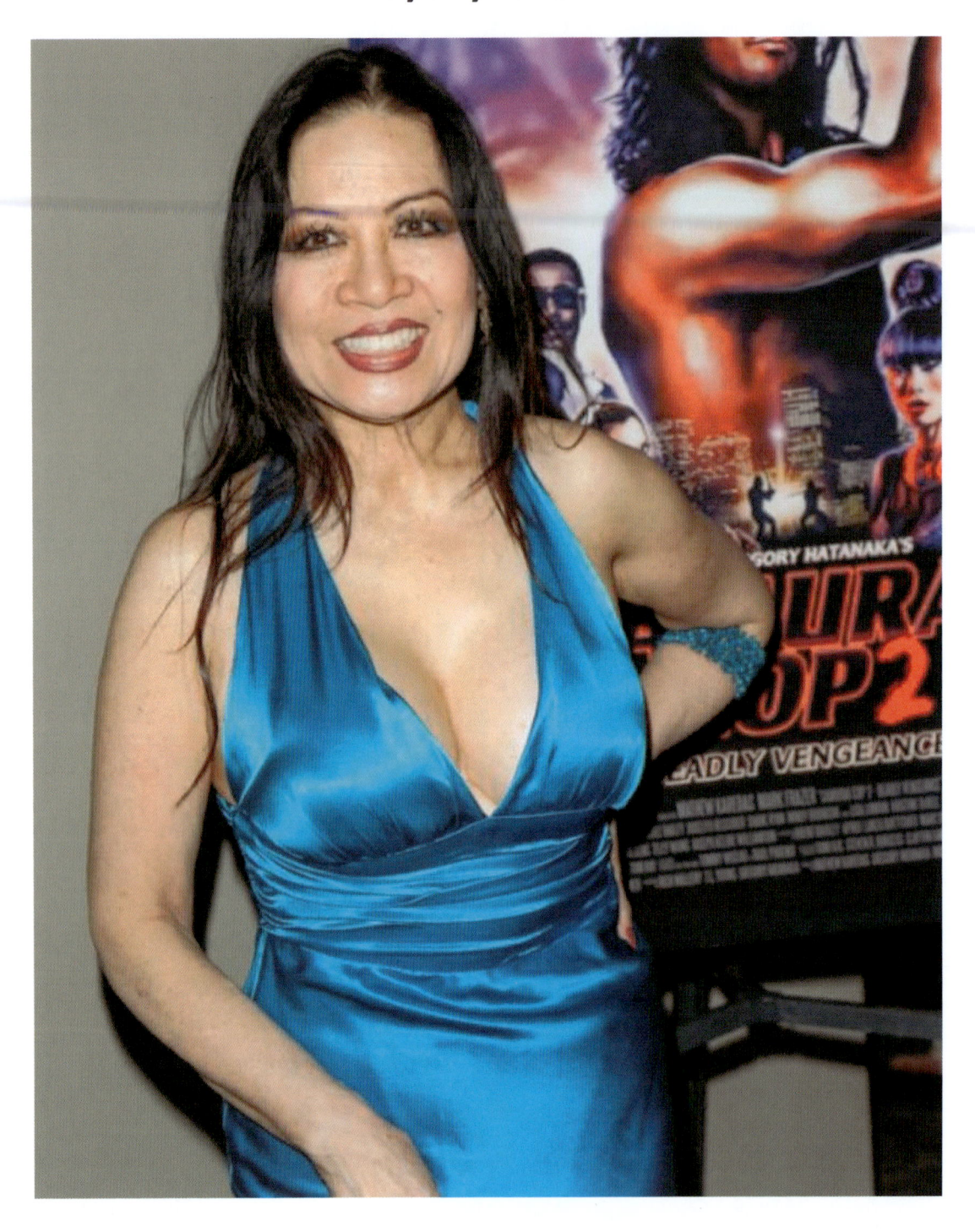

Joycelyne was a child actress at four, singing with Humphrey Bogart in "The Left Hand of God. "She won the role of Princess Ying Yaowalak in "The King and I and from then on has garnered over 100 film and tv credits. By spending days on set of "Big Trouble in Little China," she encountered the world of martial arts.

Her mentor is Eric Lee, the King of Kata. She's been in Hardbodies

II, Inside Kung Fu magazine and models a yearly calendar. She hosts "Cooking In with Joycelyne," and writes a food blog for Rama Newsletter. Her focus is on non-processed foods that provide nutrition on a budget.

Joycelyne voiced the Rambo cartoon series and currently does voices on Neptune 9 and Radio Vault Mystery Theater and acts in two web series; Señor Leche and Pepito's Mamadas.

She loves comedy and has a stand-up act as Mae East, the Asian version of Mae West. She performs at The Magic Castle and did burlesque at the Edinburgh Fringe Festival in Scotland.

She reteamed with Gerald Okumura in "Samurai Cop 2-Deadly Vengeance." She's been inducted three times in the USA martial arts Hall of Fame, and her next action film will be "Fatal Needles of Death," A martial arts/action acupuncture film.

she encountered the world of martial arts.

She earned the largest female role as Kem in the "Kung Fu" series with David Carradine. She played Miss Wong with Jackie Chan in "The Big Brawl." On location, she learned her side kick from Pat Johnson, the stunt coordinator who also did all the "Karate Kid" films.

Her mentor is Eric Lee

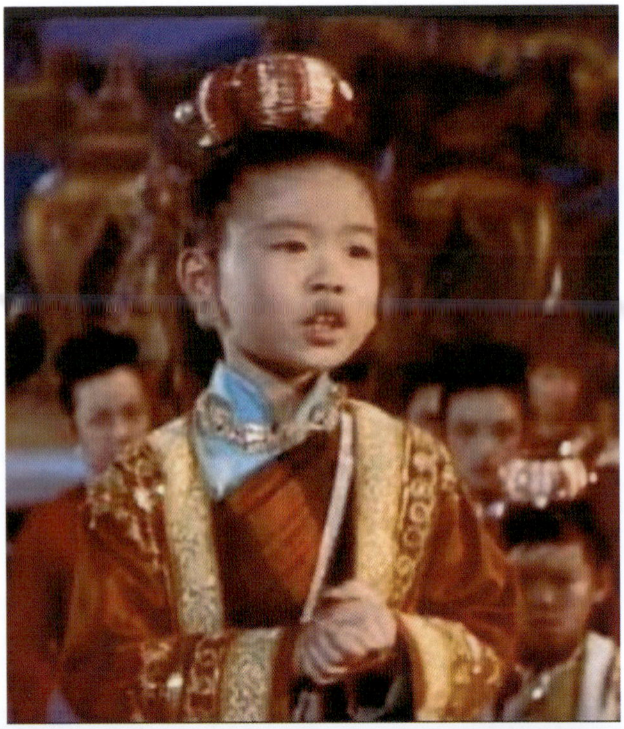

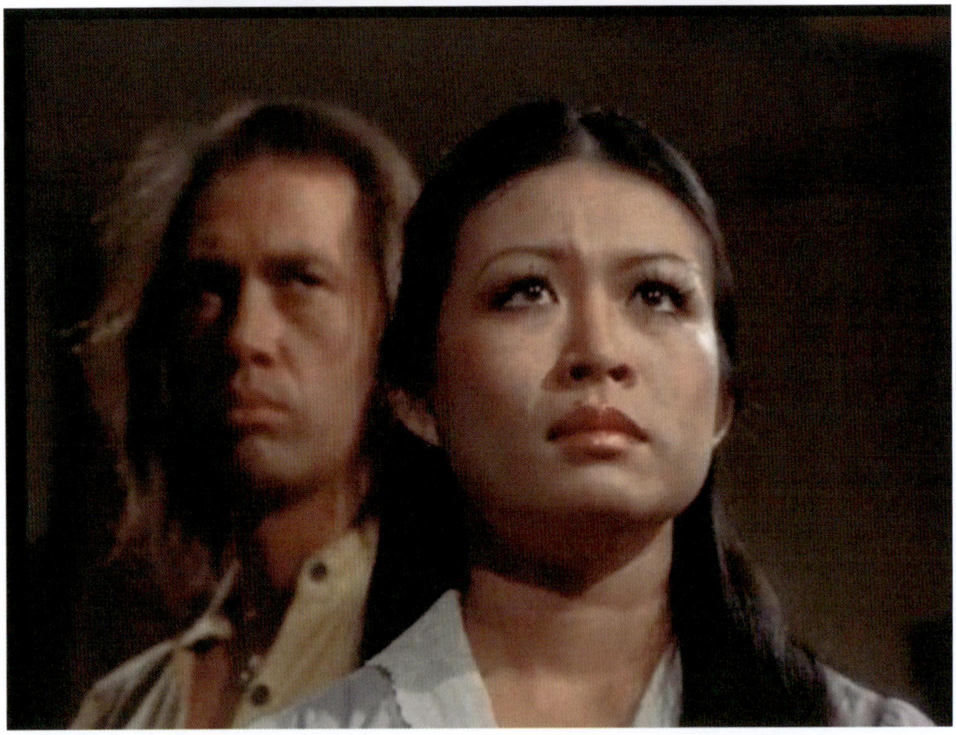

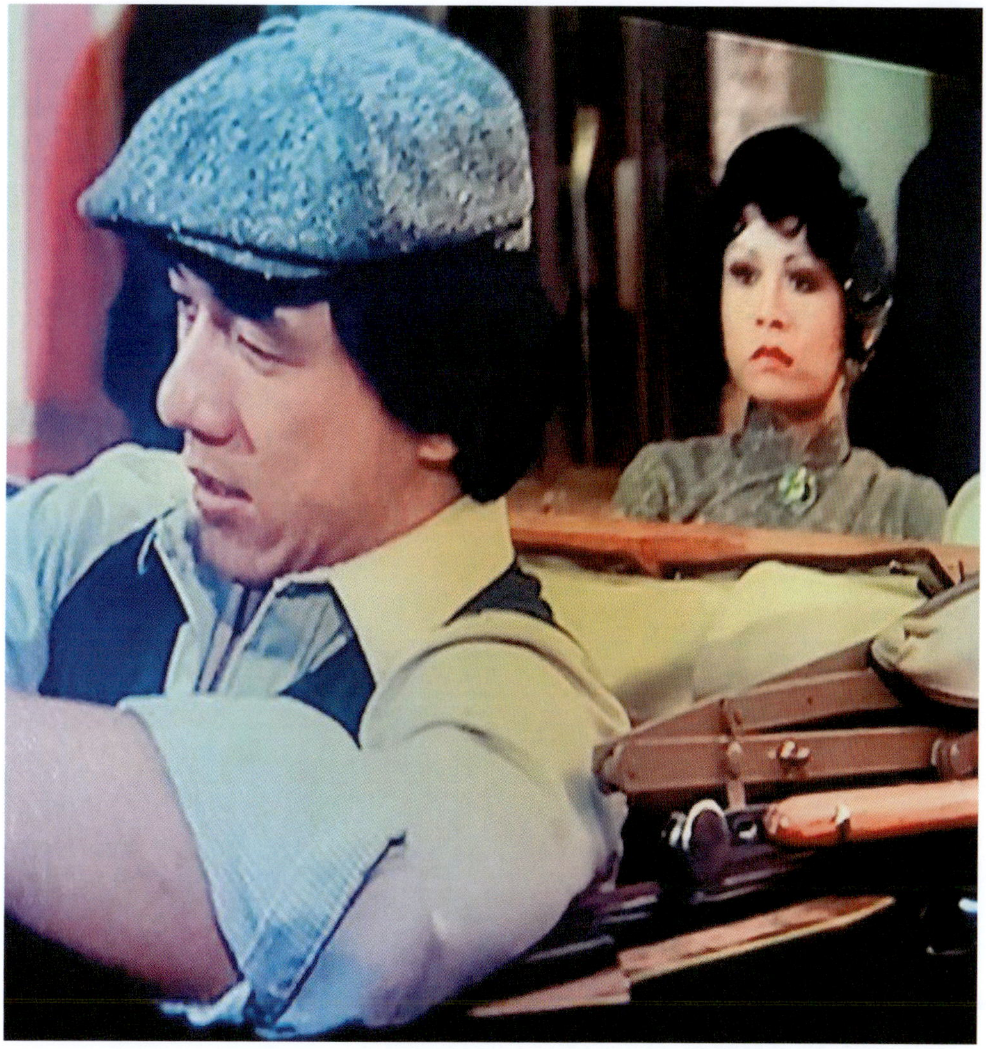

Ron Van Clief

Ron "The Black Dragon" Van Clief is a martial arts legend. Born in Brooklyn, New York in 1943, he started martial arts training in his early teens. At 5 feet 10 inches and 190 pounds, Van Clief was fast, powerful, and tough. He won 10 New York State Full-Contact Karate Championships. He won multiple Karate Point-Fighting Titles. By the early 1970s he had earned his 10th Degree Black Belt. His karate record was reported to be 110-8.

In 1994 at age 51, he launched a comeback on December 16, 1994, fighting former World Jujitsu Light heavyweight and Ultimate Fighting World Champion Royce Gracie. The Black Dragon landed one good punch but was taken to the canvas where after a valiant battle was choked into submission, He continues to compete at the age of 72 recently competing in a BJJ Tournament winning a silver medal. Thus his competitive career still goes strong.

Jeff Langton

Jeff was born in Pasadena, California and raised between San Jose, California and Brooklyn, New York. His father was a member of the Marine Corps Boxing Team and later trained young Langton in the "sweet science." When Langton was 13, he joined the Police Athletic League and trained as an amateur boxer with Gus Spencer. He also trained at Garden City Boxing Club and Bath Beach Health Club in Brooklyn New York. As a young man he also trained in martial arts as well as boxing. He trained in Tae Kwon Do with Dan Kyu Choi. He became the captain of Choi's Institute of Tae Kwon Do Championship Team and then went on to be California State Tae Kwon Do Champion. He also received a black belt in Tae Kwon Do from Master Byung Yu. He was also the first and original member of the world-famous Ernie Reyes West Coast Demo Team and introduced gymnastics and acrobatics to martial arts demonstration. This legacy continues on, as the format Langton introduced is still used today by West Coast Demo Team in shows all around the world.[1]

After making his way through the competitive world of martial arts, he moved on to film and television. He moved to Los Angeles to pursue acting. In L.A. he training extensively with six-time World Champion Kickboxer Benny Urquidez. He was also a trainer at Benny's school, The Jet Center. During this time he also did live action stunts for Universal Studios.

He began doing stunts for Sylvester Stallone and then acting in movies such as *Lionheart*, fighting on screen with stars like Jean-Claude Van Damme. After this he starred in films such as *Final Impact* and *Maximum Force* and continued to work on films and television shows like *Price of Glory*, *Matlock*, *Buffy the Vampire Slayer*, and *Las Vegas*. His background in boxing came in handy as he was asked to train and coach Tommy Morrison in *Rocky V*. Langton also appears in the movie itself as one of the fighters Tommy Gunn knocks out. In fact, his name appears in the marquee in a montage depicting Tommy Gunn rising through the ranks. Although in the video game, *Rocky Legends* his character looks nothing like him and his name is changed to Kofi Langton.] His most recent role is in the movie *Mind Polish: Master Hubbard's Special Reserve*, where he plays a scientology spiritual counselor who suffers from Tourette's syndrome.

Jeff has worked the corner in over 40 world championship title bouts including Ricardo Mayorga (WBC, IBF), Freddie Pendleton (IBF, WBA), Tony Tucker (NABF, WBC, WBA, WBO), Byron Mitchell (IBF, WBA), Uriah Grant (IBF), Kingsley Ikeke (NABA, WBC), William Abelyan (NABO), and Will Grigsby (IBF).

Jeff Langton has trained world champions of his own such as Terry Davis (NBA, IBA Champ) and Young Dick Tiger (Nigerian Commonwealth Champ). Langton has also trained Hector Pena (6-time world kickboxing champion) and Danny "Hard As" Steel (6-time world kickboxing champion). He learned how to be a cut man from his uncle Al Bonanni who has trained many world champions for Don King. He is a licensed trainer by the State of California and by the Nevada State Athletic Commission. He also owns a private gym for professional boxers and celebrities.

FILMS

- 1986 *Cobra* (Stunts)
- 1988 *Rambo III* (Stunts)
- 1989 *Roadhouse* (Stunts)
- 1989 *Tango & Cash* (Stunts)
- 1990 *Lionheart* as Cynthia's Fighter
- 1990 *Die Hard 2* as Blue Light Team #2
- 1990 *Matlock* (1 episode "The Narc) as Narc #2
- 1990 *Rocky V* as Boxer
- 1990 *Lethal Games* as Huey
- 1991 *Future Kick* as Andrews
- 1991 *College Kickboxers* as Gary Carlisle (uncredited)
- 1992 *Final Impact* as Jake Gerrard
- 1992 *Batman Returns* as Clown (uncredited)
- 1992 *Maximum Force* as Ivan
- 1994 *Street Fighter* (Stunts)
- 1997 *Hollywood Safari* as Neal
- 1997 *Buffy the Vampire Slayer* (1 episode, "Ted") aa Vampire
- 1998 *Almost Heroes* (Stunts)
- 1998 *Jane Austen's Mafia!* as Bodyguard (uncredited)
- 2000 *Price of Glory* as Referee
- 2000 *Intrepid* (Stunts)
- 2002 *Deuces Wild* as Gangster (uncredited)
- 2003 *Las Vegas* (1 episode, "Blood and Sand") as Boxing Referee
- 2004 *El Padrino* as Secret Service Agent (uncredited)

- **2006** *Mini's First Time* as The Auditor
- **2008** *Mind Polish: Master Hubbard's Special Reserve* as Frankie Carbo, Mobster #2
- **2010** *Taken by Force* as Cop
- **2011** *Brando Unauthorized* as Al Silvan

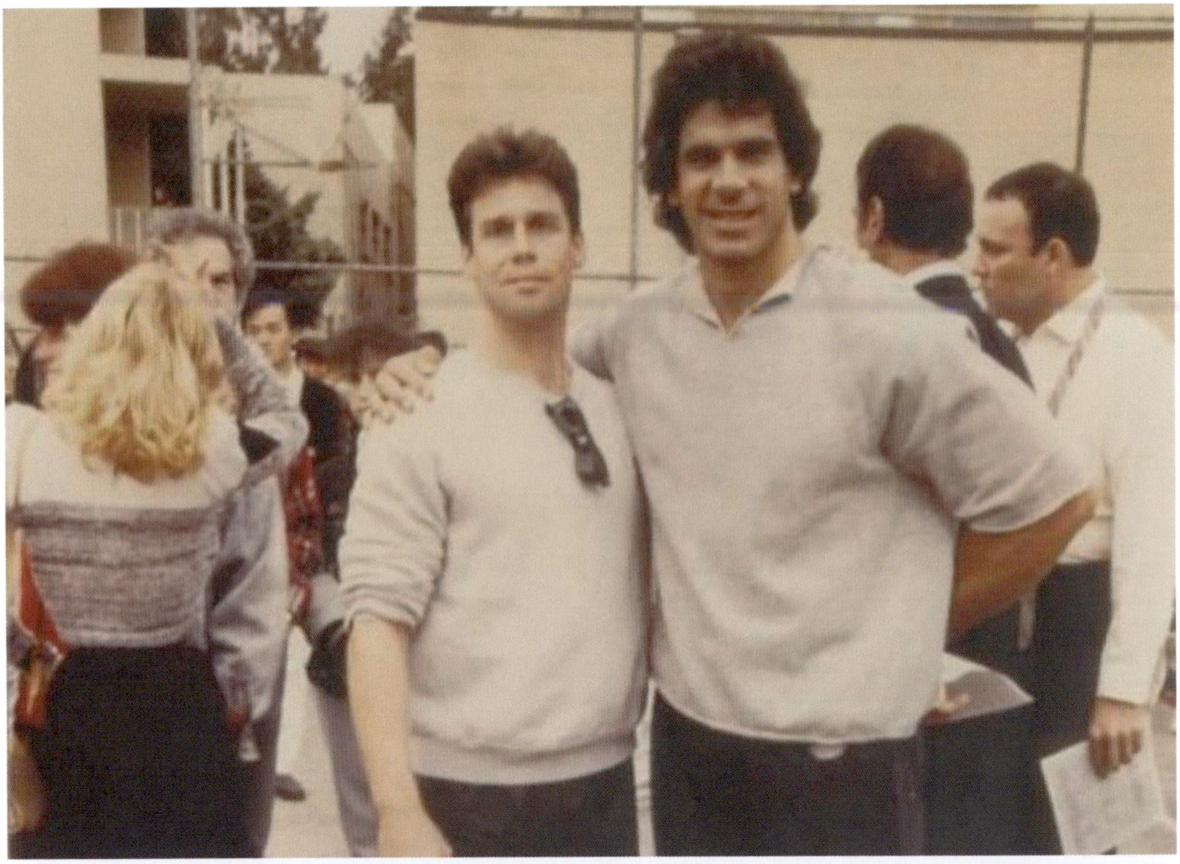

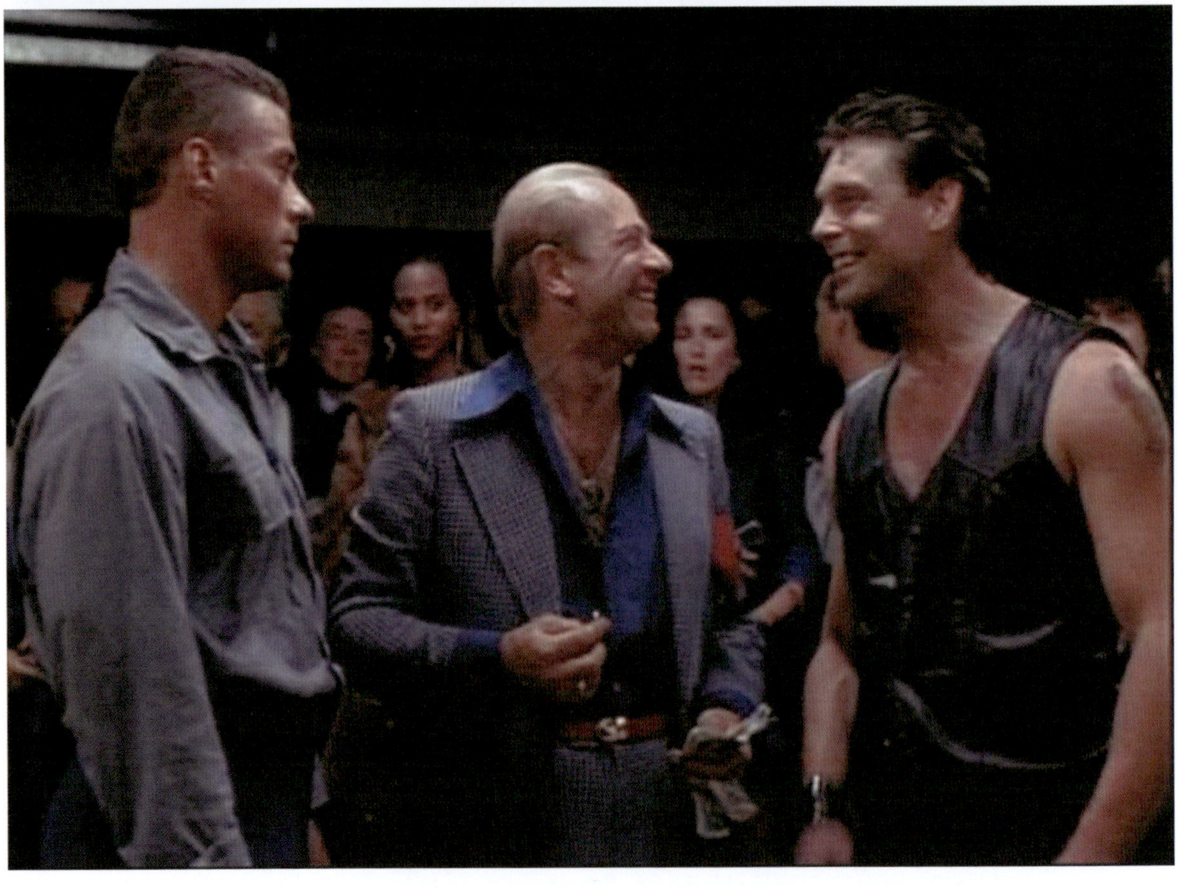

David Kurzhul

David Kurzhal (aka the "Viking Samurai") is a lifetime martial artist and natural bodybuilder. He runs the popular Viking Samurai YouTube Channel (Podcast) where he talks about action and martial arts movies, primarily from the 80s and 90s. Some of his more popular guests have been Mark Dacascos, Lorenzo Lamas, Benny "The Jet" Urquidez, Don "The Dragon" Wilson, Scott Adkins and Michael Jai White.

Growing up an army brat, David got his first taste of martial arts at the age of 6 when his parents enrolled him and his older brother in Judo on an army base. He spent a year there; however, he really wasn't that interested in it at the time as he felt he was really just "wrestling much bigger kids."

It would be many years later, at the age of 13, when he would finally get serious about the martial arts. Inspired and motivated by movies such as "Bloodsport" and "Best of the Best," along with threats of being bullied at school, was more than enough to make him seek out the local Taekwondo school. It would also be at this time that he would take up weightlifting. When reflecting back on the two activities he says, "it really was the best thing I ever did for myself, as it helped keep me out of trouble, built my confidence and completely transformed my body."

After several years of dedicated TKD training, David would meet his next serious instructor while lifting weights at the local 24-Hour Fitness. "I was doing the splits in the gym one day and this guy approached me and told me about his Kenpo school down the road," says David. That started a journey for several years that consisted of private one-on-one training for a mere $80 a month. David says, "I was a poor college student at the time, so he was generous enough to work with what little money I had to pay him. In exchange, I did help teach his classes for him." David continues, "a year or so after meeting him, I would also work at a private weightlifting club in order to help pay my way through college."

David has continued training in the martial arts and lifting weights his entire adult life and more recently took formal classes in Krav Maga. "At this stage, and for a long time now, I'm much more interested in movement as opposed to styles, which is why I identify as a 'martial artist,' as opposed to a 'taekwondo guy,' a 'krav maga guy,' etc," says David.

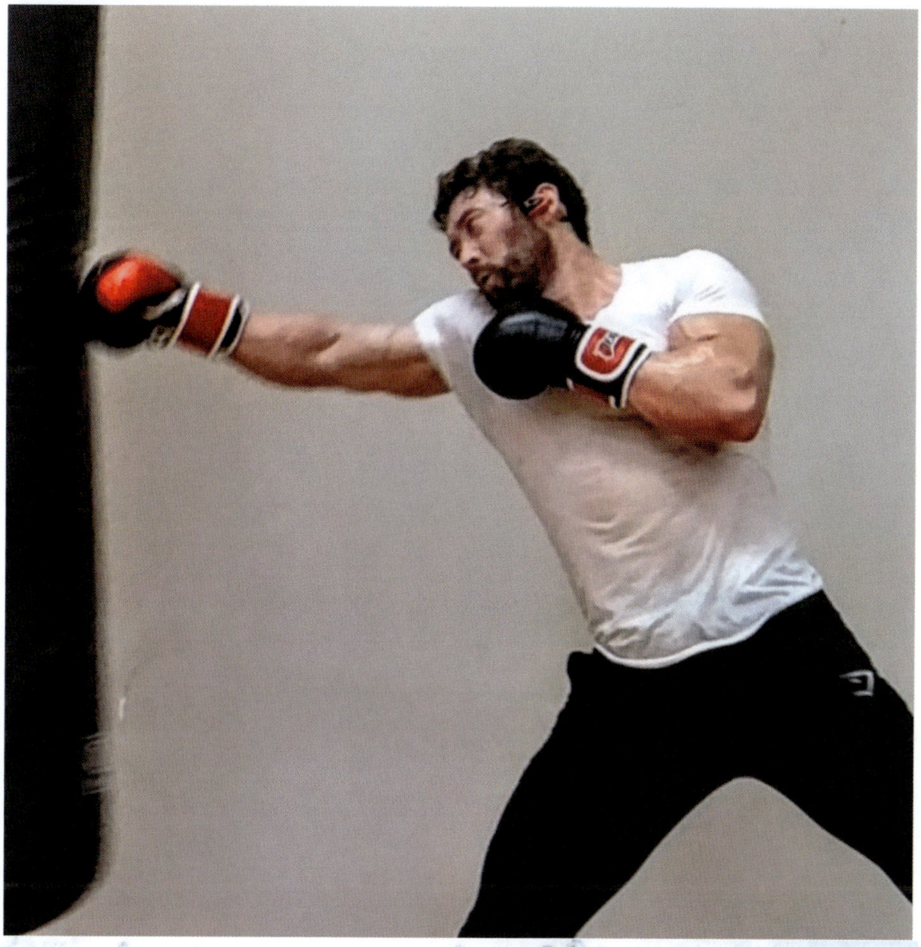

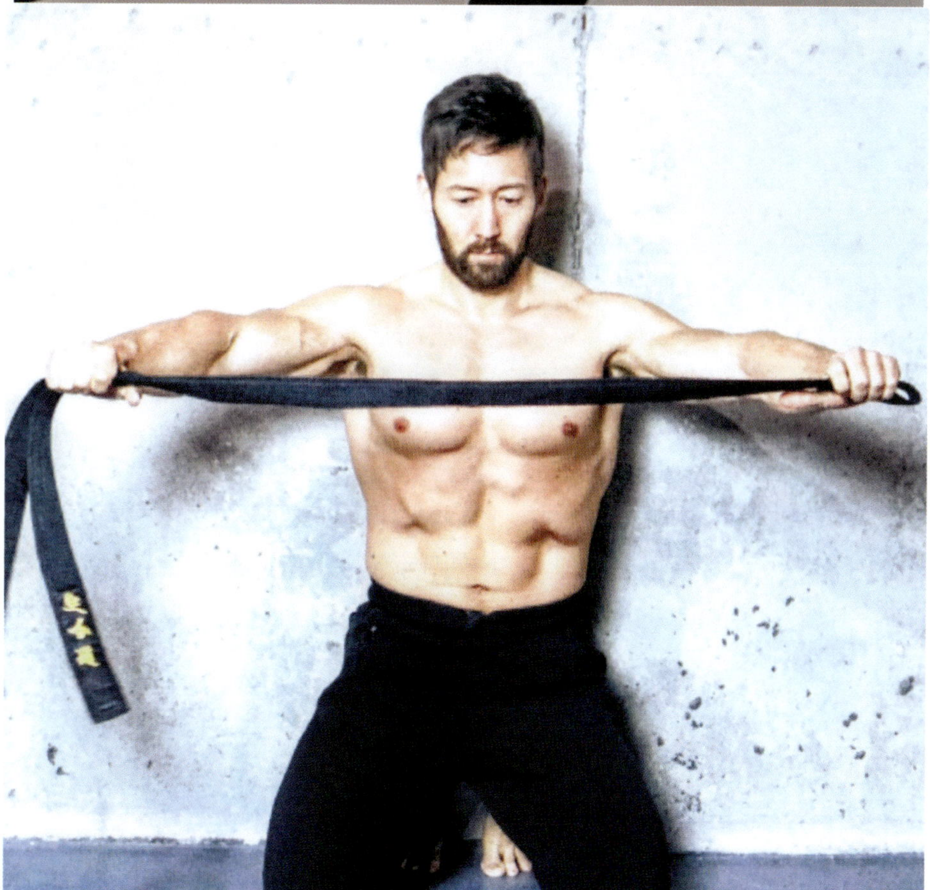

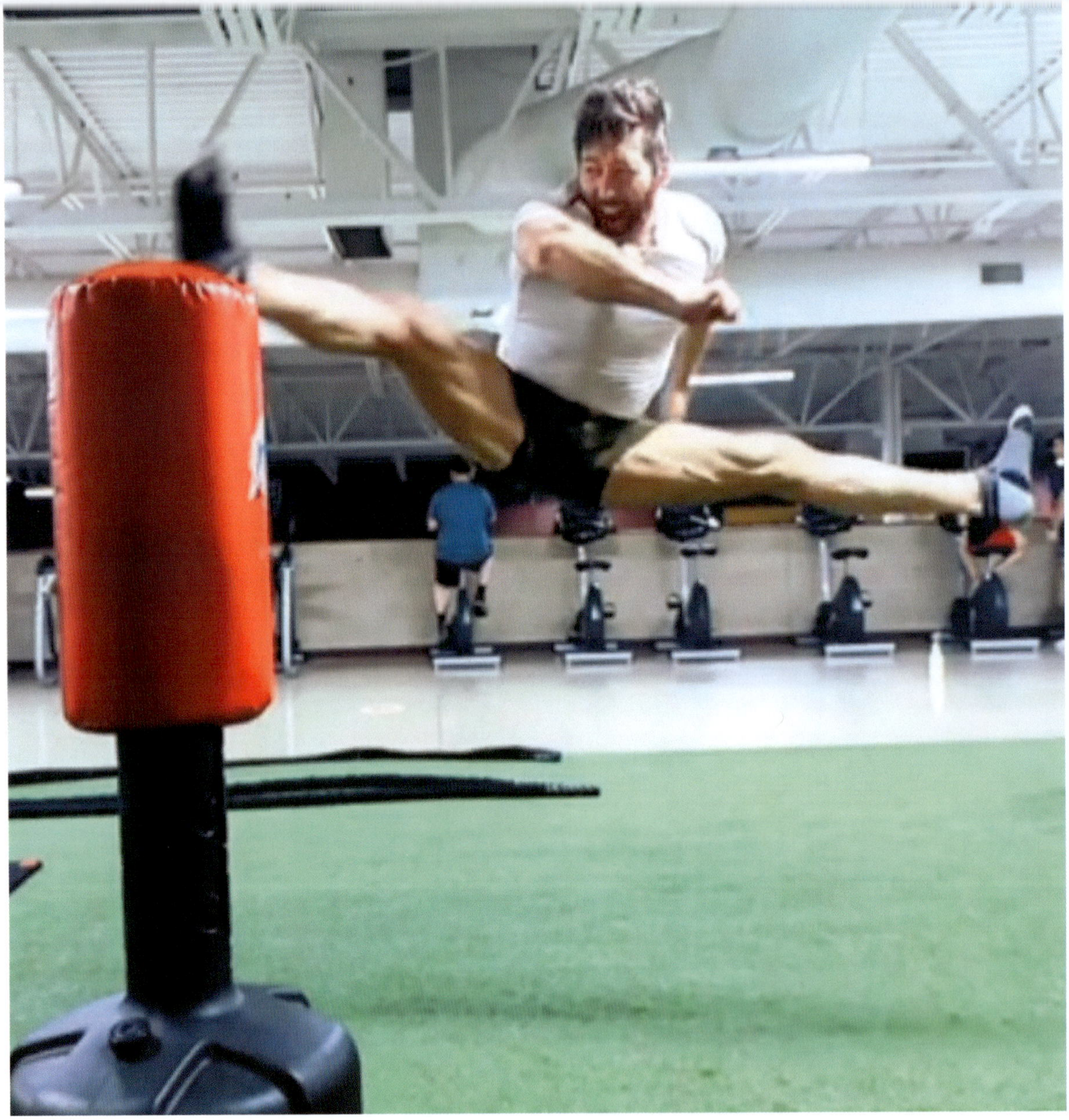

Bill (superfoot) Wallace

Bill "Superfoot" Wallace is a living legend in the world of martial arts and professional kickboxing. A pioneer in the sport, he began his martial arts career as a Karate point-fighter. He competed along with such immortals as Bruce Lee, Chuck Norris, Joe Lewis, and Skipper Mullins. After an incredible career in point-fighting, Wallace made his professional debut as a kickboxer in 1972. He quickly captured the World Middleweight Championship and retired as the undefeated champion after compiling a record of 23-0. With the urging of his friend Chuck Norris, Wallace has appeared in a number of motion pictures, mostly as the "heavy" in martial arts films. Wallace, a college graduate, continues to give exhibitions and trainings around the world.

Bill Wallace retired as the undefeated Professional Karate Association (PKA) middleweight champion after defeating Bill Biggs in a 12-round bout in June 1980. The victory, Wallace's 23rd straight, signaled the end to an illustrious 15-year career in tournament and full contact fighting.

Known to the Karate world simply as "Superfoot," symbolic of his awesome left leg, which was once clocked in excess of 60 mph, Wallace left a string of battered and bruised bodies along the martial arts fighting trail.

He used his foot as others would use their hands, faking opponents with two or three rapid fake kicks and following with one solid knockout technique. His power was amazing, his precision astounding.

Wallace, a 5-foot, 10 1/2-inch native of Portland, IN, began studying Karate in February 1967 after suffering a right leg injury in a Judo accident. The injury left him without the use of the leg in Karate competition. Some observers said Wallace was committing martial arts suicide. Wallace, however, had other ideas.

In the next seven years, "Superfoot," named after his manager saw an advertisement for a "super foot long hot dog" at a sporting event, dominated the point-tournament circuit.

As a national champion point fighter three years in a row, Wallace captured virtually every major event on the tournament circuit. The more prestigious victories included: the U.S. Championships (3 times), the USKA Grand Nationals (3 times), and the Top Ten Nationals (2 times).

He was such a dominant figure in martial arts that Black Belt magazine, the bible of industry publications, named him to its Hall of Fame three times in seven years -- twice as "Competitor of the Year" and once as "Man of the Year."

In 1973, Wallace, whose education includes a bachelor's degree (1971) in physical education from Ball State University and a master's degree (1976) in kinesiology (the study of human movement) from Memphis State University, suffered what many considered a career-ending injury. However, one of Wallace's friends, the late Elvis Presley, flew in a Los Angeles acupuncturist to treat the Karate champion at Graceland Manor.

A year later, Wallace turned professional and captured the PKA middleweight Karate championship with a second-round knockout (hook kick) of West German Bernd Grothe in Los Angeles. He relinquished the crown in 1980, undefeated and respected around the world.

Despite his retirement, Wallace continues to be one of the martial arts' most popular figures. He is the author of three books: Karate: Basic Concepts & Skills, Dynamic Kicking & Stretching, and The Ultimate Kick.

A former member of the President's Council on Physical Fitness, Wallace has also been active in the film industry.

His credits include: A Force of One, with Chuck Norris; Kill Point, with Cameron Mitchell; Continental Divide and Neighbors, with John Belushi, for whom he acted as trainer and bodyguard; Protector, with Jackie Chan; A Prayer for the Dying, with Mickey Rourke; Ninja Turf; and A Sword of Heaven.

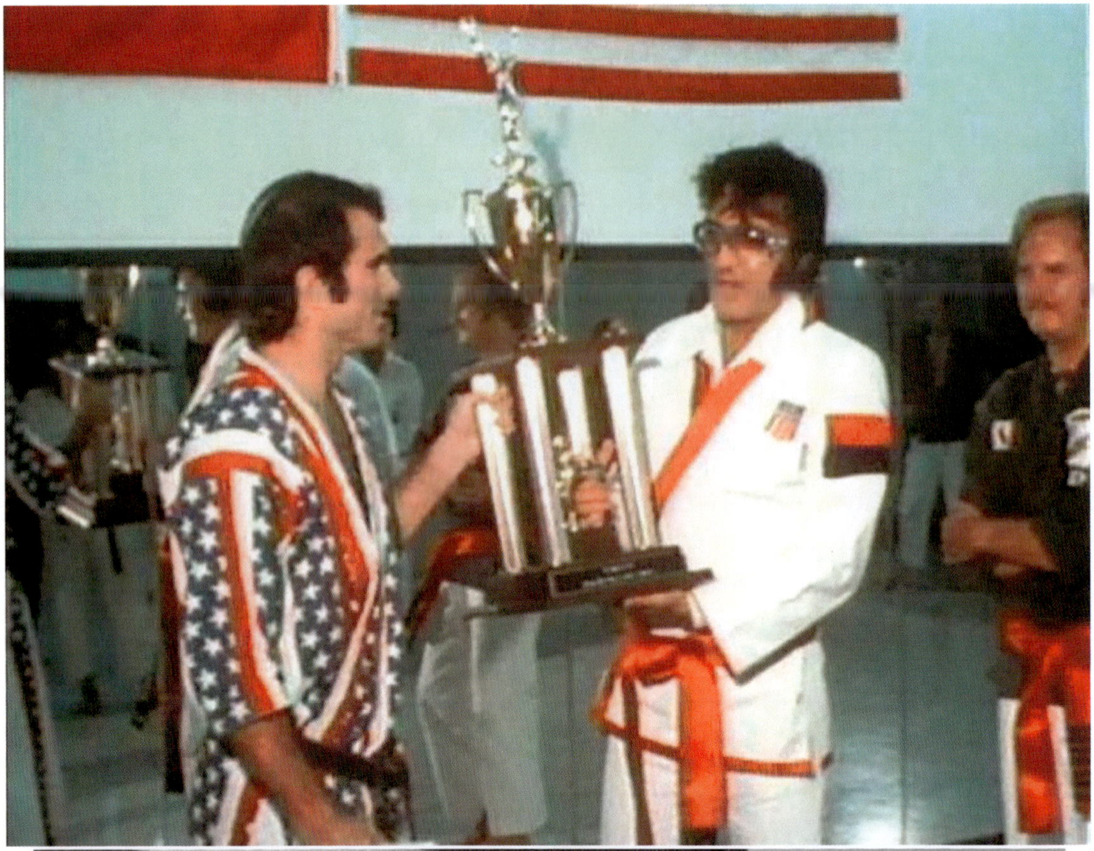

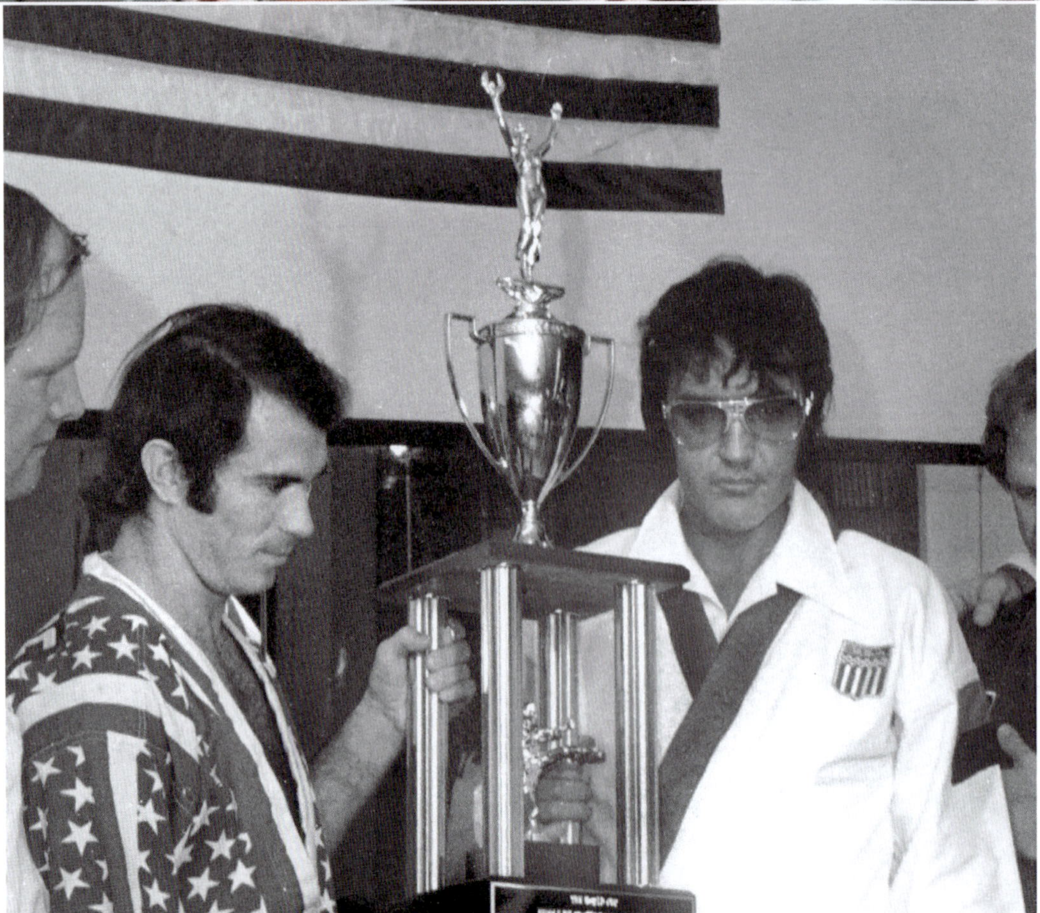

IN LOVING MEMORY OF
FUMIO DEMURA

Fumio Demura is possibly the world most celebrated, beloved, and revered Master of Martial Arts.

The arts for which is most known are Shito-Ryu Karate-Do, Kobudo (weapons), and Batto-Do (sword), although his training and knowledge span uncounted arts and applications. Mr. Demura's life, his childhood in Japan, his development and emergence as a Martial Artist, his many experiences and adventures teaching in the United States since 1965, growing his organization, Shito-Ryu Karate-Do Genbu-Kai, and the innumerable contributions he has made to Martial Arts and to our society, could fill volumes, and are held dear by his many students and followers. This Martial Arts Master is celebrated with titles and awards too numerous to count, but he is known simply as Sensei Demura to millions of people. He has spent his life bringing Martial Arts to the American people and to people all over the world, fueled by his desire to help people everywhere have happy, successful lives. For 75 years, he has trained in Martial Arts – a near unparalleled achievement. Today, Mr. Demura continues the further development of the arts of Karate-Do, Kobudo, and Batto-Do, as well as his ongoing efforts to teach them to as many people as he can reach. Fumio Demura's contributions and accomplishments are an essential legacy in the World of Martial Arts.

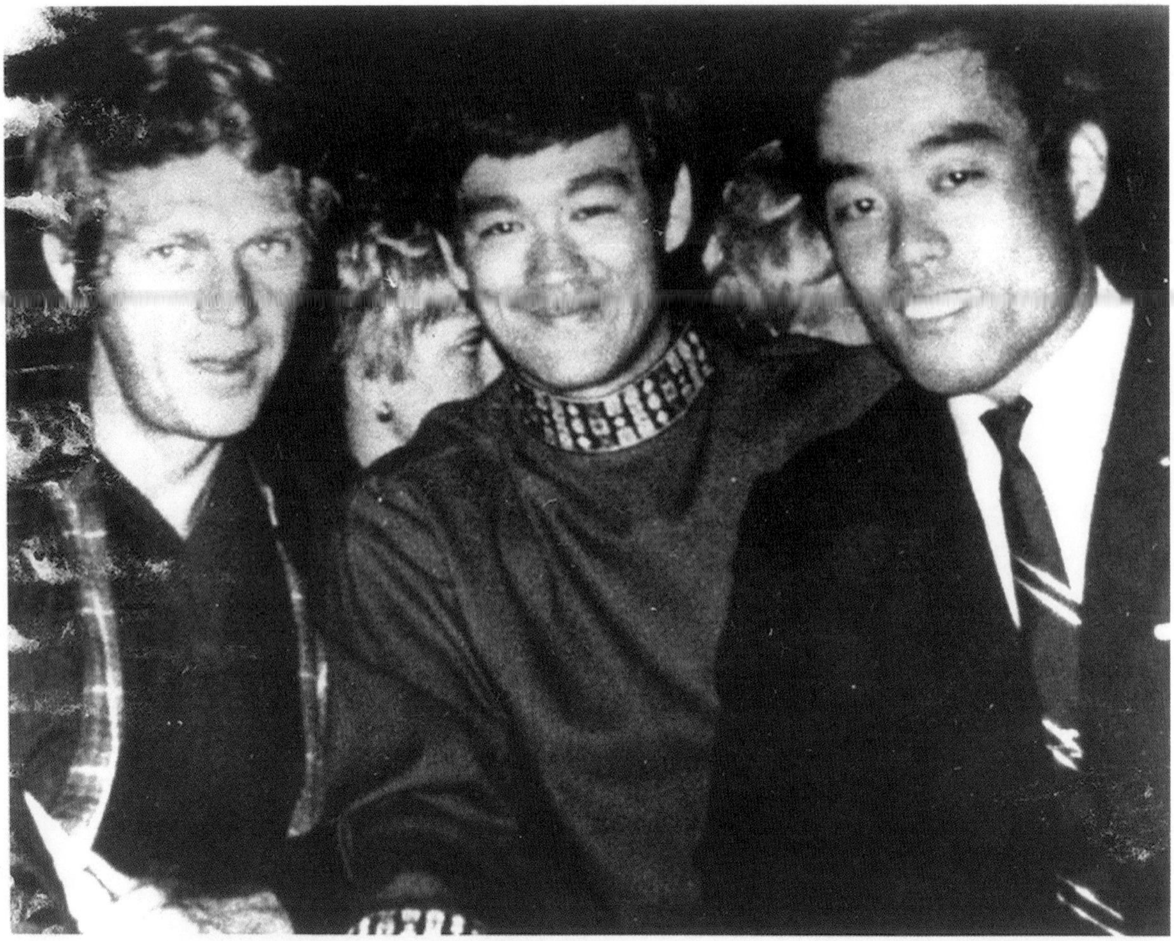

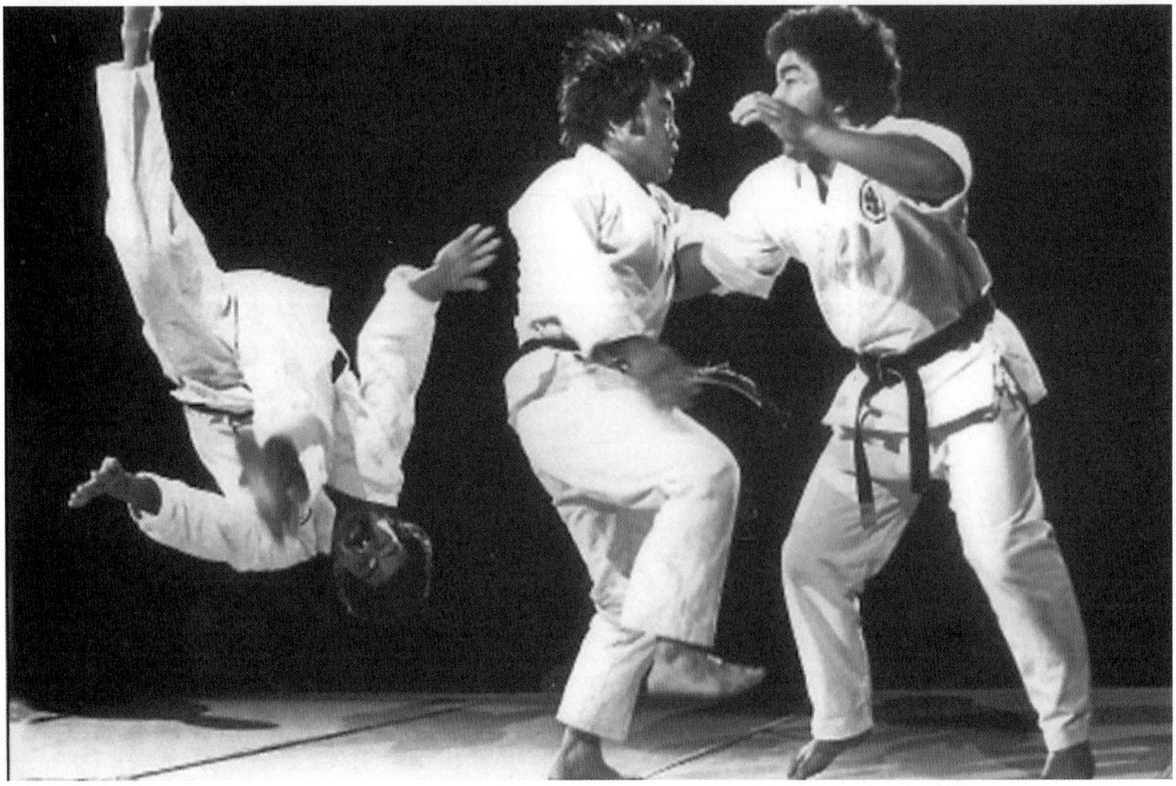

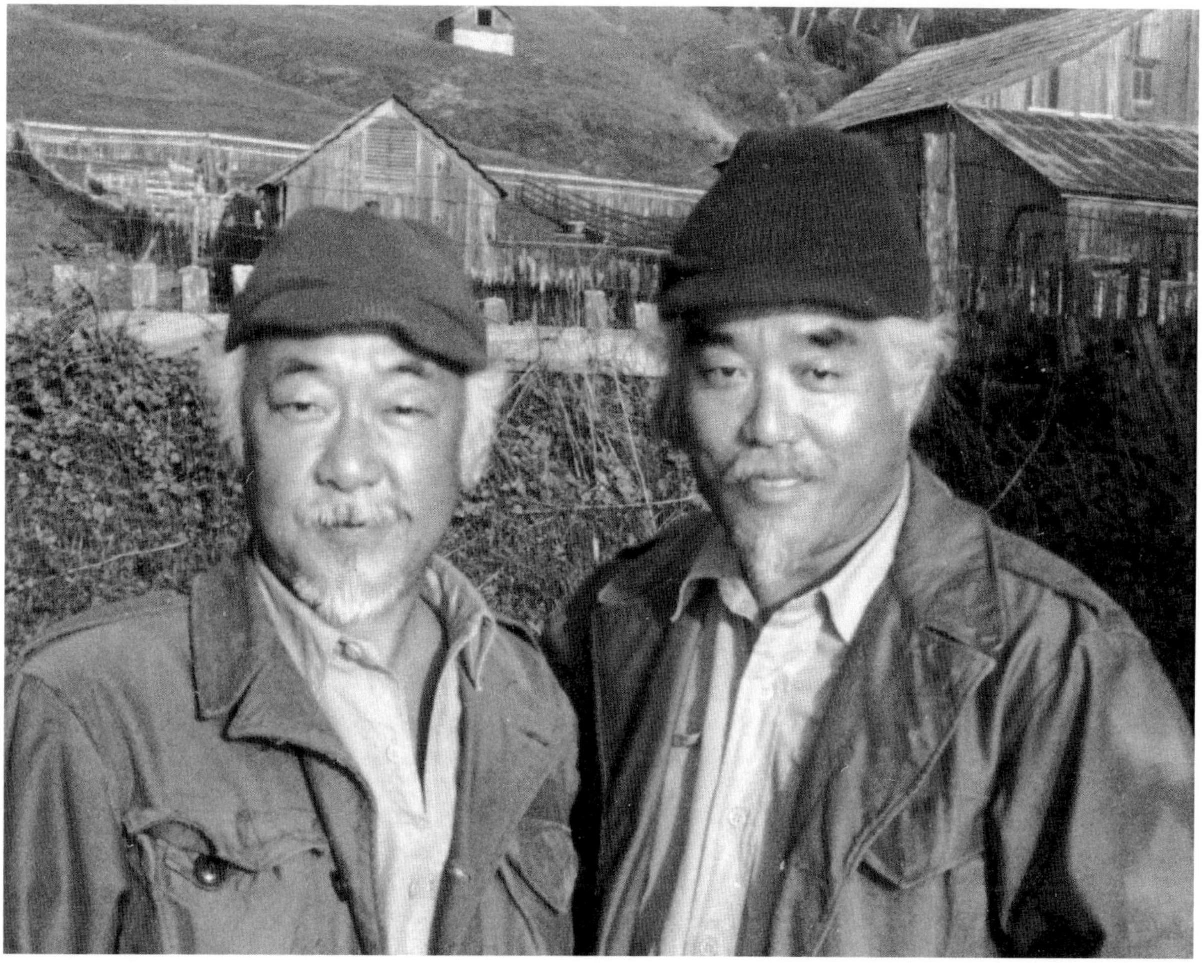

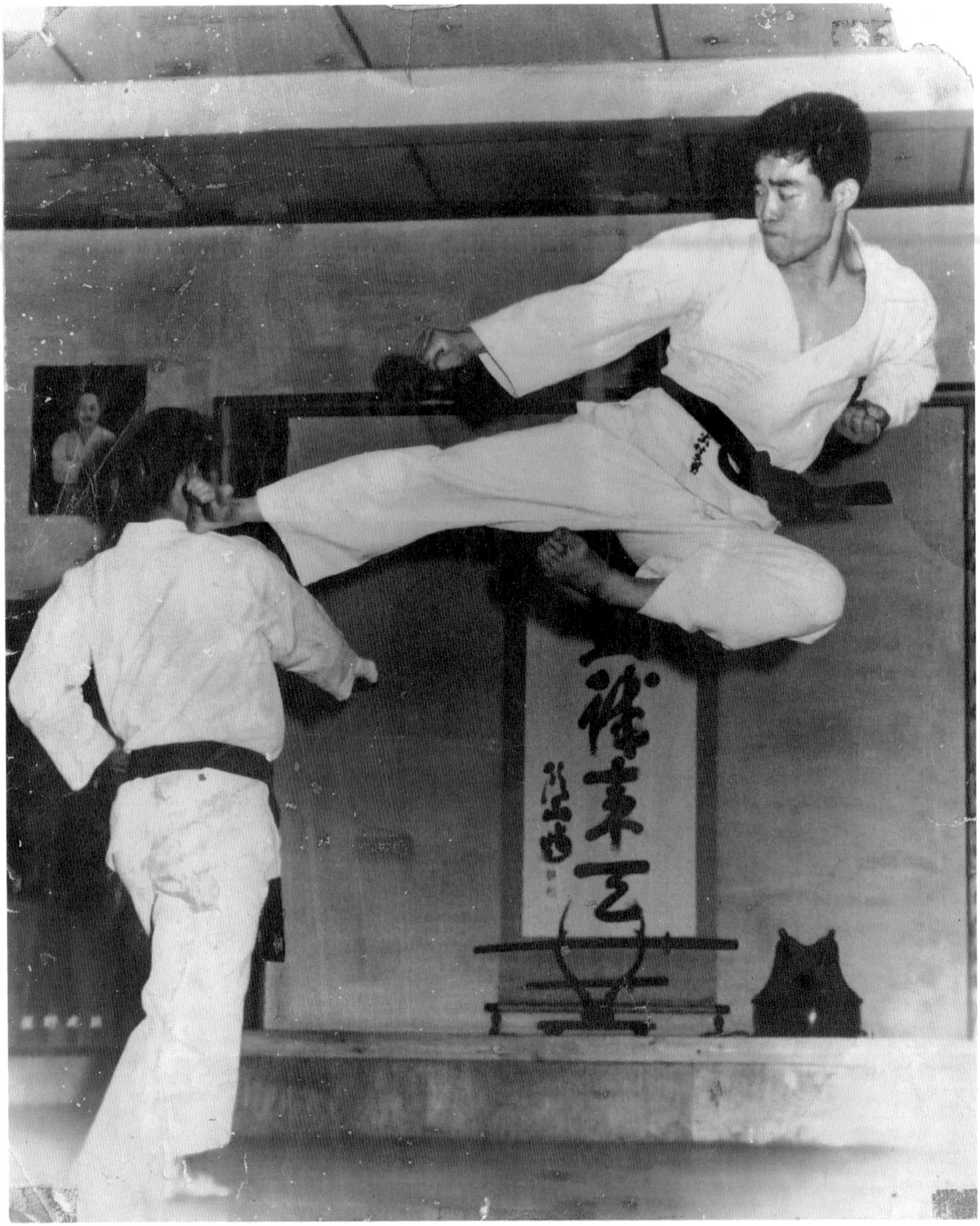

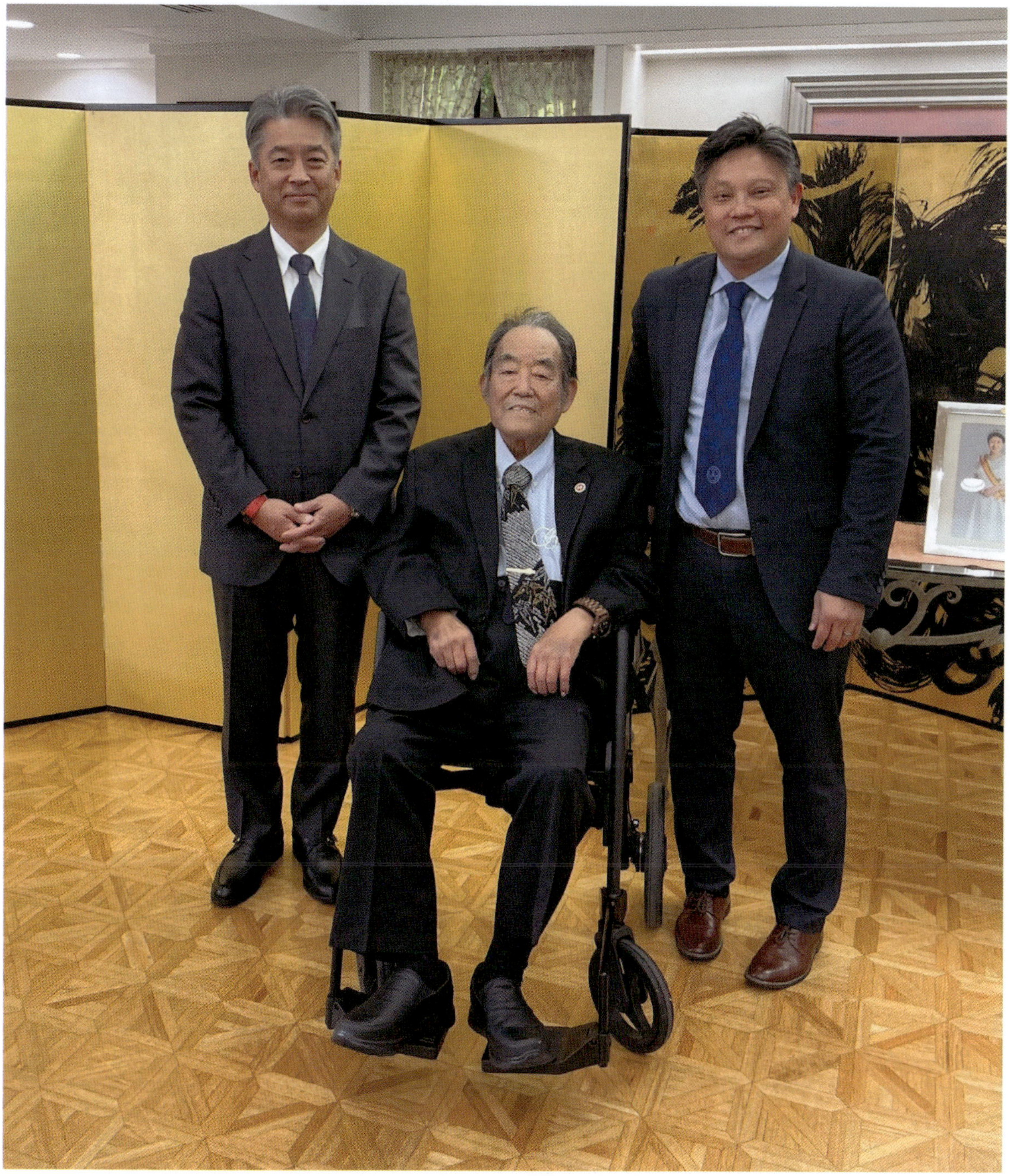

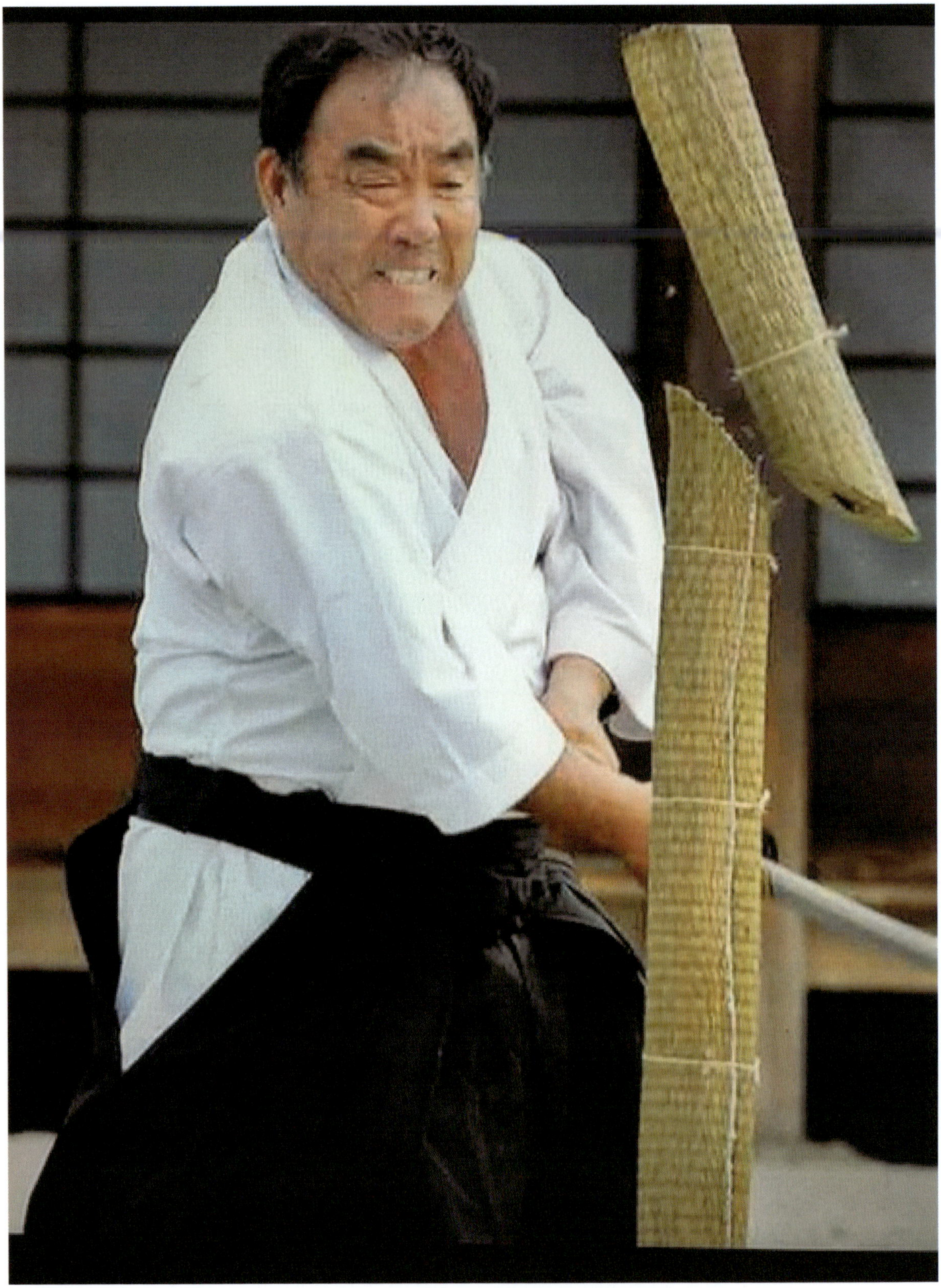

Sensei Thanh Nguyen

Sensei Thanh Nguyen has been a martial artist for nearly all of his life. As a 13-year-old youth, he began training with the internationally renowned Shihan Fumio Demura. Even as a teen, Mr. Nguyen displayed an extraordinary ability to both learn and develop his own expertise, and also to train others to help them develop their expertise. Over the last 35 years, Mr. Nguyen has trained in Shito-Ryu Karate-Do and Okinawan Kobudo (weapons), as well as Toyama-Ryu Batto-Do (sword), flourishing in the rich martial arts training environment provided by Fumio Demura, and demonstrating his exceptional abilities. As a leading member of the Shito-Ryu Karate-Do Genbu-Kai International and its affiliated organizations, Thanh Nguyen continues to expand his expertise, and devotes his time to training others within the organization and for other students, throughout the United States and all over the world.

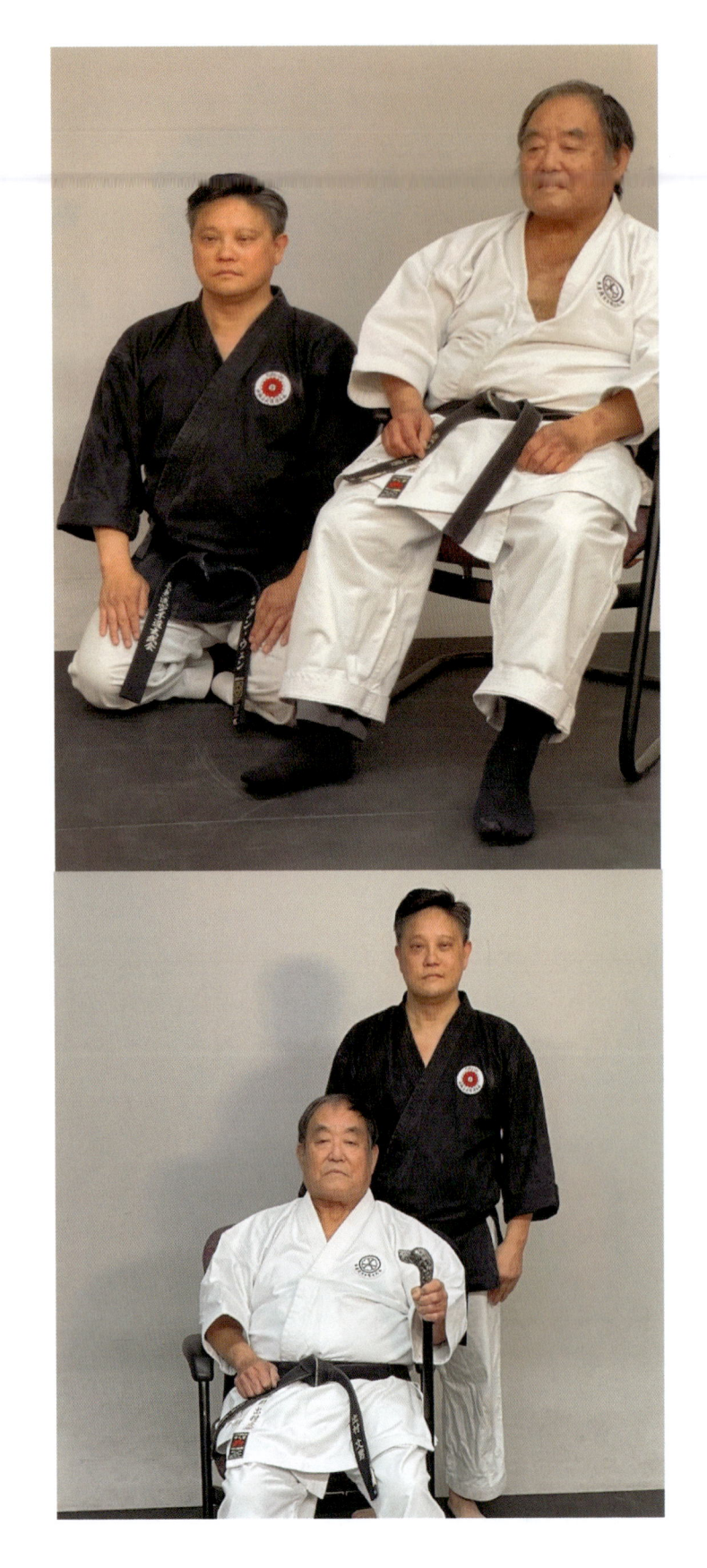

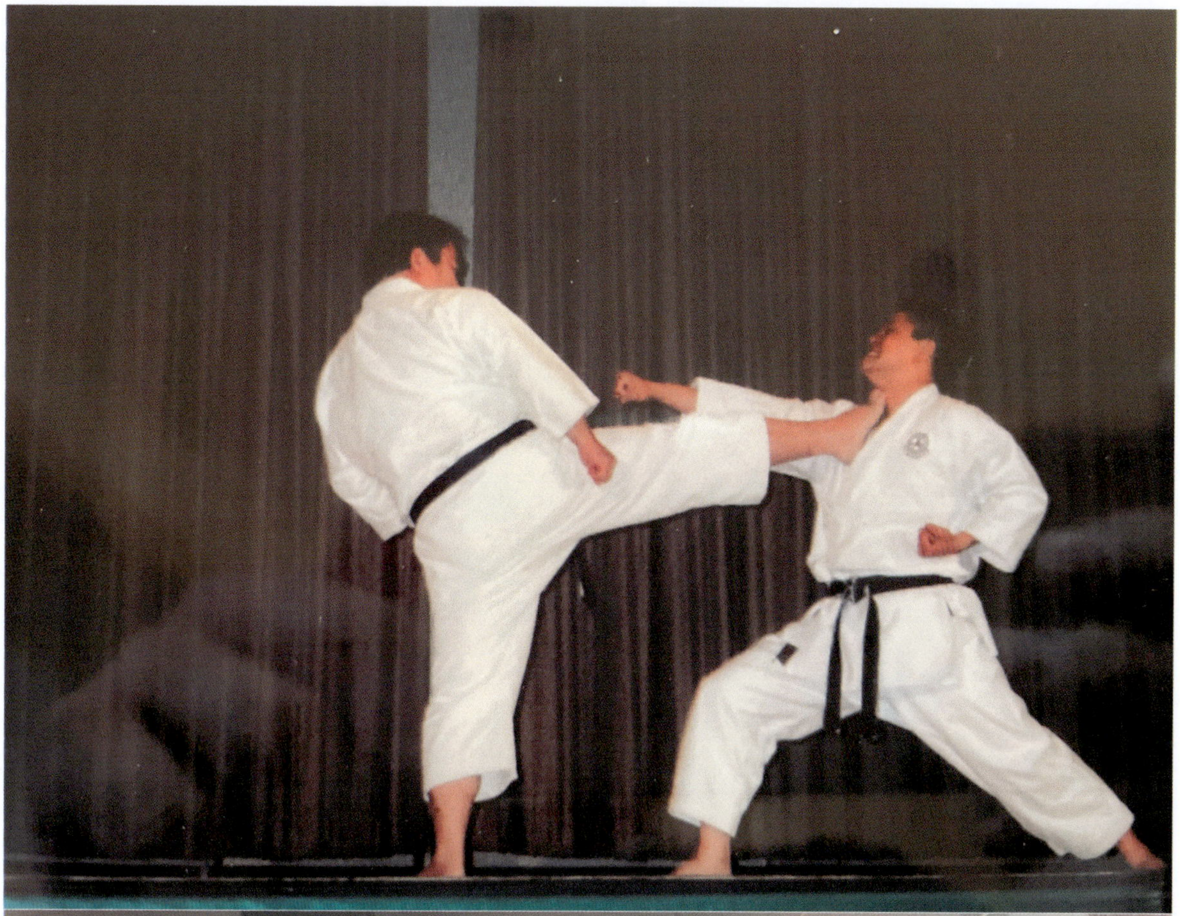

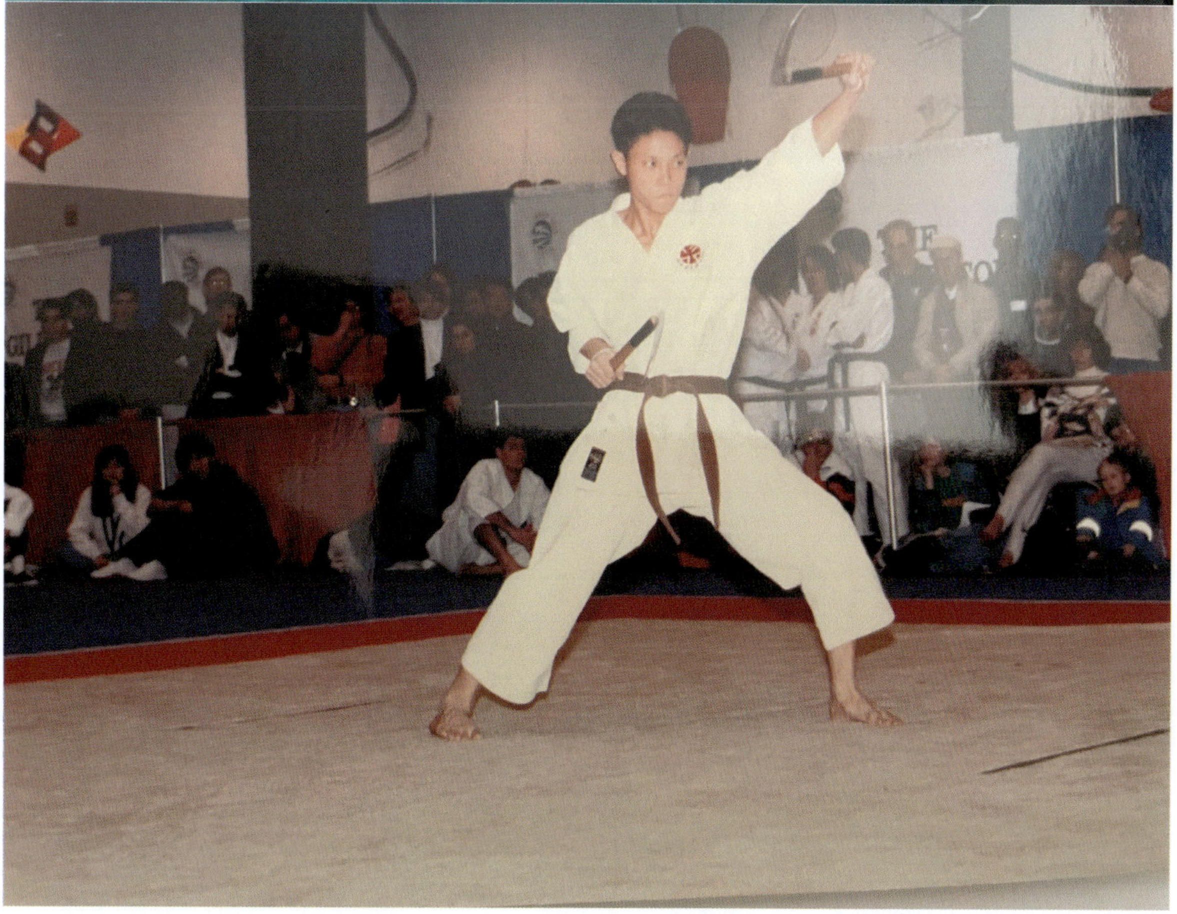

JAPANESE BUDO 武道

MAGAZINE #5 | JUNE 2021

THE BEGINNINGS OF KATA

A PHILOSOPHICAL LOOK AT KATA

LOREM IPSUM

LOREM IPSUM

INTERACTIVE

THANH NGUYEN

Following in the footsteps of my Master *FUMIO DEMURA*

Simon Kook

I previously studied and worked with Tony jaa for almost 20 years after that I turned myself into an actor and had the opportunity to work with iko and lewistan and many other films working with Tony jaa and other Hollywood stars. and had the opportunity to be invited to receive awards in many countries regarding the martial arts of Muay Thai.

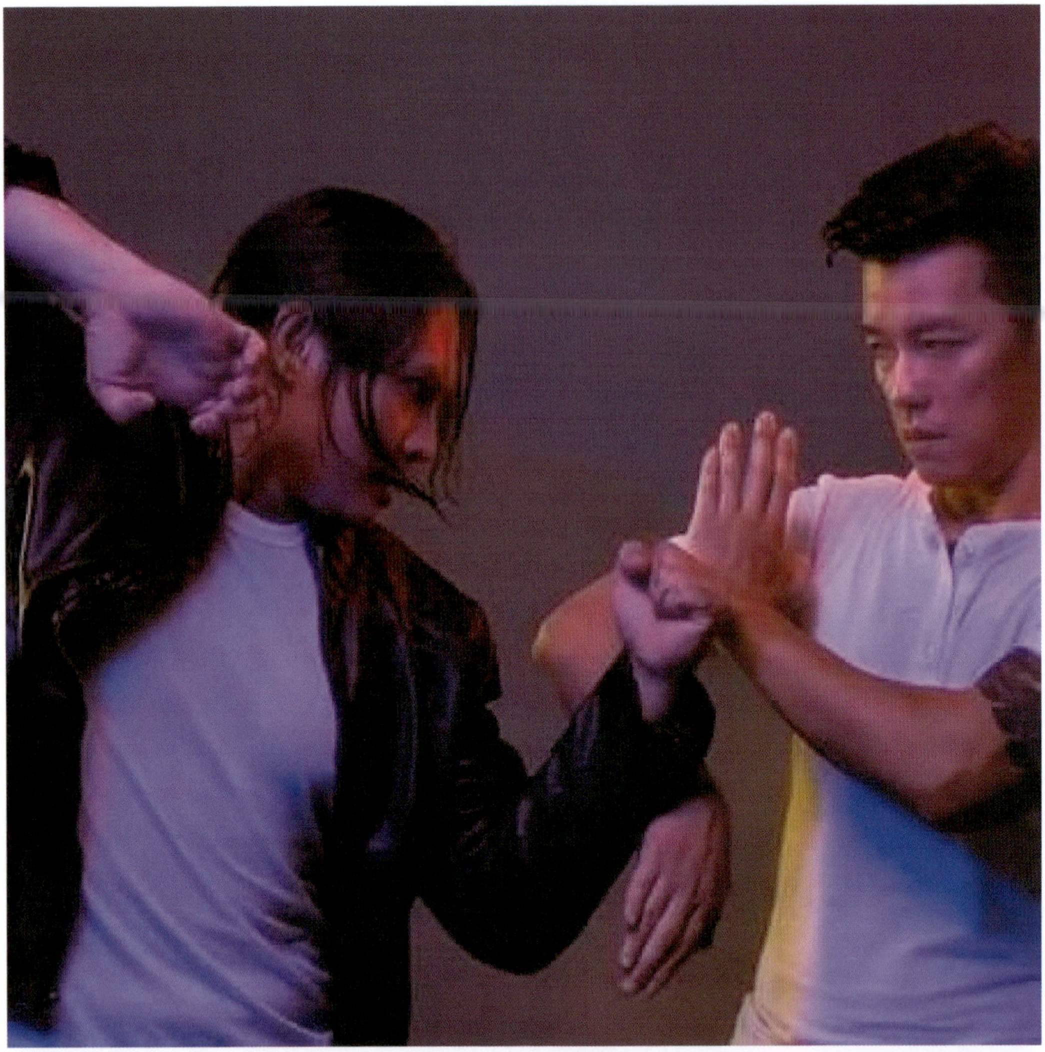

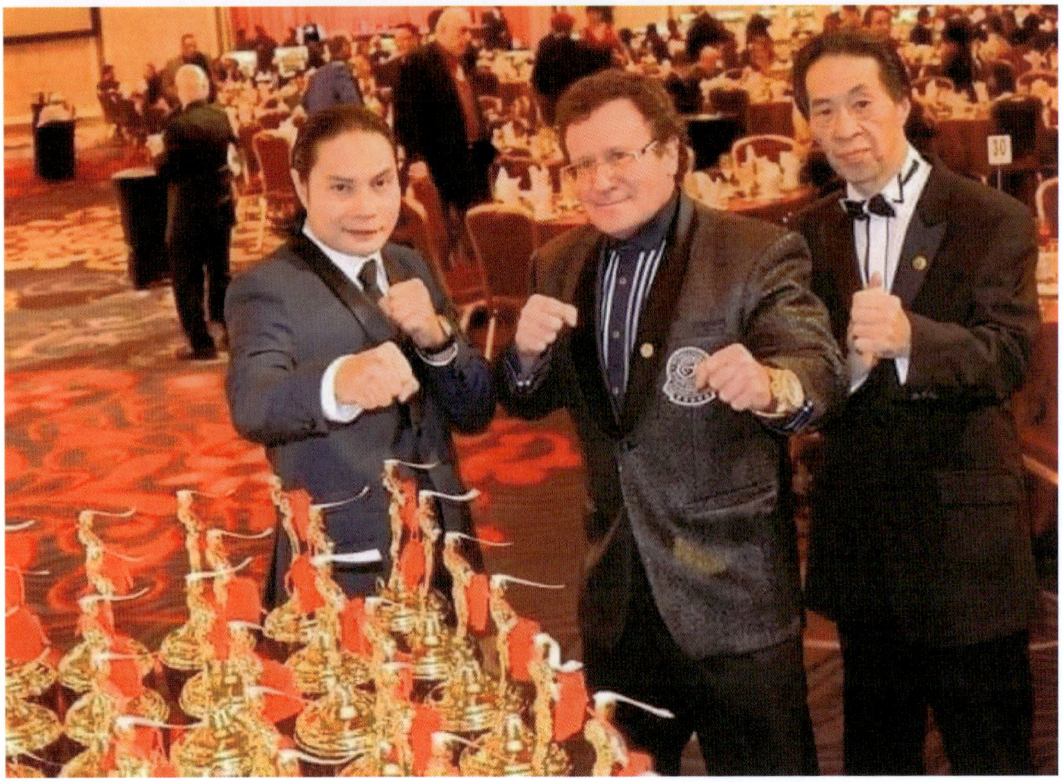

Samuel Kwok

My name is Samuel Kwok I was born in Hong Kong 6th April 1948 I have spent 45 years training and promoting the art of Wing Chun Kung Fu . Was trained by two sons of Ip Man and other students of GM Ip Man .Bruce Lee's teacher aim protect and preserve Ip Man Wing Chun . To improve people's health and help people to apply the principle and philosophy of Wing Chun in life. Went to more than 36 countries to teach , taught and trained many famous Martial Artists GM Rondy McKee , GM Cynthia Rothrock , Carl Van Metten Peter Constertine . World Champions like Paddy Monaghan , Quentin Chong . Worked and did joint seminars with Grandmaster Carlson Gracie (BJJ) . Taught famous director and stunts Art Camacho, actor Steven Seagal, Dr Robert Goldman, Action Actor Muay Thai fighter Simon Kook Crystal Santos etc .Was in the movie Assassin X (The Chemist) with Grandmaster Eric Lee Using pure Wing Chun Kung Fu and helped with Ip Man movie , documentary 40 years anniversary of Bruce Lee's Enter The Dragon . Author of 5 books and many DVDs . Made a Ip Man Wing Chun App to help people to learn Wing Chun Became inductees and revived many awards of varies Martial Arts Hall of Honours . Will be doing more action movies with Wing Chun in the near future .

©FOTOCROSS-ART
PHOTOGRAPHY

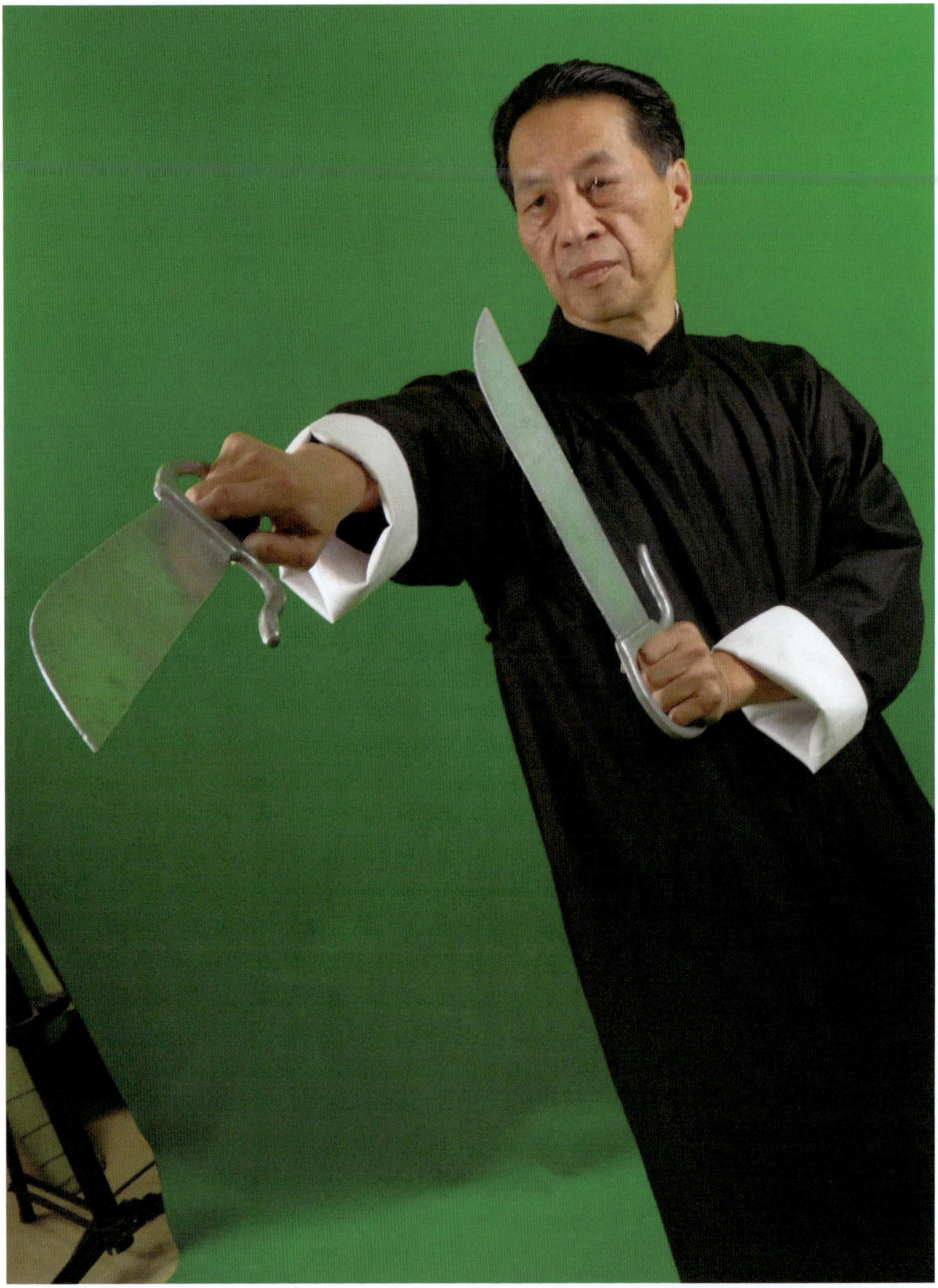

Lewis Tan

Lewis Tan is a half Chinese half English, film, television and theatre actor. He played as the series regular Gaius Chau on season three of AMC's "Into The Badlands" ; Lu Xin Lee on Netflix's first Asian American original series "Wu Assassins" and many films including the record-breaking Marvel film "Deadpool 2" and most recently the lead role in James Wans Warner Bros reboot of "Mortal Kombat"

Born in Manchester, England to a fashion model Joanne Cassidy and national champion martial artists Philip Tan. Lewis moved to Los Angeles at a young age as his father was making a mark on action cinema as a stuntman and fight choreographer working on legendary films like "Indiana Jones and the Temple of Doom", "Batman" and "Tango and Cash". Lewis began learning martial arts from his father while at the same time attending theatre school. Lewis had multiple honors in school as well as winning many amateur fights in kickboxing and Muay Thai.

After graduating Lewis began his professional career guest starring in TV shows from "CSI:NY", "CSI:Miami", "Hawaii 5-0" to his first major films including "Pirates of the Caribbean 3", and "Den of Thieves".

At the same time Lewis gained notable fame as a fashion model. He signed with Wilhelmina modeling agency and secured a contract as the face of Nivea in Asia for a few years doing numerous campaigns and commercials. He did many editorial ads including Diesel, Dolce and Gabanna, Puma and Levi's.

Lewis was then picked by Forest Whitaker to play the lead in the indie drama "Sacrifice", this was the start of his film career. The film won awards at many film festivals, it was then that Lewis received worldwide attention for his guest role in Marvel's "Iron Fist" where he played the drunken master "Zhou Cheng", the scene was top ten most paused Netflix moments of the year and the scene received a viral campaign with fans asking for a more prominent role.

Lewis is known for performing his own action scenes and got the attention of the show runners Al Gough and Miles Milar of AMC's "Into the Badlands", securing him a lead role in season 3 of the show, led by famous choreographer from "Kill Bill" and "The Matrix" Master Dee Dee. His role on the show and his action ability gained him more critical acclaim.

In 2018 Lewis began filming a lead role in Netflix's Asian American action series "Wu Assassins" alongside Kathryn Winnick and Iko Uwais. He plays the flamboyant gangster Lu Xin Lee, the show premiered to great reviews both with fans and critics.

Lewis continues to be a strong voice in the Asian American media as an advocate for diversity and original story telling.

In 2019 Lewis was cast as the lead role in James Wan's reboot of "Mortal Kombat" for Warner Brothers and New Line. The film was released April 23, 2021, in theaters and HBO Max on the same day. The film's trailer broke the record for most watched R rated film of all time and is the most watched WB film.

In 2021 Lewis will star in the Netflix action film "Fistful of Vengeance" and alongside Emma Roberts in the romance comedy "About Fate". He is also producing and starring in the spy series "Quantum Spy" with partner Tony Krantz and is in development for his first feature film as a director.

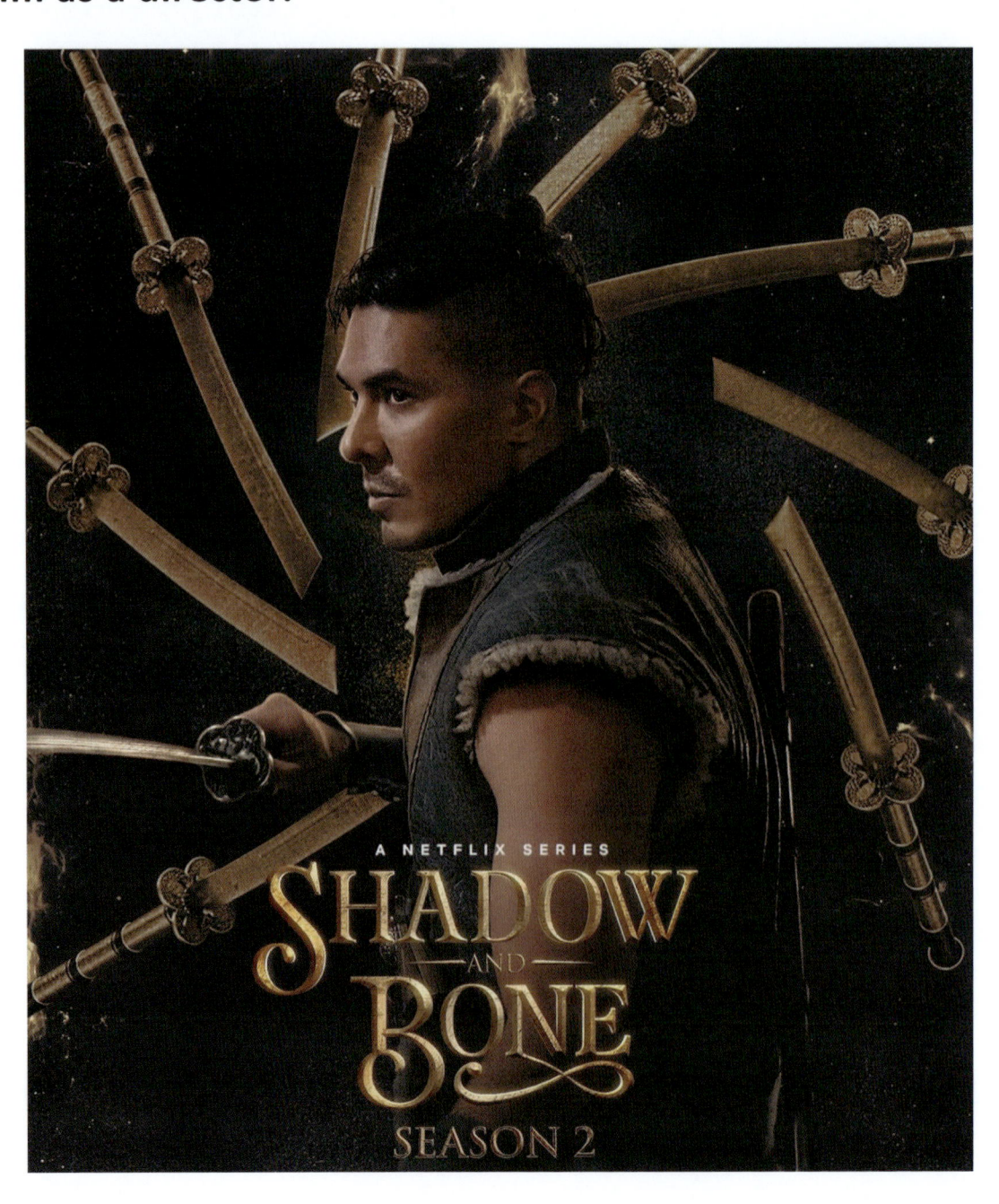

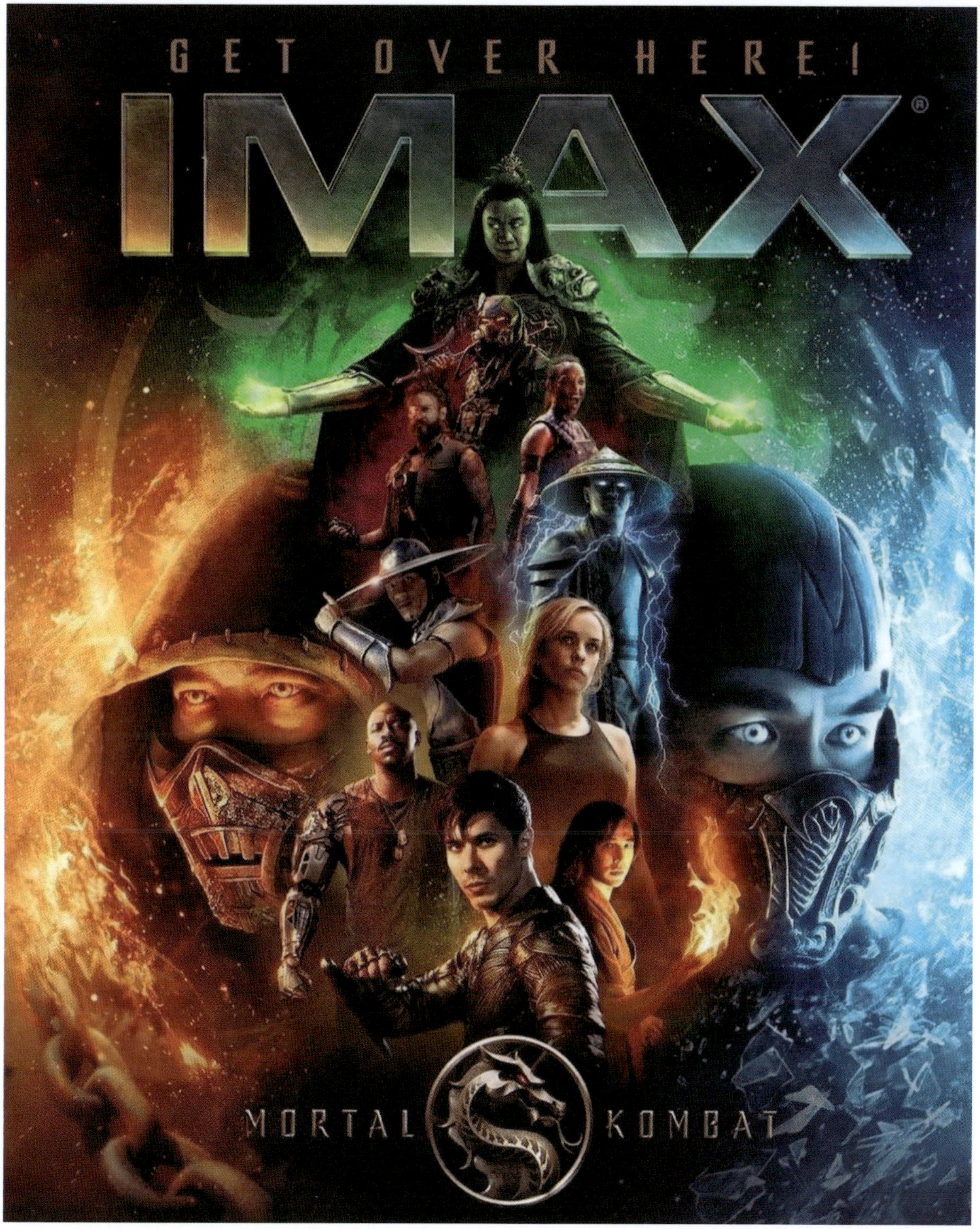
GET OVER HERE!
IMAX®
MORTAL KOMBAT

Steven lambert

Steven Lambert was born in Brooklyn, New York on October 28, 1954. He is the second of four children born to a housewife mother and a restaurant owner father. A second generation American, his grandparents emigrated from Russia to Ellis Island. He began studying the fundamentals of Shotokan and Tae Kwon Do at the age of 9. In the sixth grade he received the John F. Kennedy Award for Physical Fitness. At 13, his parents took him to his grandparents in Chatsworth, California while they returned to New York to prepare to move to California a few months later.

Blindsided by the move and in unfamiliar surroundings, he became directionless. He found a martial arts school so he could continue his Shotokan training for two more years, and then the school closed. By chance, he stumbled upon a Sil Lum Kung Fu Five Animal style Northern and Southern systems school, which later became the White Lotus system. The discovery of the school, and Kung Fu itself, became a life changing experience for Steven, and King Fu immediately became his passion, giving him focus and direction. Lambert soon reached the Master level along with expertise in Praying Mantis, Sticky Hands and several other styles.

At age 19, he competed in his last tournament as Hollywood had come knocking and he answered the door. He was discovered by casting agents after he took second in Weapons, Hand Forms, and Fighting divisions at a tournament. They asked simply, "How would you like to fight Chuck Norris?" Uncertain at first, he promptly changed his mind when he was offered $500 under the table for the opportunity. Since then Lambert, as a stuntman, has amassed 35 years of experience with a resume every martial artist dreams about. He has worked on some of the biggest films and with the some of the finest talent both in front of, and behind, the camera.

Steven Lambert has done stunts, choreographed, or coordinated countless movies including American Ninja, Revenge of the Ninja, Always, Indiana Jones and the Last Crusade, Dragon: The Bruce Lee Story, Remo Williams: The Adventure Begins, Casino, The Ocean's 11 Trilogy, Total Recall, Titanic, and most recently, White House Down.

He has worked as James Woods' stunt double for the past 25 years and has also worked alongside icons such as Arnold Schwarzenegger, Sylvester Stallone, Al Pacino, Harrison Ford, Sharon Stone, Richard Dreyfuss, Julia Roberts, and Jack Nicholson; martial arts legends including: Chuck Norris, Jean Claude Van Damme, Brandon Lee, David Carradine, Sho Kosugi, Michael Dudikoff, Steven Segal, and Jet Li; and directors including: Sam Firstenberg, James Cameron, Roland Emmerich, Paul Verhoeven, Richard Donner, Philip Noyce, Steven Soderbergh, Martin Scorsese and Steven Spielberg.

His work has garnered him with two Stunt Awards: one for Best High Work in *Remo Williams: The Adventure Begins*, the other for *Best Fight Sequence*. He was inducted into the Stuntman's Hall of Fame in 1986 and was a member of the Stuntman's Association for 33 years. He had the honor of appearing in the very first issue of Premiere magazine as well as appearances in *American Cinematographer* magazine, *Inside Kung Fu* and *Karate Illustrated*. Lambert also holds the distinction of the first stuntman to ever perform on the Statue of Liberty, only a stone's throw away from where his grandparents had first landed on Ellis Island two generations before in search of the American Dream. In looking back on his life and career, he paraphrases an old Chinese proverb

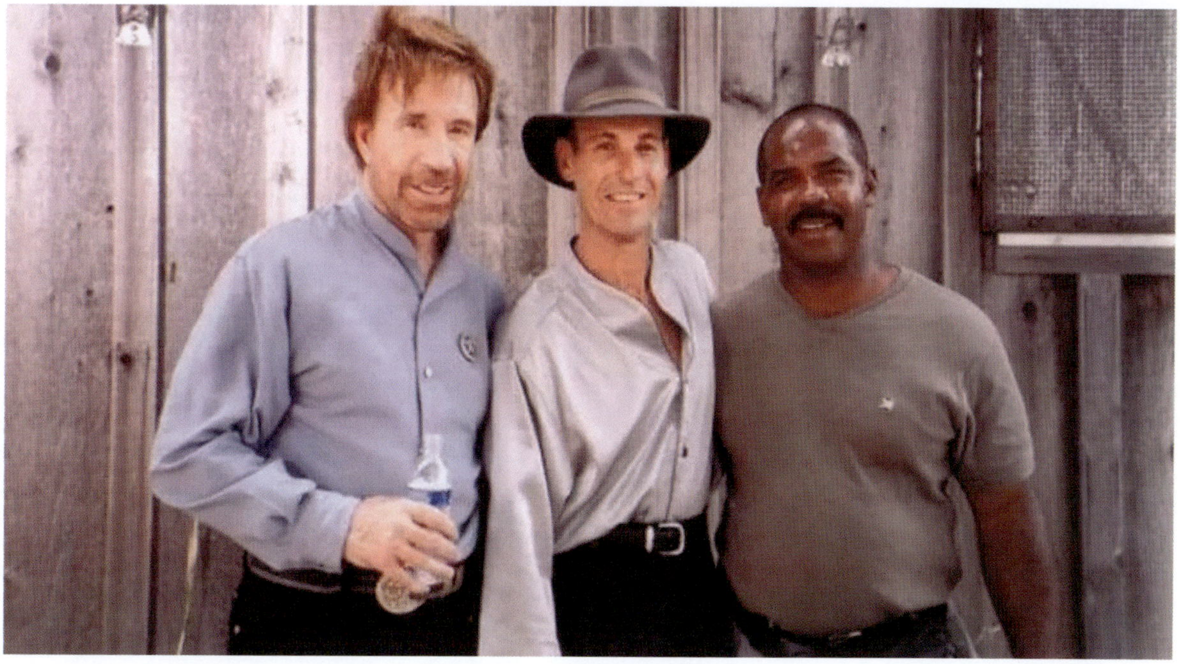

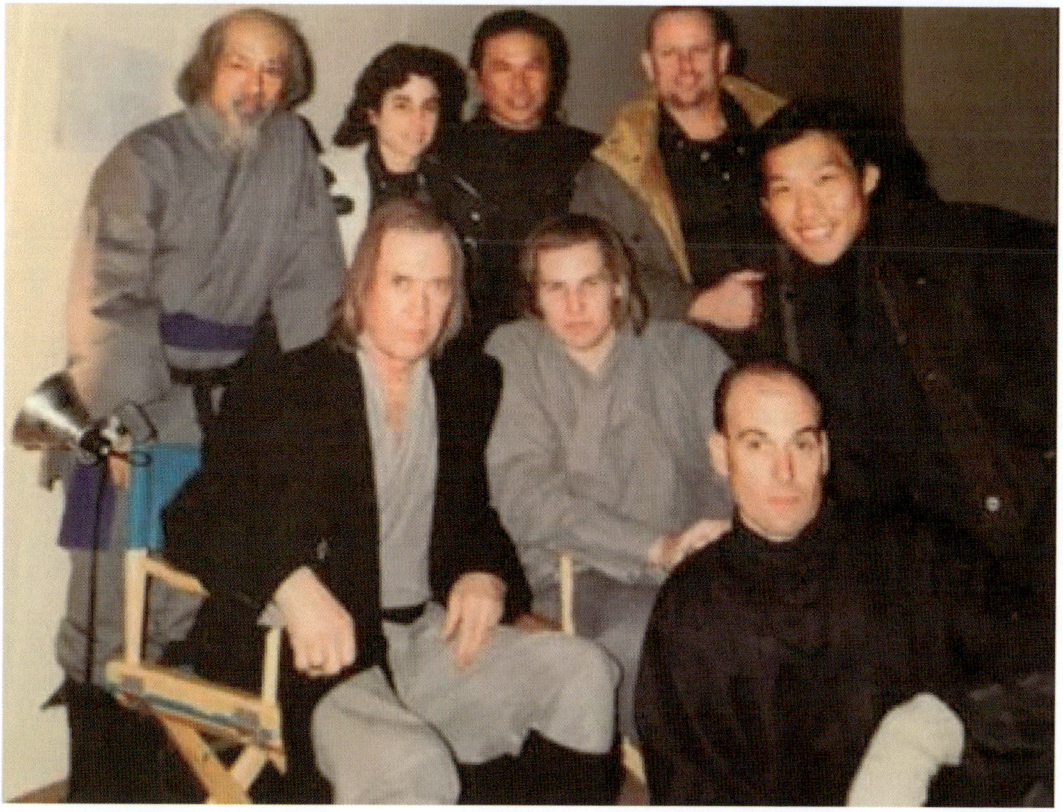

Steven Seagal

Steven Seagal is one of the most successful and renowned international action heroes in recent history, with over 40 movies, two major television series and more than $3 billion in box office revenues. Some of his films include *Hard to Kill, Marked for Death, Under Siege, Under Siege 2, Executive Decision, Glimmer Man, Exit Wounds and Machete.*

Seagal's success as an action movie icon derives from his real-world experience with special security operations and as a sworn Deputy Sheriff in three states. He is also an acclaimed producer, writer, martial artist and musician.

As a young teenager, Seagal traveled to Japan where he studied Zen and sought out every great master, he could find to perfect his martial arts earning black belts in Aikido, Karate and Kenjutsu. A 7th-dan black belt in Aikido and Karate, Seagal was the first foreigner to operate a dojo in Japan.

Seagal spent 18 years in Asia, studying Eastern philosophy, acupuncture, herbology, bone manipulation and choreographing martial arts fight scenes in movies. When he returned to the United States, he opened a martial arts academy and became a sought-after Master for other teachers and the like.

Agent Michael Ovitz introduced Seagal to Terry Semel of Warner Bros. who produced and distributed his first film, *Above the Law. Hard to Kill* soon followed along the unforgettable *Under Siege* and *Under Siege 2* where he played Navy SEAL counter-terrorist operative, Casey Ryback. Seagal made his directorial debut in the film *On Deadly Ground*. He followed with a dozen other action movies such as *Executive Decision, The Patriot, Glimmer Man, Exit Wounds* and Robert Rodriguez's *Machete*. He also starred in and produced the A&E Network's hit television series *Steven Seagal: Lawman* and Reelz hit series *True Justice*.

To date, Seagal has produced over 30 movies, acted in over 40 movies, written over 10 screenplays and toured with his Blues band throughout the world. A lifetime humanitarian, Seagal recently arranged an official U.S. Congressional

Delegation to Russia, including visits with top government officials.

Seagal has tirelessly devoted countless times and effort to various causes but with particular focus on children who are suffering. From Cancer to AIDS to Human Trafficking to Child Slavery, he continues to aid in the fight. He has also received major awards for Animal Rights activities that have made a difference and made two of the most important environmental films ever made.

Steven Seagal is currently working as a Special Representative and Envoy of the Ministry of Foreign Affairs of the Russian Federation.

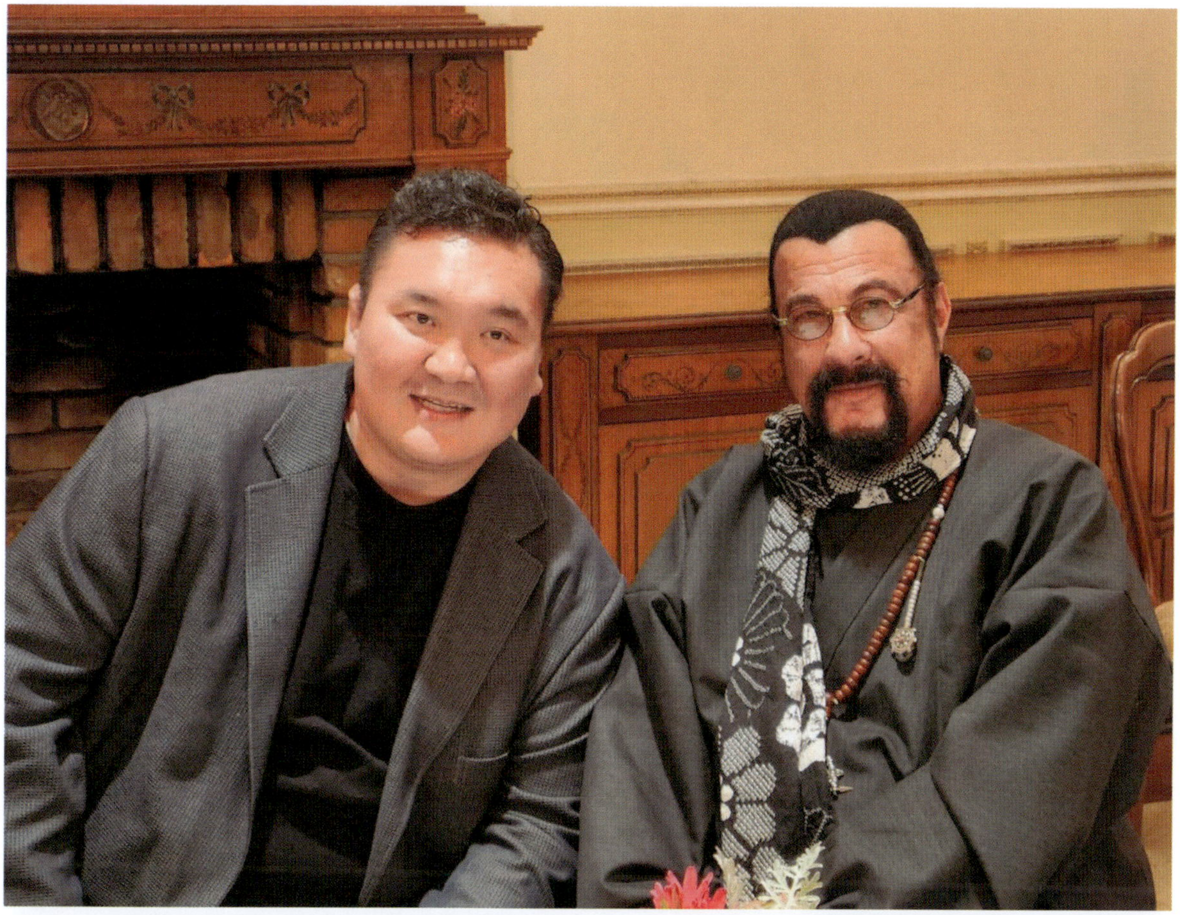

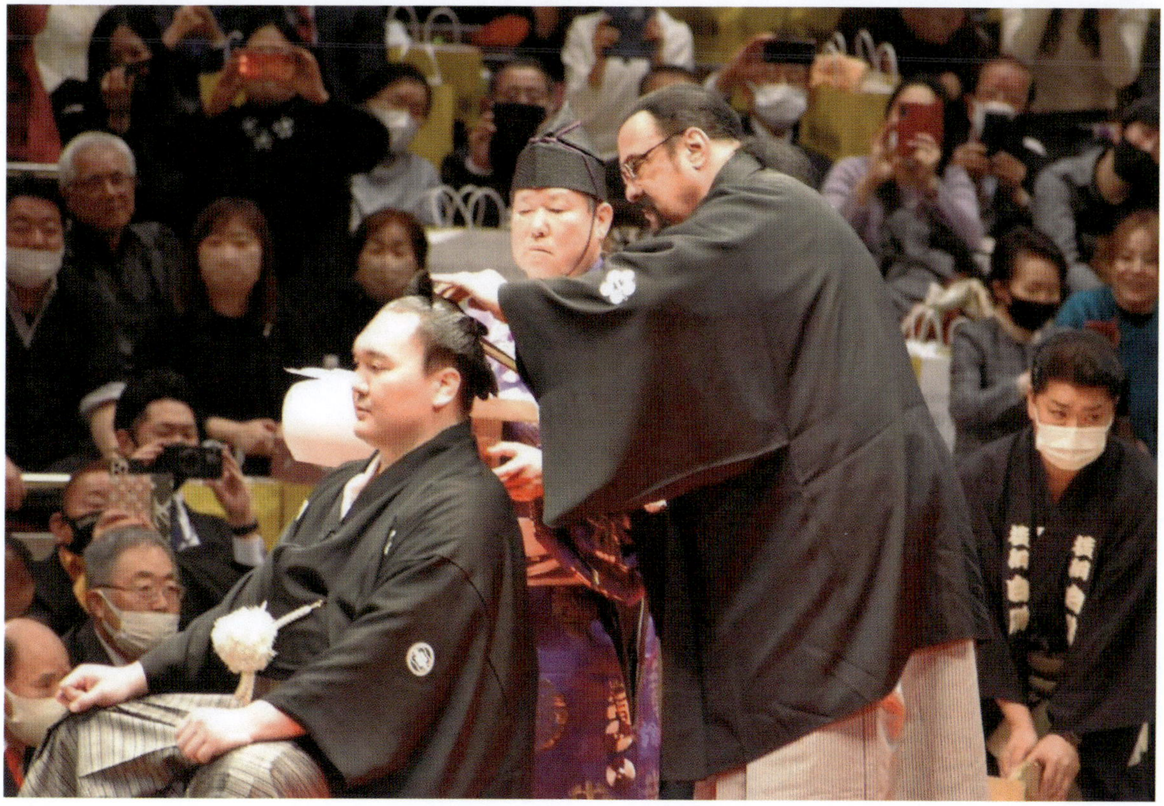

RON RON MURREY

The fighting arts have long been a passion for me. My grandfather was a professional boxer and my dad was a Judo Instructor and I grew up and probably held the record for the most fist fights in our community. It wasn't until my younger son Kyle took an interest in Martial arts that we began our formal training. Kyle was diagnosed with Autism and had many struggles in everyday life. He did not have the ability to speak or to interact with people. We enrolled him in a karate class. We did have many expectations but he did show interest and excitement. After several months of lessons, he began to make a remarkable transformation. He became much more alert and excited to go to classes. His instructor Shihan Tom Ingargiola informed us Kyle was learning skills at an incredible level and had us come in to watch his progress. Kyle went through his combinations and pinions with an incredible flow and ease. We were truly astonished. Within several months, a miraculous transformation took place. We witnessed his motor skills develop his social skills excelled and he began to speak. By year's end, he was able to go attend kindergarten class. Kyle continued to excel in karate and continued on to become the youngest blackbelt that the system has ever had. At only 9 years of age, he was granted permission to test for blackbelt as an adult and pass with flying colours. He continued to win many tournaments and competitions including 2 USA kickboxing titles and 4 other regional championship belts. He is currently a 4th Degree Blackbelt and continues as a Kickboxing Instructor. Looking back, did we witness a miracle? I say maybe we did. Something about his commitment to the arts magically transformed him and changed all of our lives in an incredibly positive way. When Kyle wanted me to join his kempo school, I readily agreed. Kyle's words were "dad please join karate, that way we would be able to do it together for the rest of our lives." I did indeed join the school. I happened to break my ankle within the first 10 minutes of class. Shihan Tom came to my house during my recovery providing me with tapes to watch and drills I could do while recuperating. Over the years, I have cherished the times spent with my martial arts family whether it was teaching self-defence seminars, kickboxing classes, competing in karate tournaments or working each other's corners in the ring. In 1999, Kyle and I branched out on our own and opened Kiaiki Dojo in Long Island, New York. At this point, my daughter Dorian began training and developing her fighting skills. We trained and began taking full contact kickboxing bouts in the ring. After attaining success with many good fights, we began of dream of possible kickboxing titles. With incredibly hard work and dedication, we pursued this quest with a vengeance. This resulted in Kyle Murray "Like Whoa" winning 2 USA championships and 4 other regional title belts. Dorian "Braveheart" Murray won 4 championship title belts and myself "Iron" Ron Murray collecting 3 world title belts. In 2008, I was inducted into the World Professional Martial Arts Hall of Fame by the legend Aaron Banks. To this day, I get to teach alongside my wife Tracy and we watch the transformation of our students before our eyes in our IKTA Kickboxing and Kempo Classes in Laguna Woods, California. Periodically, we hold belt advancement tests in our program and Kyle assists us during the belt testing. We remain that family that kicks together and sticks together through the wonder of Martial Arts.

Highlights –

- 2000 – Won Heavy Weight Division of the NE Kempo Continuous Point Sparring Championship
- 2000 – New England fought first bout on the card Kickboxing, remained in ring and fought the second bout boxing (won both fights)
- 2004 – Professional Kickboxing Federation Middle Weight World Champion
- 2004 – USKBA Super Middle Weight World Champion
- 2004 – Recipient of the Bushido Spirit Award from Kempo Master Thomas Ingargiola
- 2005 - Professional Kickboxing Federation Cruiser Weight Division World Champion
- 2007 – Professional Kickboxing Federation Light Heavy Weight World Champion
- 2008 - Inducted into the World Professional Martial Arts Organization Hall of Fame in Madison Square Garden, New York
- 2020 - Became IKTA California Director
- 2021 - Sensei Ron and wife Tracy began teaching IKTA Kickboxing and Kiaiki Dojo Shaolin Kempo classes in Laguna Woods, California

** Current 2nd Degree Black Belt in Kempo
***Current 3rd Degree Black Belt in IKTA

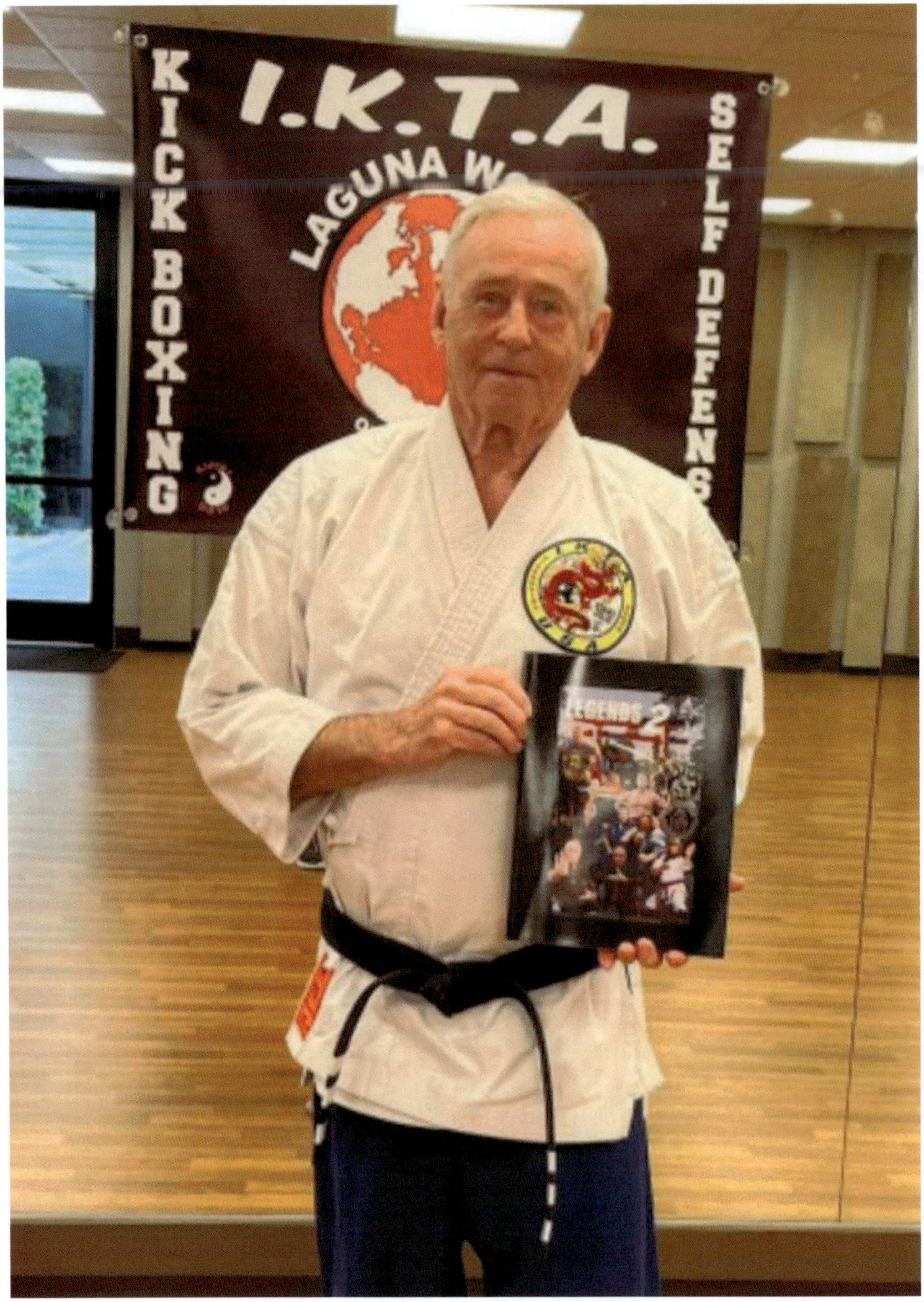
I.K.T.A.
KICK BOXING
SELF DEFENS
LAGUNA W
LEGENDS 2

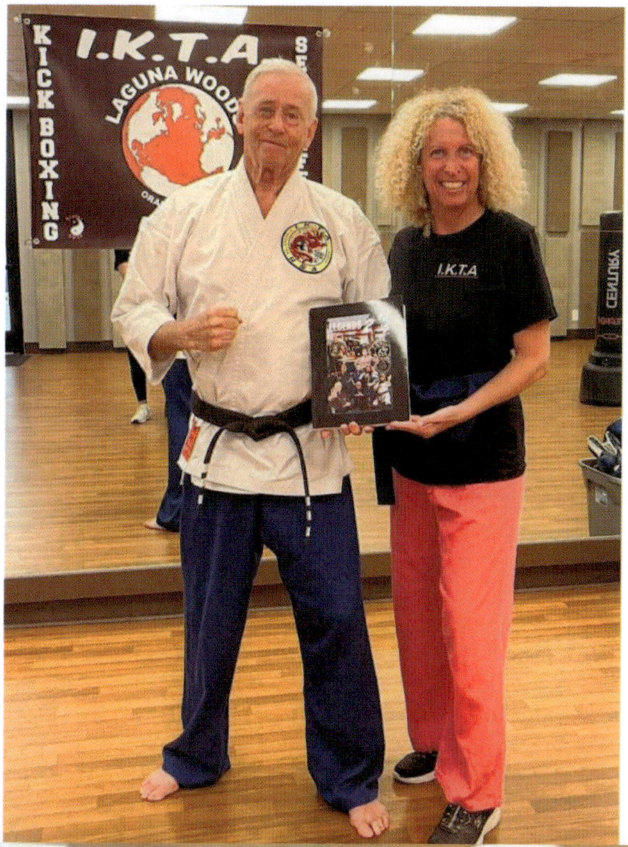
I.K.T.A
KICK BOXING
LAGUNA WOODS
I.K.T.A

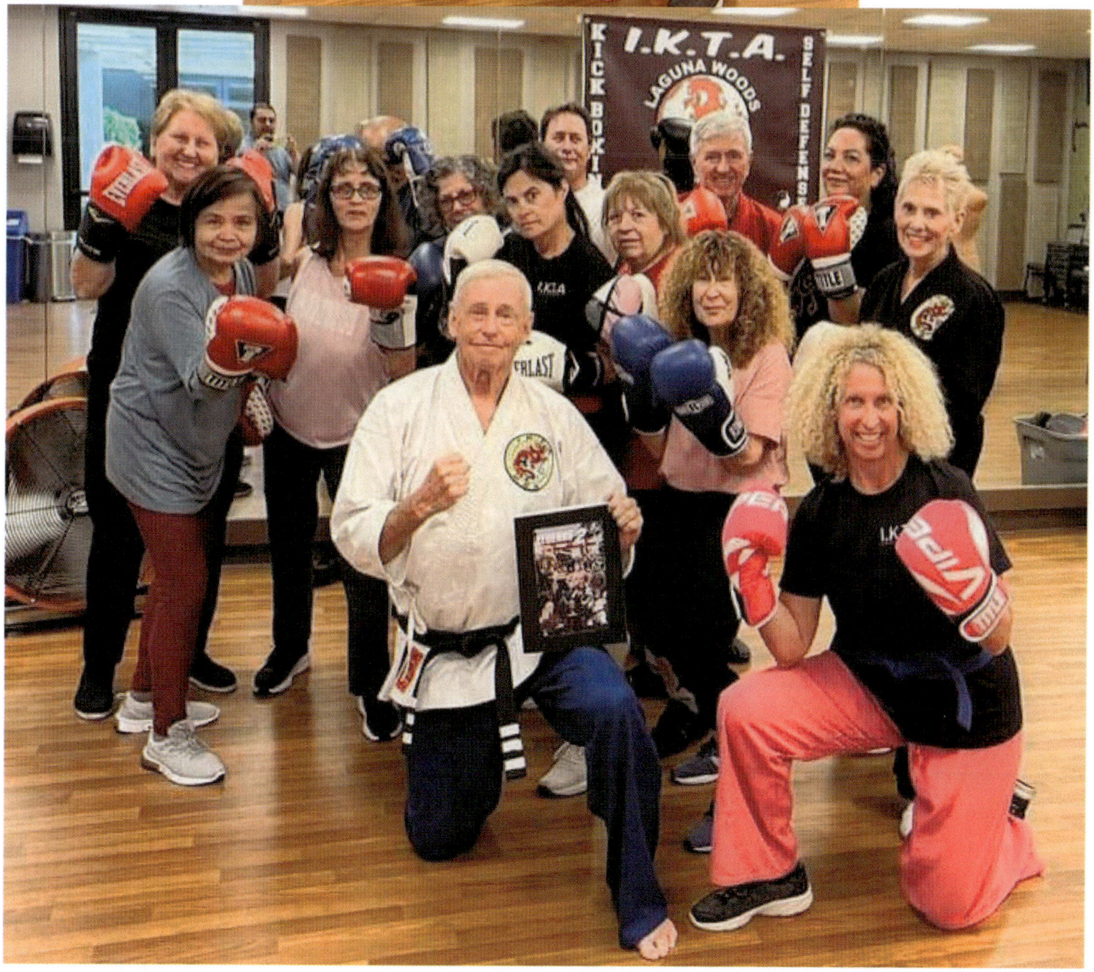
I.K.T.A.
LAGUNA WOODS

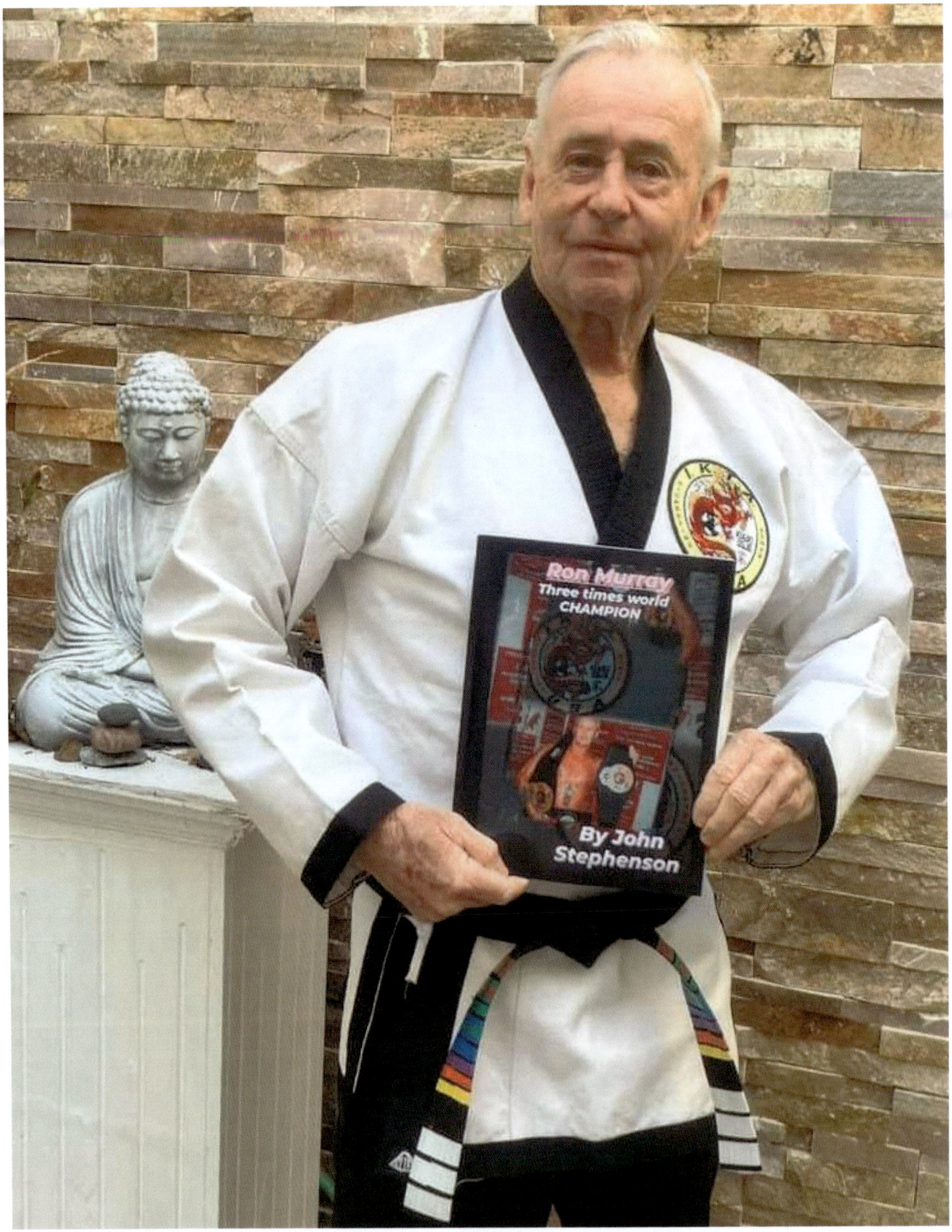
Ron Murray
Three times world
CHAMPION
By John
Stephenson

CHAD BLEVINS

In 1993 I started kickboxing with dreams of being the next Bruce Lee. In 1999 I was told to meet Rick Rossiter and train in the Burmese Martial Art of Bando. I competed in the American Bando Association nationals that same year and I won. That same Nationals, I met my future coach and a man I call my uncle and family in a man named Sam Jones. From 1999 -2007 I won 7 ABA national kickboxing titles and the Uskba Ohio state title. Later in 2007, I would become a team member for the New Jersey Tigers in the World Combat League. Over the next few years of competing professionally, I got the chance in 2015 to fight for the ISKA North American Kickboxing Title belt. I won the fight via tko in the 4th round. In this year, I'm hoping to compete In June for the WKPO World Title in kickboxing.

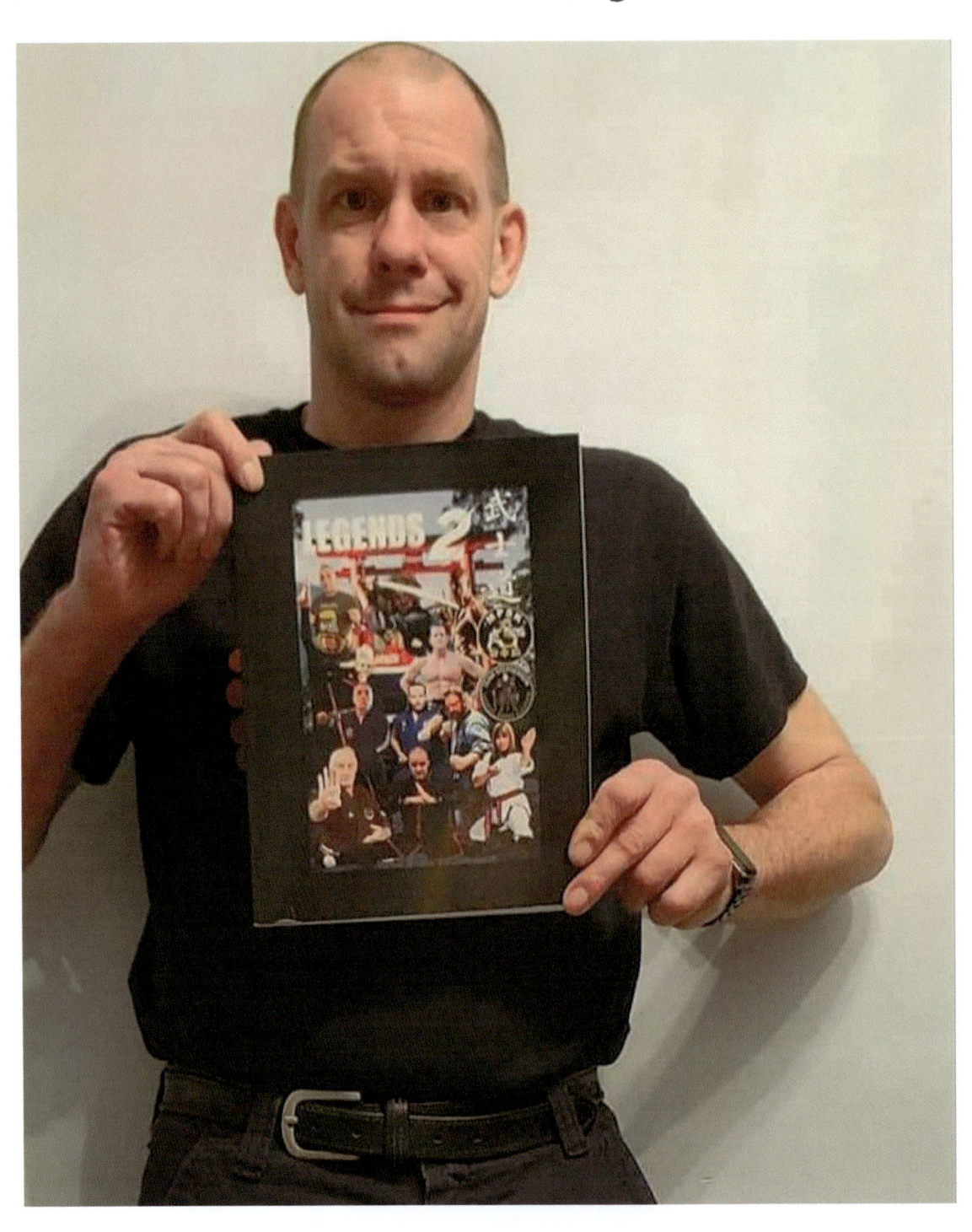

JAMES TURNER

James "The Dragon" Turner

James "The Dragon" Turner is the IKTA European Light Heavyweight Kickboxing Champion. As well as being an experienced professional fighter, James is an in-demand Kickboxing instructor, having just co-authored his first book 'Full Contact Kickboxing: A Complete Guide To Training And Strategies' with Andy Dumas, and being a regular featured seminar instructor at the UK Martial Arts Show, the biggest martial arts expo in the UK.

James is one of only four Black Belts worldwide to be personally certified by Massimo Brizi: legendary World Champion and Italia / Vice World President of the Intercontinental Kick Thai Boxing Association (IKTA). James represents the IKTA in the UK as its Great Britain President. As well as training extensively with Master Brizi, James has spent considerable time working with his friends, American Kickboxing legends Don "The Dragon" Wilson and Bill "Superfoot" Wallace, and regularly consults Curtis Bush and Sensei "Iron" Ron Murray, among others, who he is proud to call his close and trusted friends. When training for his international title fights, James combines the training methods he has learned from legends of Kickboxing, Boxing and the martial arts world at large, with his knowledge acquired through his degree in sports science to formulate a technical, physical and nutritional program to maximise his own skills and attributes. When in England, James trains himself, but acquires sparring partners, pad holders and trainers to assist him that he knows and trusts are of the required standard of quality. Additionally, James regularly travels to Italy to train under Master Massimo Brizi along with James' peers, Kickboxing Champions Alessio Crescentini and Andrea Rinaldi at IKTA Gym Civitavecchia, the HQ of the organisation in Europe. James has been recognised numerous times in the UK Martial Arts Hall Of Fame and is passionate about sharing his knowledge and experience with like-minded people who enjoy training and developing as martial artists. James teaches Kickboxing at the Absolute MMA Gym in Cornwall, England; working alongside Master Mohammed M. Afzal, Scott Paterson and the other 'Absolute MMA' instructors to provide a first class martial arts learning and training experience for all. As well as his martial arts and fitness knowledge/skills, James is also a trained and experienced actor and singer. James is an avid enthusiast of the iconic American Chevrolet sports car, the Corvette. Expect to see him arrive at a martial arts event near you in his 1992 red Corvette C4!

James is honoured to be selected by Master John Stephenson for inclusion in 'Legends' Vol. 2, and would like to thank Master Stephenson and all in the martial arts for their support as he continues the quest to achieve his ultimate goal: IKTA World Champion!

CERTIFICATO
I.K.T.A.
CERTIFICATE
REPRESENTATION
PROFESSIONAL
EUROPEAN CHAMPION
LEGENDS 2
HALL of FAME
2022

FULL CONTACT
KICKBOXING
A complete guide to training and strategies

AMANDA WILDING

Jeet Kune Do Instructor

My first experience with martial arts came in 2006. When I went along to a class as moral support. I totally fell in love with it on my first lesson and never looked back. I continued to attend the classes Even through my divorce, training In the class with my ex-husband even though we didn't speak. I found a strength inside of me to keep attending as I was addicted to the training and couldn't imagine not being able to train, it's where I found myself. It became my journey. I have been honored to have been mentored but some of the best martial artists around, I was honoured to be taught by Sigung Richard Bustillo who was the owner of the IMB in California and was a student of Bruce Lee. This was one of the highlights of my training. I had the opportunity to train yearly with him when he was in the UK. Over the years he was not only an idol and a teacher he became my friend. His guidance and support were one of the reasons I opened up my own training class. Since Richards passing I have been fortunate to continue my IMB journey with the mentoring of Steve de la Cruz, who has taken on the IMB in California. The IMB has been the core of my training, Andy Gidney who is the IMB Instructor in the UK has been one of the most supportive mentors, he has helped me every step of the way and in the process has become one of my good friends. I've had the privilege to train under some of the best instructors in the UK. Mo Teague, Chris Kent, Eddie Quinn, and Geoff Thompson, these instructors have also been big influences in my life, these guys have helped me so much. Another big influence on my martial arts training was Antony Pillage, who is no longer with us, he gave me his time and friendship. Both Tony and Richard helped to motivate me in setting up my own classes. They supported me, advised me, and encouraged me when I didn't think I would be able to do it. These guys gave me the courage that I needed, and I will be forever grateful for that. Warriors Within Martial arts started in April 2017 which started with adult classes, based in Belper Derbyshire. Which was to teach my interpretation of Bruce Lees Jeet Kune Do. The class focused on the techniques, principles, and concepts of Jeet Kune Do. The class also incorporated elements of boxing, kickboxing, wing chun, self-defense, and weapons. I've been fortunate to host special guests Mike and Steph Knight, Nasser Butt, and Steve Timperley. Lee Bown and Rob Watson. In my journey, I've had the pleasure of meeting, training, and forming relationships with some amazing people.

In my journey I've achieved awards in :

2017 British Martial Arts Award

2018 British Martial Arts Award Overcoming Adversity Female Runner Up

2019 British Martial Arts Award woman of the year runner – up

2019 British Martial Arts Award To Recognise their achievements in overcoming extraordinary challenges within the field of martial arts.

2019 International London Martial Arts Hall of Fame Instuctor Award

2020 International London Martial Arts Hall of Fame Spirit Award

2021 International London Martial Arts Hall of Fame Masters Award

2022 UK Martial Arts Hall of Fame

2023 UK Martial Arts Hall of Fame

Im presently doing a degree in Health Sports, and Fitness.

Being a woman in the martial arts world is tough, it takes a lot of dedication and training to be able to prove that you deserve to be there. Over the years I've trained in the circuit of marital arts, you see a lot of women attend but don't carry on, you saw a handful that will see it through. My journey has taught me that whatever you put your mind to you can achieve, it may take a bit of time, and it may be hard work, but you only get back what you put in….

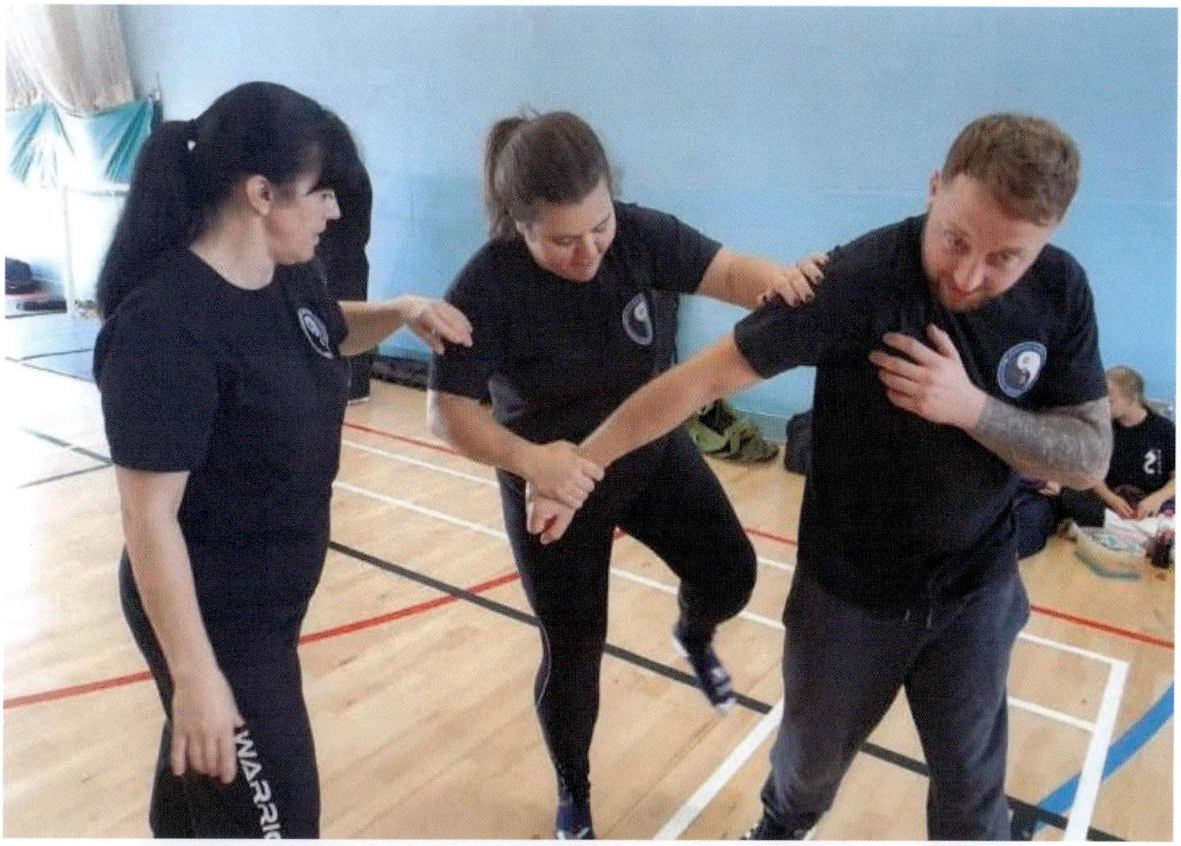

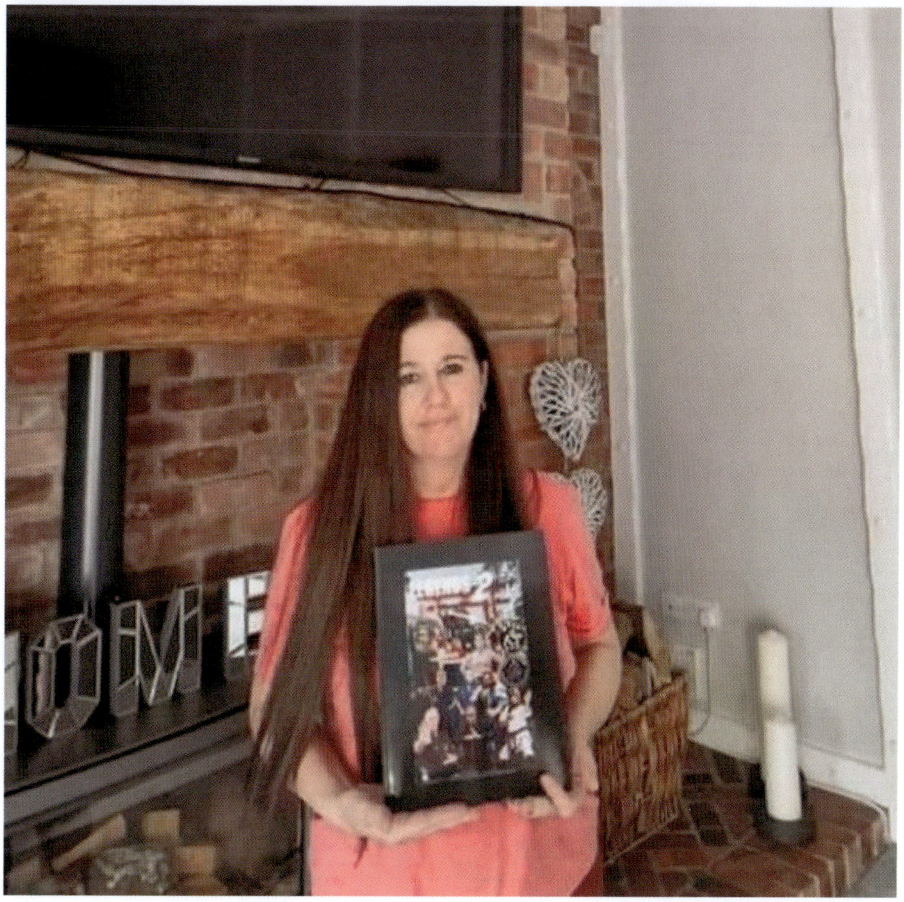

DEAN TANYA WILLAIMS

Dean Williams Welsh Road Warrior born and bred in Merthyr Tydfil Wales. Started boxing at age 8 1980. Welsh National Champion! 2001 Cruiserweight World Boxing Federation champion. Was a sparring partner for legends Larry Holmes, Thomas "Hit man" Hearn's, Tim Witherspoon, Saoul Mamby and many other Champions! Trained and worked with Manny Steward, Kevin Rooney, Hector Roca and more.! Was part of team Drago in the blockbuster movie Creed2! Worked with Dolph Lundgren, Sylvester Stallone & Michael B Jordan."

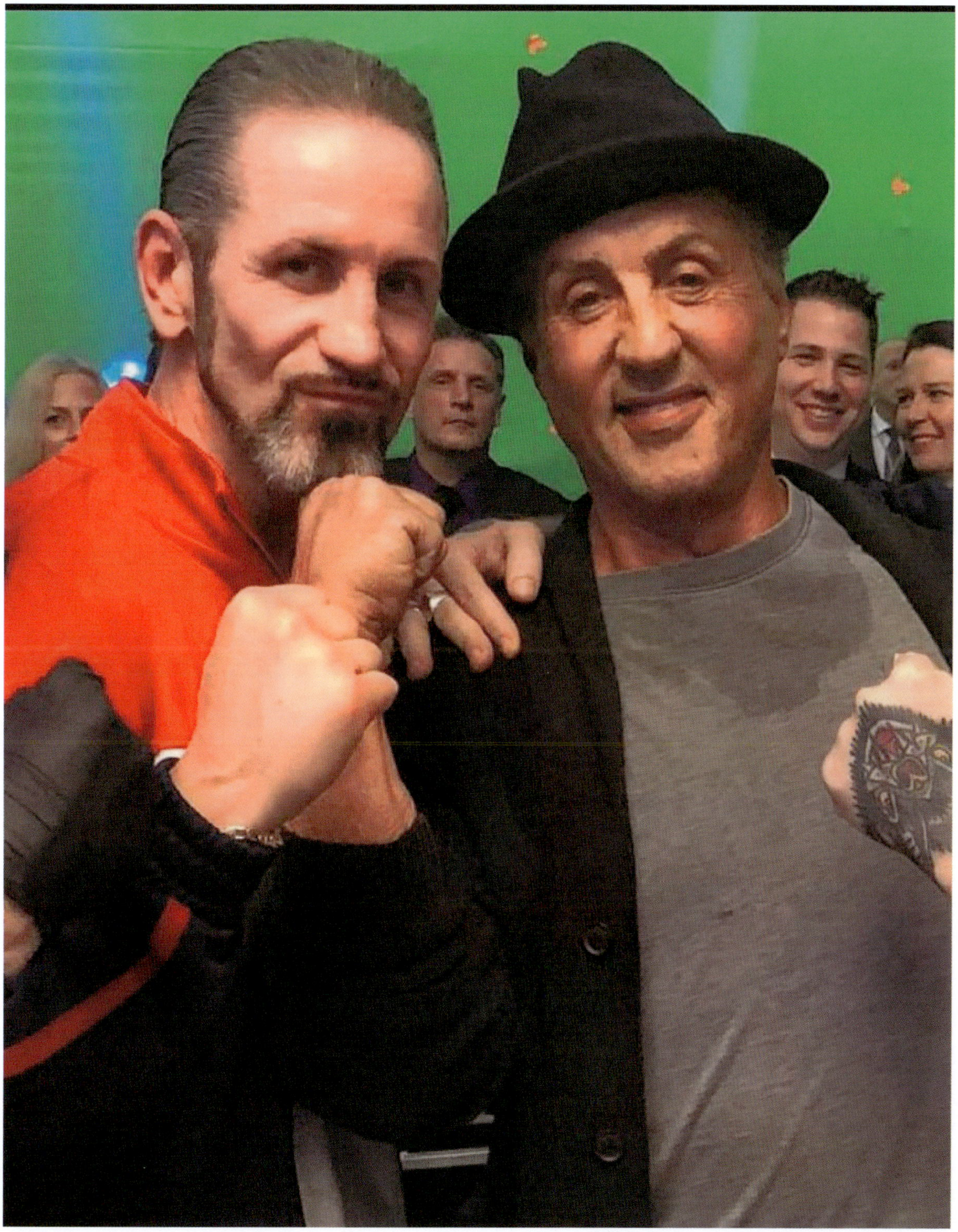

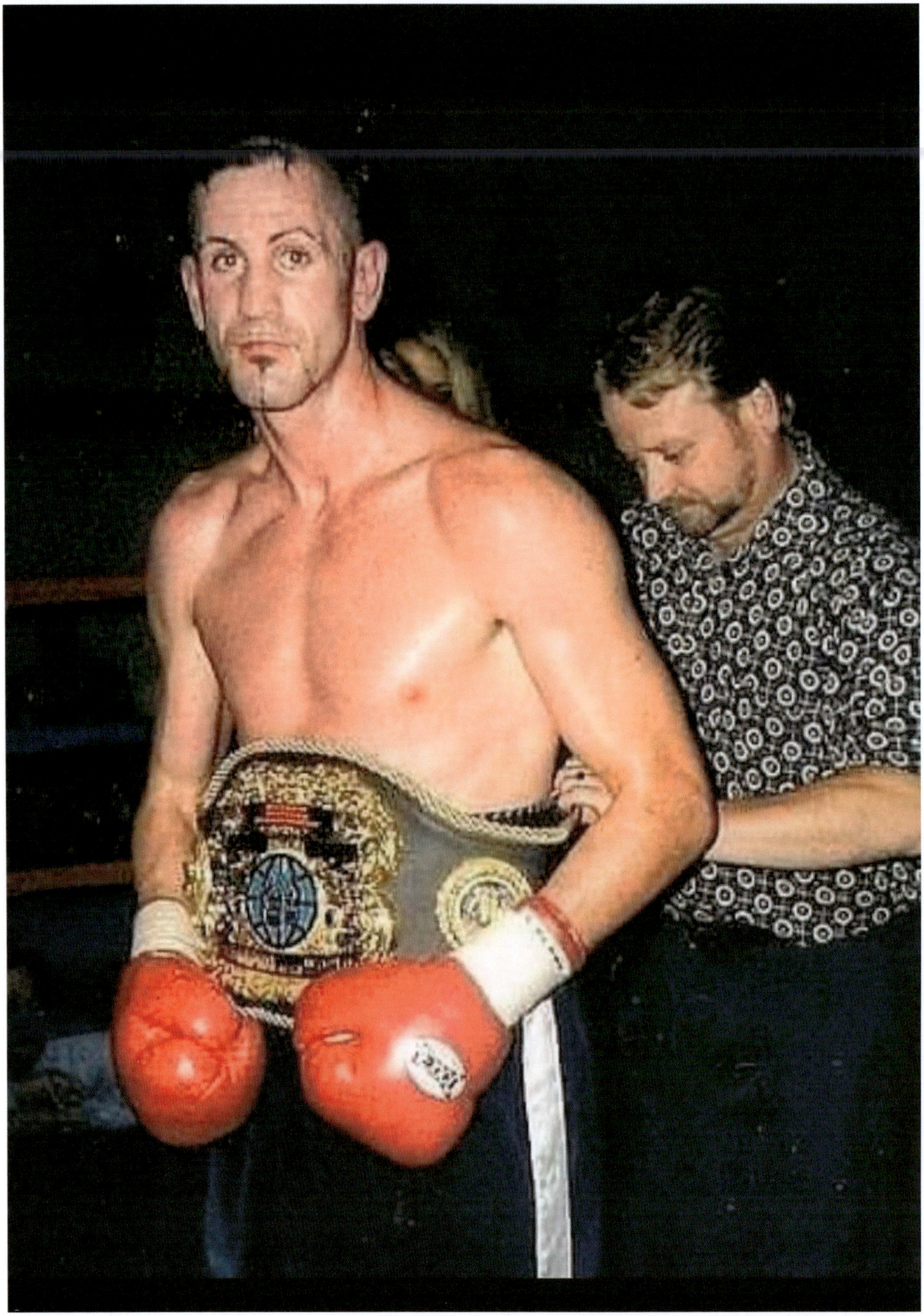

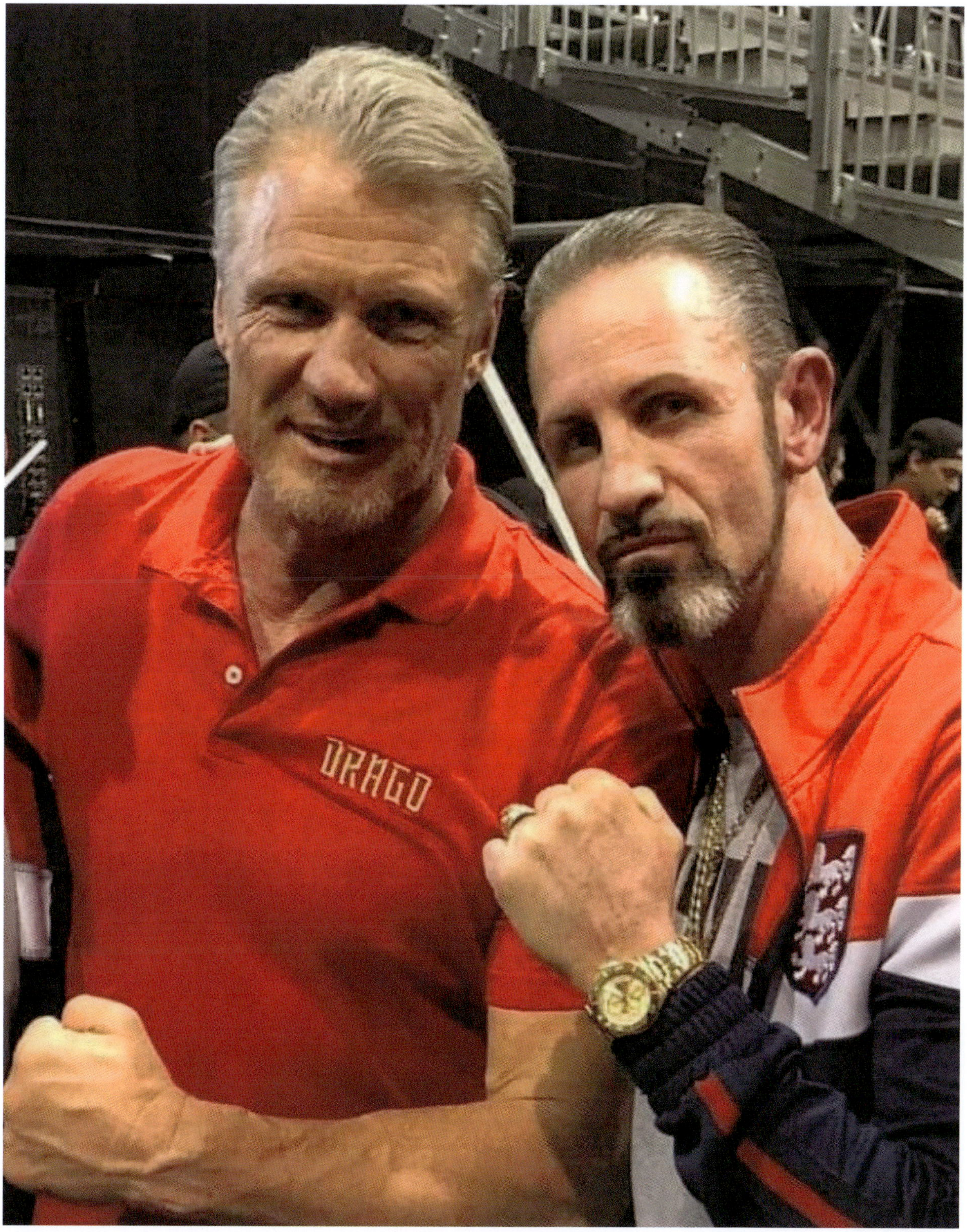
DRAGO

COLIN BOXSHALL

Started training in 1983 age 14
First Dan grade in Wado Ryu Karate aged 18
Started kickboxing at 19
and then TKD with the TAGB under GM Kenny Walton.
Competed until 2018 retired at 50 years old due to injury.
Won 15 World Titles in Karate, Kickboxing & TKD
Sparring Patterns/Kata
36 National/British/UK title & 7 European.
Dan grades in three different styles
Now runs Humberside Tae Kwon Do in Grimsby Lincolnshire.
Still with the T.A.G.B.
Enjoy training the students and helping them achieve their goals.

Loves meeting Famous Martial artists & Film Stars.

I have my Kumite gloves from my last world title win in 2018.
Signed by karate legends Chuck Norris and Dolph Lungren.

HUMBERSIDE
TAEKWONDO
태권도

1984 ALL VALLEY
KARATE

HUMBERSIDE
TAEKWONDO
태권도
空手

HUMBERSIDE
TAEKWONDO
태권도

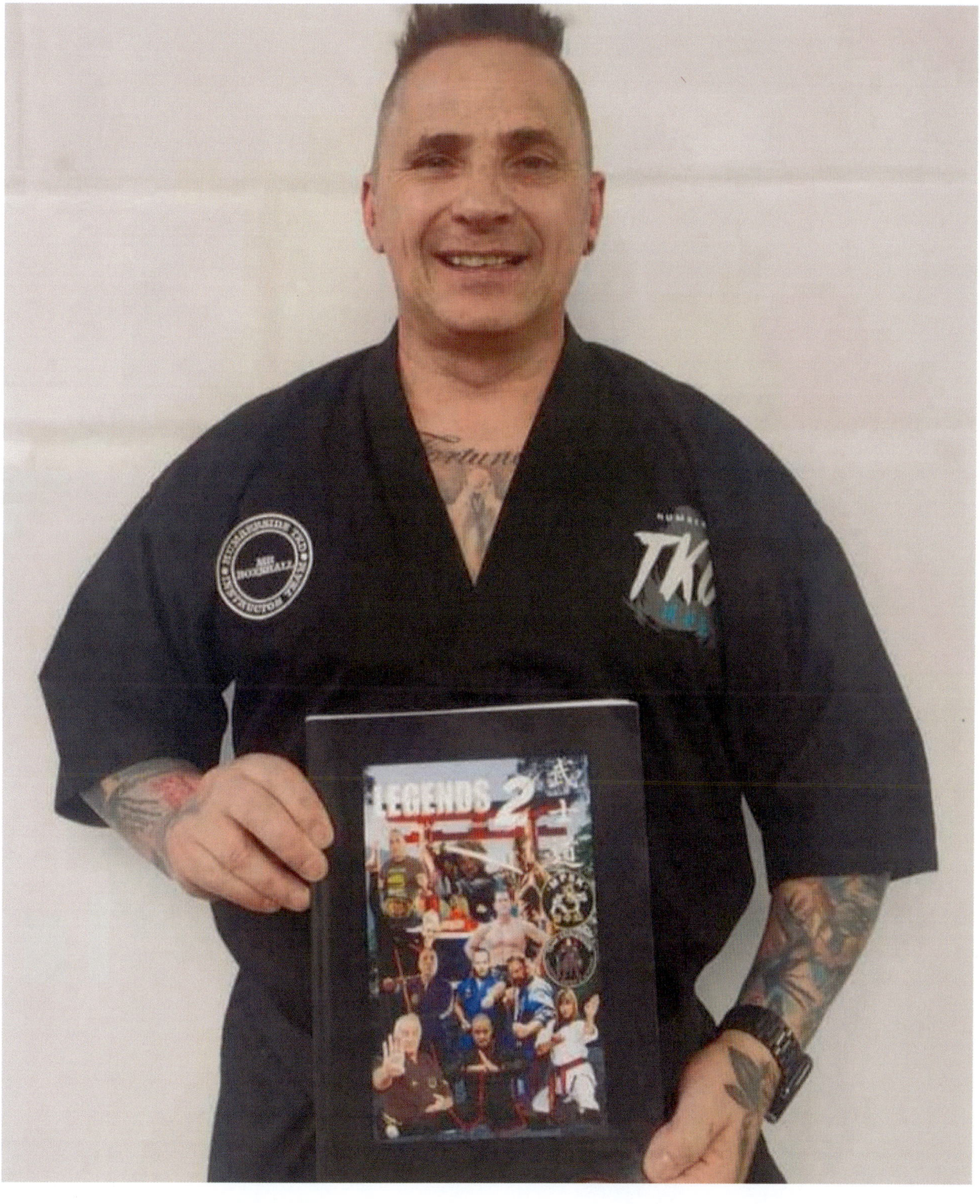
LEGENDS 2

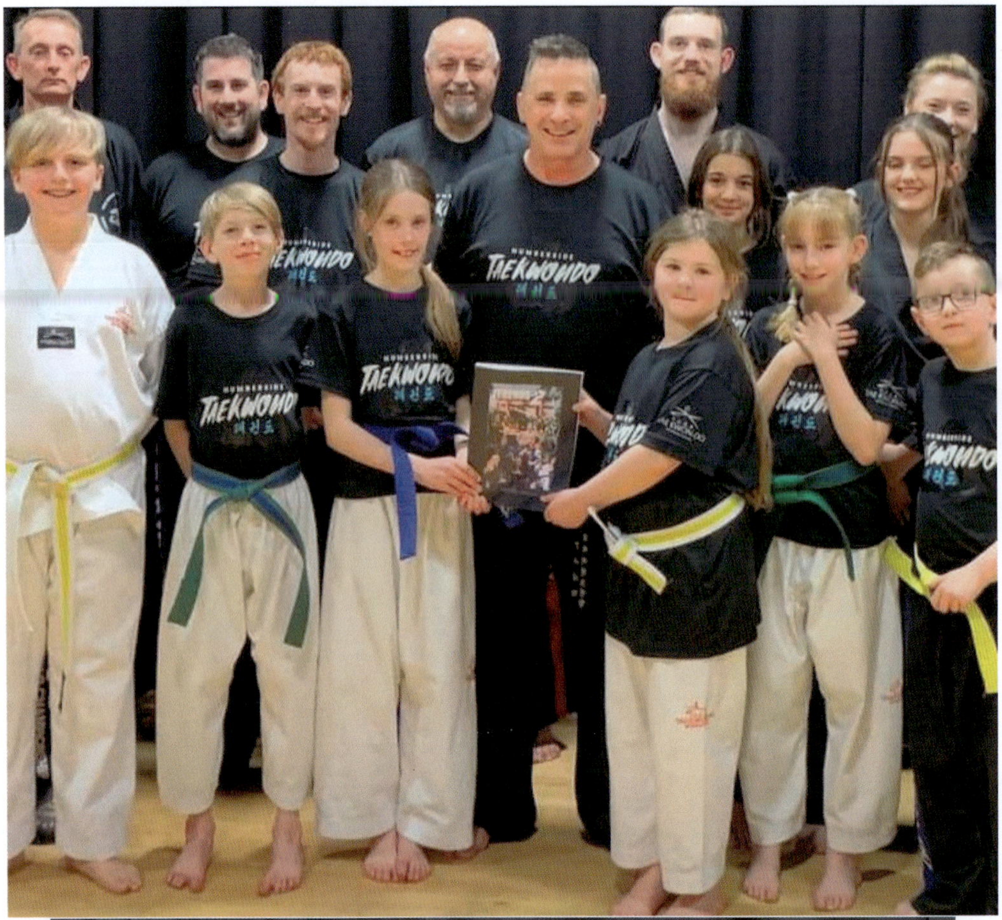
HUMBERSIDE
TAEKWONDO
태권도

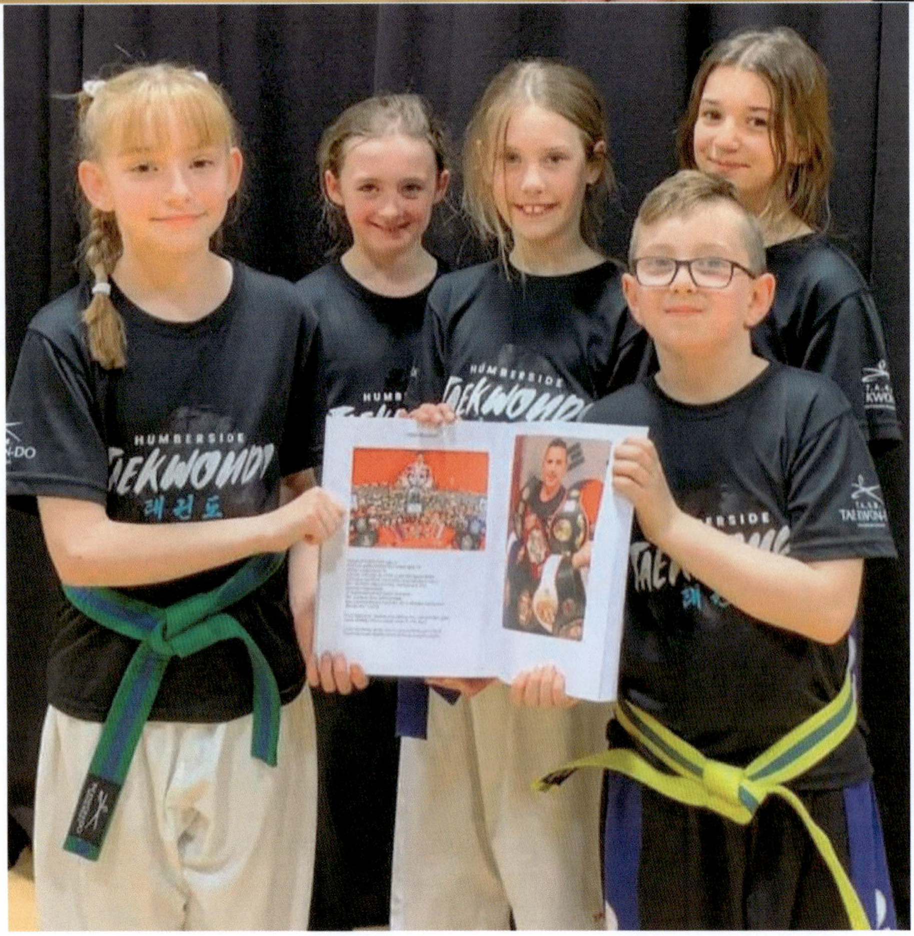
HUMBERSIDE
TAEKWONDO
태권도

DAZ STIRRAT

Renshi Daren Stirrat 7th Dan
Chief instructor Hampshire Academy of Shotokan Karate
I have been training for 44 years.
I teach traditional Shotokan Karate and self-defence.

I have also trained in Capoera, Boxing, Wing Chung to mention a few.

I have trained with many Karate Legends all over the country throughout my career.

My goals are to promote not just Shotokan Karate but all Martial Arts and teach the true values of the Martial Arts and remind the world that we should be one big family.

I competed in the late 80s and the best result was becoming the English Karate Organisation National and European Kata Champion for 10 years .

And my squad in the last 8 years have been super and we have competed at the FSKA World championships 3 times and have had great results taking Golds, Silvers, and bronze medals in all 3 competitions.

I have been Nominated 2 times for awards at the ukmas Martial arts Hall of Fame run by bob sykes and Paul Barnett . I have been nominated again this year. I also got nominated for an international hall of fame award in January this year 2023.

Man's Health
magazine

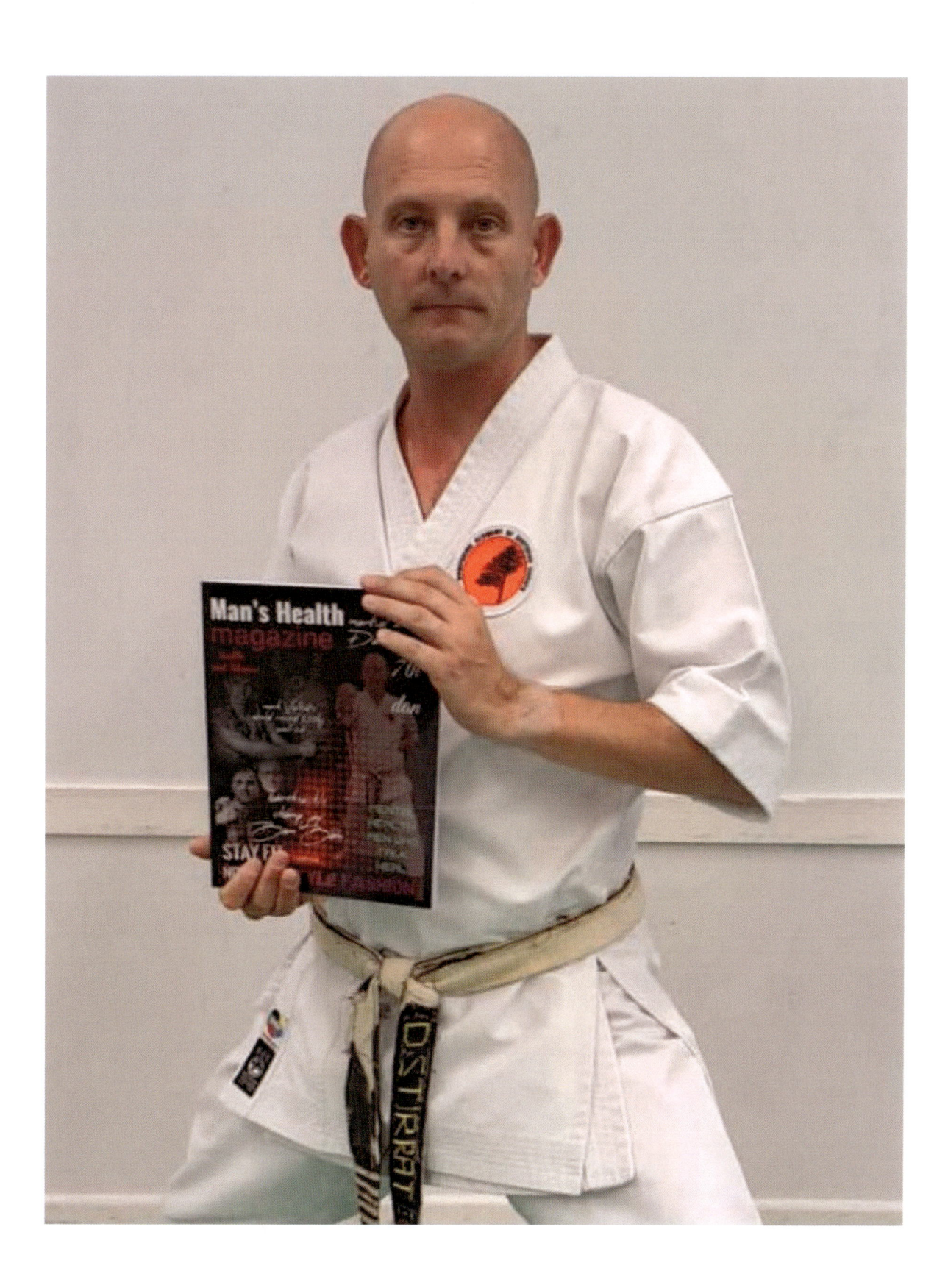

STAY FIT

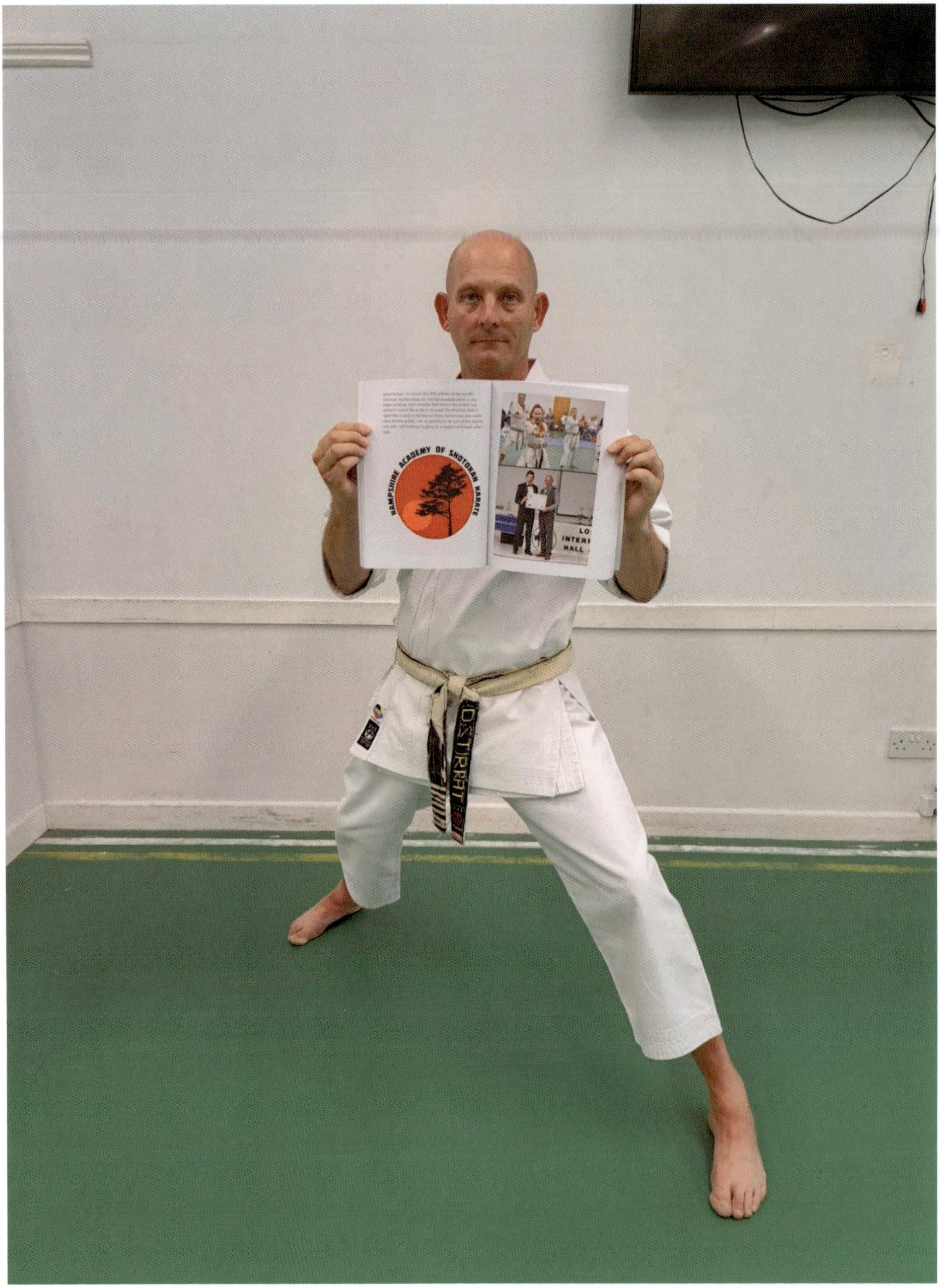
HAMPSHIRE ACADEMY OF SHOTOKAN KARATE

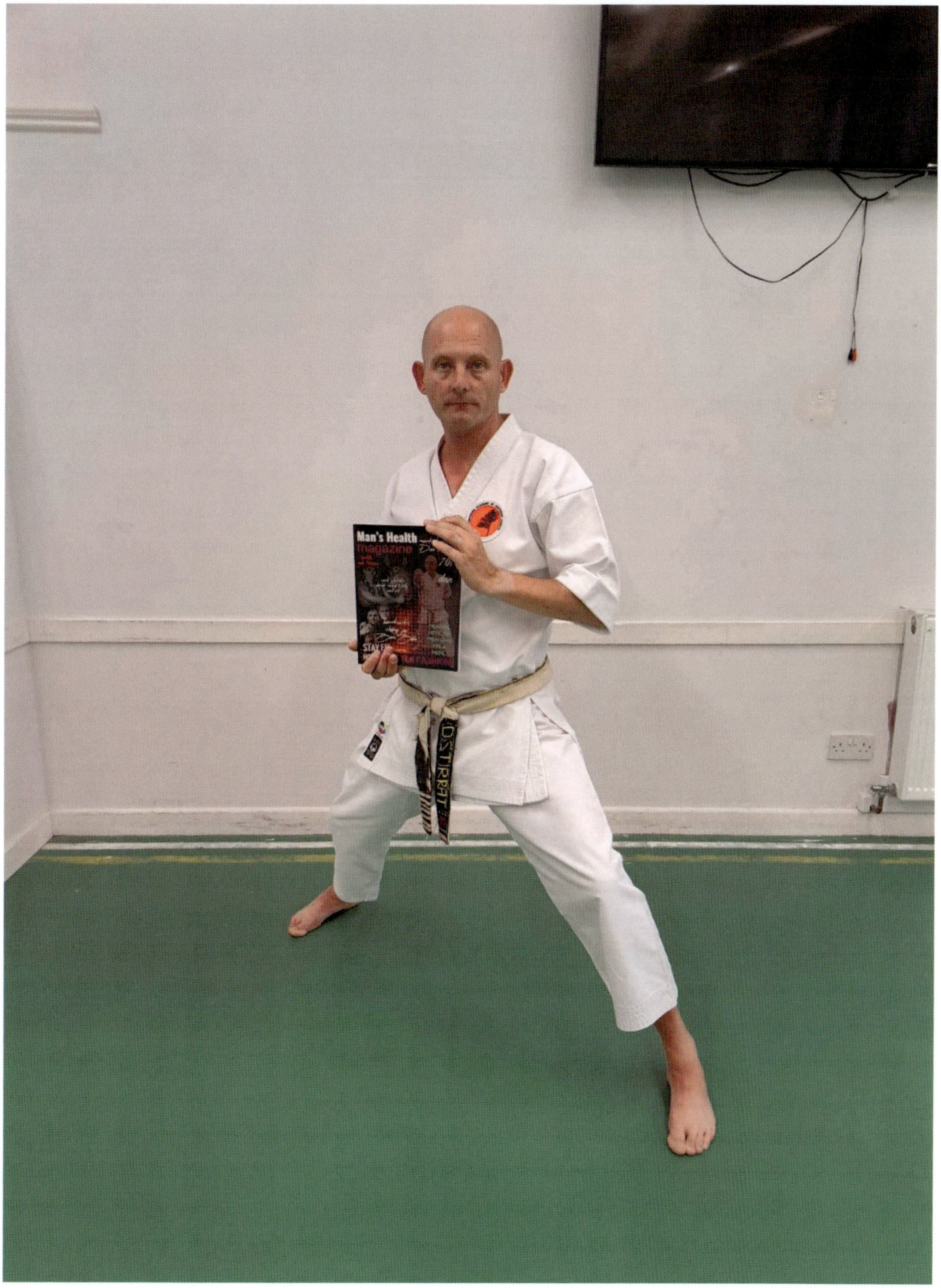
Man's Health
magazine

DAVE GENTRY BCA

Grandmaster David Gentry BCAe.   14-11-1961. Age 61.

8th Dan Black Belt RSK Kickboxing

8th Dan Black Belt Haider Academy of Martial Arts

6th Dan Black Belt in PKA Kickboxing.

6th Dan Black Belt IMAF.

London Regional Instructor for RSK Kickboxing.

IMAF Great Britain kickboxing Commissionaire and technical director, (International Martial Arts Federation.)

BTEC Level 3 Advanced Award In Self Defence Instruction (NFPS National Federation for Personal Safety)

YMCA Qualified Gym Instructor.

LA Muscle Sponsored Athlete.

32 YEARS training under PKA and RSK kickboxing. 1st Dan – Oct 1998, 2nd Dan - April 2000, 3rd Dan – Nov 2002, 4th Dan – Feb 2005, 5th Dan – April 2009 and 6th Dan April 2015, 7th Dan November 2016 8th Dan July 2018.

List of achievements.

LONDON INTERNATIONAL MARTIAL ARTS HALL OF FAME:

2006- Special Merit Award.

2007- Master of the Year.

2008- Master of the Year.

2009- Humanitarian Award (Related to Pride of Britain Nomination for saving a boy's life.)

2010- Martial Arts Spirit Award.

2011- Excellence Award in Martial Arts.

2012- Media Award.

2013- Community Spirit Award

2016- Humanitarian Award

2017- Grandmaster Award

2018- Community Spirit Award

2019- Gold Award

2020- Excellence Award

2021- Martial Arts Spirit Award

AMERICAN ACTION MARTIAL ARTS HALL OF FAME:

2009- Outstanding Dedication to the Martial Arts.

2010- Exemplary Contribution to the Martial Arts.

2011- Goodwill Ambassador to the Martial Arts.

Martial Arts Illustrated Magazine Fighters Hall of Fame:

May 2014- Fighter of the Year Award

October 2014 Legend Award

May 2015 Gold Award

April 2016 Black Belt Hall of Fame Award

May 2016 MAI Show Hall of Fame Award

November 2017 Contribution To Martial Arts Award.

May 2018 Instructor Award.

November 2018 Grandmaster Award

2019- Lifetime Achievement Award

2020,2021,2022. Top Instructor Award

2022- RSK Kickboxing Top Club Award.

Haider Academy Of Martial Arts London Hall Of Fame Awards

June 2018 Worlds Martial Arts Heroes Award

August 2018 Contribution To Martial Arts National And International Award

February 2019 Lifetime Achievement Award

July 2019 Heroes Award for Conquering Challenges and Inspiring Others.

July 2022 Second Lifetime Achievement Award.

Seminars

Emden, Antwerp Cala Mount Joi for IMAF.

Seni Martial Arts Show London, MAI Martial Arts Show Doncaster 2015 and 2016, Brunel University, Yearly London regular seminars at 8 schools in London re anti-bullying and anti- street and knife crime.

British Citizen Award BCAe

Awarded the British Citizen Award for Education in January 2020 at Westminster Palace London, for 30 years working in schools educating youngsters about the effects and dangers of bullying and street/knife crime. Also for raising over 30,000 pounds for various charities.

Pride Of Britain Nominee.

In 2009 I was short listed for a Pride of Britain Award for saving a young boy's life when I found him hanging on a washing line around his neck, got caught in it when playing action man at 4 years old, pulled him off moments from death, right time, right place, FATE!

Hillingdon Borough Local Hero Award 2013.

In 2013 I once again saved a young man's life after he suffered an anaphylaxis shock after eating a Prawn curry, due to 1st aid training I recognized the symptoms, reacted quickly which resulted in saving his life. For this I received a local hero award from my local Borough of Hillingdon.

Hiingdon Borough Local Hero Award 2022.

In 2022 I once again received this award for keeping my Hillingdon Borough active through Covid Lockdown through zoom classes and for raising funds for the NHS Charity.

Awarded International Budo Spirit Award by IMAF Germany 2010.

2009 awarded Grand Master status for reality-based combat fighting instructors (GBNRF) America.

Have appeared in 3 books:-

The Kickboxing Handbook by John Ritschel.

The Warrior Within by John Ritschel.

The Martial Arts Guide by Claire Bone.

Currently authoring my own book called Fate! Hero? Or Jinx?

Have appeared many times in Combat Martial Arts Magazine and was a feature writer for Fighters magazine where I had my own column called ASK DAVE for a year.

Was a feature writer for online fitness magazine www.famouslyfit.com owned by pop star from Steps Lee Latchford Evans. Authored articles based on martial arts techniques and training exercises.

Have trained pop stars and movie stars, Lee Latchford Evans from Steps, currently 1 of my Black Belts, Stacey Cadman star of Cavegirl CBEEBIES AND Sky's Mile High. Caire Richards from Steps and Scott Adkins martial arts movie star and 1 of my Black Belts, who has appeared in Unleashed With Jet Li, Wolverine with Hugh Jackman, played weapon 11, The Shepard with Jean Claude Van Damme, Expendables 2, The Medallion with Jackie Chan and his own films Undisputed 2 and 3 and Ninja 1 and 2. Accident Man 1 and 2 and his latest major movie John Wick 4 with Keanu Reeves. Also Green Street 3 Underground, playing the main character and I have a small role in the film as a Tottenham hooligan.

Have appeared on TV many times and have had extra parts in films. Have appeared recently in the Steps Re-union programme on Sky, ITV'S Fat Nation and recently did a channel 4 Documentary where I mentored a troubled teenager for a month to change her ways, yet to be aired. Was an extra in a program called Country Murders on Sky TV playing a policeman. Also played a policeman Special Forces in a film called Comes A Bright Day featuring Timothy

Spall. Also played a part as a hooligan in Green Street 3 with the main star Scott Adkins who was my student for 4 years in the PKA.

In 2015 played a policeman who has a fight with Lou Ferrigno (the original Incredible Hulk) in a film called Instant Death. Get taken out in a severe manner.

In 2011 AND 2012 I was an ambassador for the government for the Better Breakfast Campaign working alongside celebrities such as Lee from Steps, Alex Reid and Holly Mathews, touring schools around the country trying to get kids into healthy eating and healthy sports.

I ran the Great North Run for Leukaemia and 2012, I ran The London Marathon for The Play Barn Charity raising over one thousand pounds to help provide a safer environment for kids with cancer.

In 2013 I challenged myself in 4 major events to raise money for Diabetes UK and a local school for children with disabilities. I ran the London Bupa 10 k in May, The Prudential 100 Mile Bike Ride in August, The London to Paris Bike Ride in September and the Bupa 10-mile Great South Run in October again raising 3,000 pounds. I took part in these events with good friend and training partner Lee Latchford Evans.

In 2015 I was again completed the London To Paris bike ride and raised 6,000 pounds for local charities.

In January 2018 I raised 1,000 pounds for the London Ambulance service in 1 night after 3 of my students at ages

16 and 17 were tragically killed after being hit by a car in Hayes West London.

Anti Bullying/ street knife crime.

I have been working in schools and communities over 20 years delivering seminars about street/knife crime and anti-bullying. Trying to get youngsters away from the bad side of life, so that they can lead productive futures instead of a life of crime. Also have done many seminars at Tottenham football ground. Also deal at the same time about the effects of bad nutrition for youngsters to try getting them into a healthy fit lifestyle. It has been 1 of my personal goals in life to see martial arts taught in schools curriculum for the positive effects that it brings to students, especially in the aspect of respecting oneself and others.

I am currently 1 of a few celebrities campaigning against anti autism bullying and trying to get the hate crime laws changed for the safety of all who are affected. I have also recently taken part in a forthcoming documentary about this, now available on you tube. This campaign is ongoing and currently gone as far as the European and English parliaments.

Recently did a similar piece about martial arts in schools for Sky's London 360 community channel. That can be seen on my streetwise website. This was about the positive effect of martial arts philosophies on young children.

My first Martial Arts session began at Lau Gar Kung Fu under the tutorage of Neville Wray

My personal martial arts journey began after watching Bruce Lee's Enter The Dragon that gave me the bug. To this day this great man has been my inspiration in martial arts. Over the years I tried many styles of martial arts all great in what they have to offer, but the Introduction of Van Damme's Kickboxer set me on a new road, Kickboxing.

I am now a full-time instructor and over the years have produced over 200 Black Belts, World and British Kickboxing Champions. I have taught seminars in Europe under IMAF in my role as Commissionaire for Great Britain. I have been honoured to train with some of the world's great martial artists and stars such as Scott Adkins and Lee Latchford Evans.

I currently teach classes in West London and travel to schools in Hillingdon and London Borough's delivering my anti buying/knife crime healthy living seminars to youngsters.

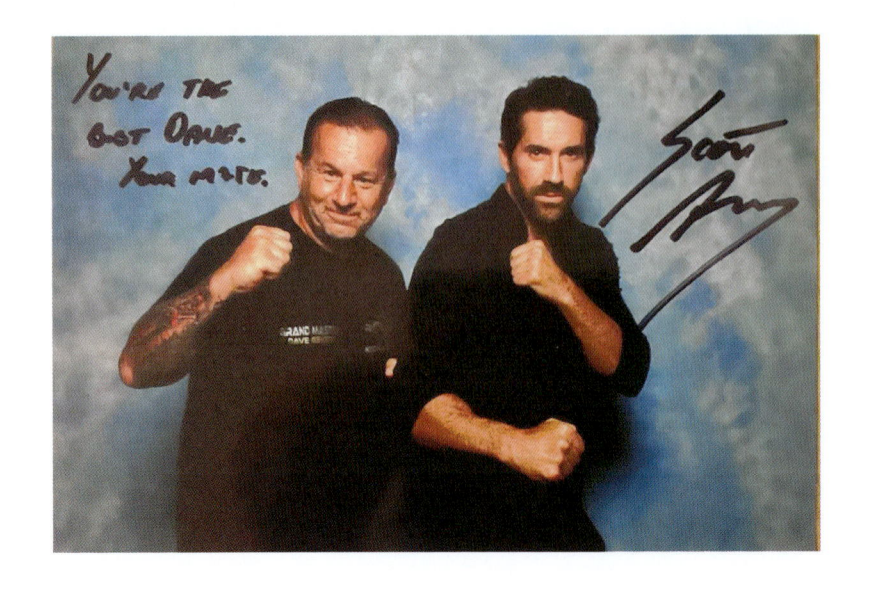

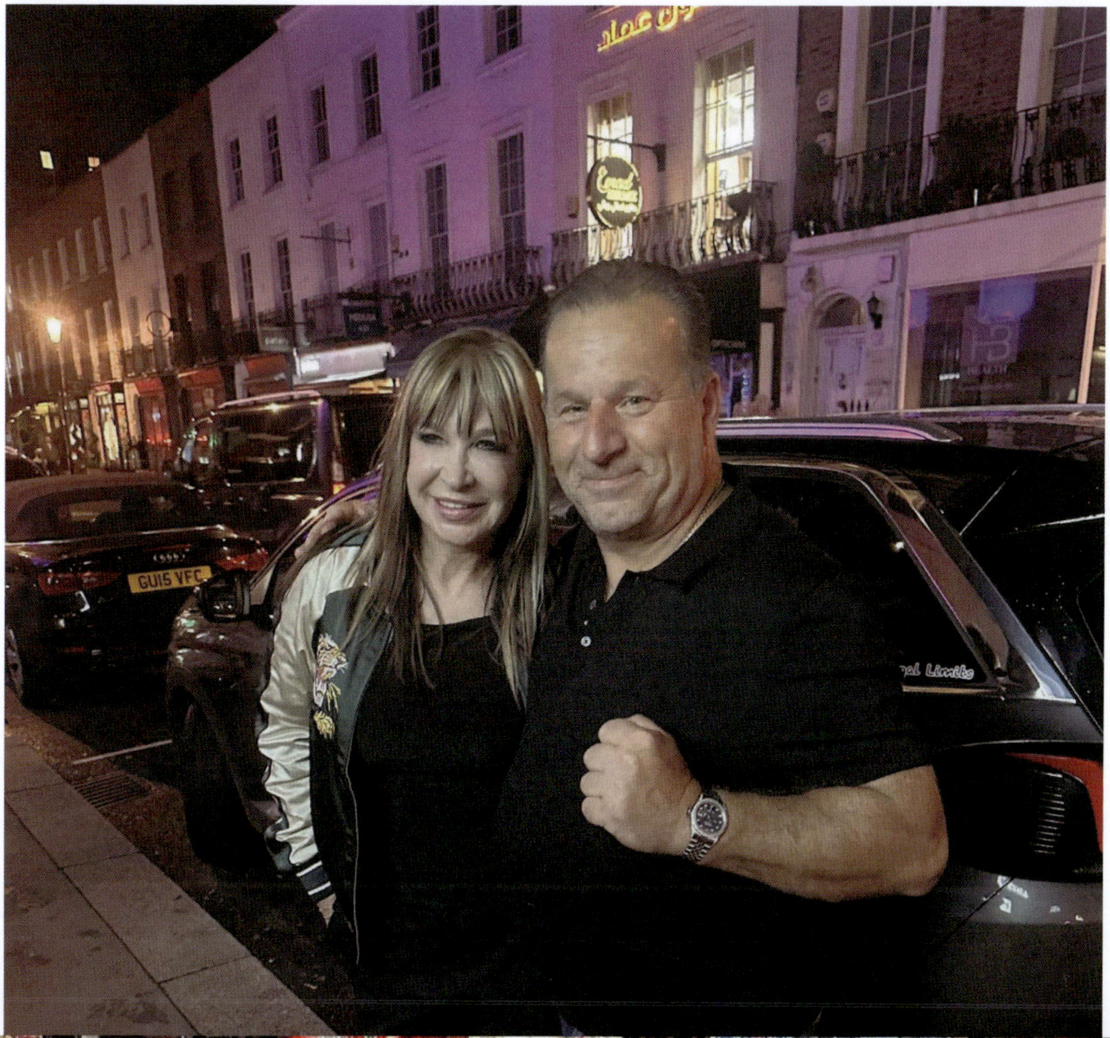
GU15 VFC

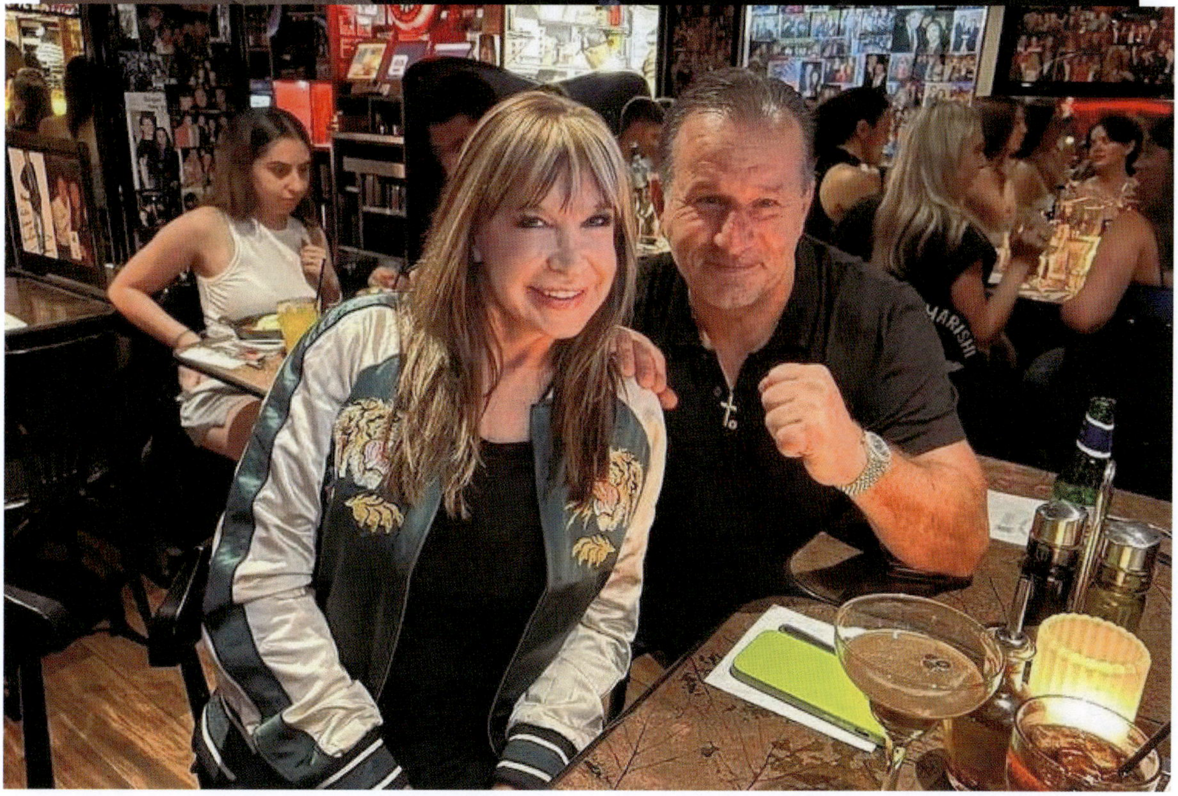

CREATED BY

@SHAOLINJAA

@CRIKEART

RADAR THOMAS

My name is Lawrence Thomas, I go under the name Radar
I have been training for 50 years this year boxing, fighting six different martial arts. I hold 4 different black belts
I have been mainly a street fighter always sticking up for harmless people!!
I have had 220 fights on the street with 202 knockouts and unbelievably won the other 18 fights but didn't win them easy! I had 1loss to a younger fella he got me one night

from behind but was on his doorstep next morning and put him in hospital for 5 days!!

I also won tough man competition after I turned 52 years of age, I am 69 years of age this year!!

I had on one occasion 7 fights in two hours in street fight anything goes except to the groin and got $10.000 cash I might have won but i was sore for 4 to 5 weeks.

I fought ex titleholders Australian titles a muay Thai man from Thailand, who for the first time in my life put me to one knee as I was waiting for my hip operation and he was my 3rd fight and had noticed I was limping on my left side but I got up and beat him anyway!! I get kids off the street ,adults women etc

And I train people still to this day for free my satisfaction is seeing them walkout of my bush gym after 4 to 5 weeks and look at me and say radar thank you very much.

Money don't buy that sort of thing with me!!

There are six of us in the family three boys three girls I am the eldest and I have always said The girls are the toughest!!

My mother and sister have passed on so I look after my father full time he held my hand when I was a kid so I will hold him back if need be !!

I am z country boy who lived on 25 acres of land with my dad we live right on the edge of town in a place called Narrabri NSW Australia!!

I have been through 2 lots of cancer which I cured myself as I refuse chemotherapy, I also have had 2 full hip replacements and was told years ago no more martial arts but here I am at 69 years of age still doing it and helping others it's a way of life and I recommend it to anyone!!

I would like to thank Master John Stephenson the Legend Himself for adding me in this book called Legends of Martial Arts!!

MARK STRANGE

Mark Strange, the highly decorated British film actor and martial artist, recently played one of the lead roles in the global action-horror film Redcon-1. The award-winning movie received a theatrical release and a global release including a Netflix and Amazon Prime release and across many US streaming sites.

After the success of Redcon-1, Strange landed a featured role in Ip Man 4: The Finale (the highest grossing martial arts movie franchise of all time and No.1 on Netflix US) in which he has an epic showdown with Bruce Lee (played by Danny Chan). In the film, Strange worked under legendary action choreographer Yuen Woo-ping (The Matrix trilogy, Kill Bill). Ip Man 4 stars Donnie Yen (Rogue One, Flash Point) and Scott Adkins (Undisputed franchise, Doctor Strange) the film went on to win a Hong Kong Film Award for Best Choreography. The movie was released internationally in cinemas and via streaming sites and in the UK by Universal Pictures.

Recently finished filming on the new movie Hounds of War working alongside Hollywood actor Frank Grillo.

Other career highlights include Avengement (starring Scott Adkins, directed by Jesse V. Johnson) currently on Netflix. Stan Lee's Lucky Man starring James Nesbitt, Christopher Nolan's Batman Begins and working alongside Jackie Chan in Twins Effect and The Medallion.

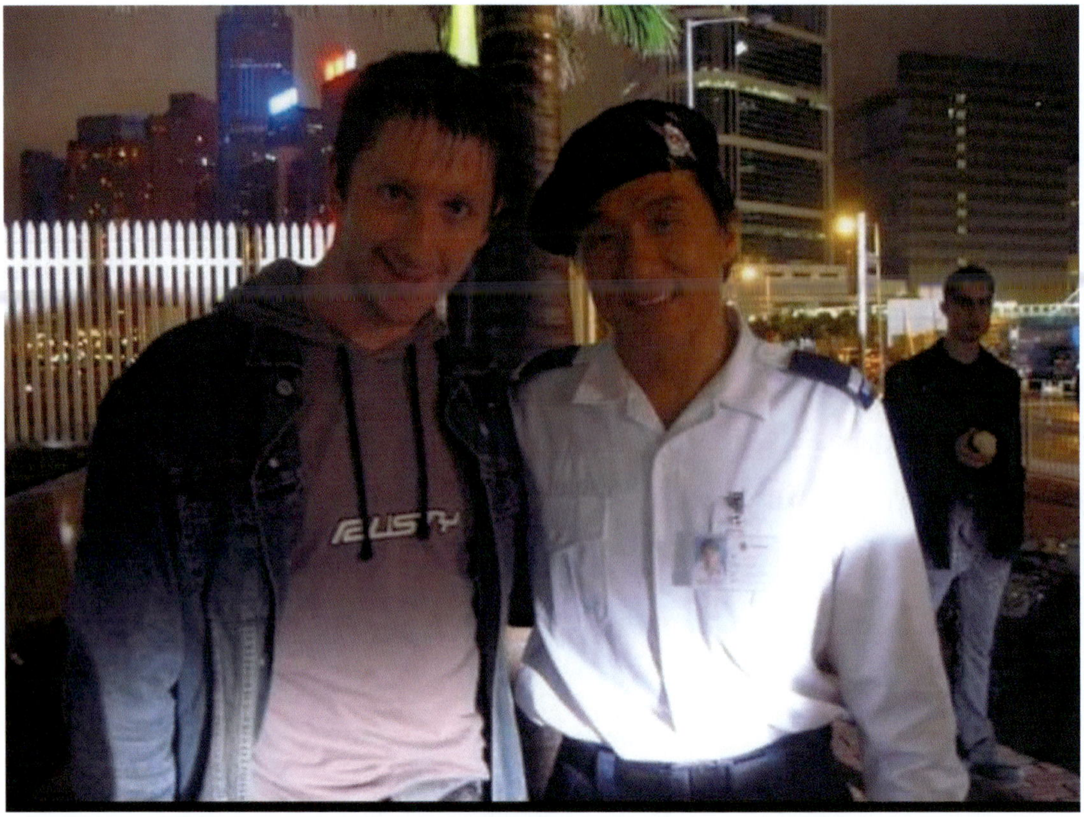

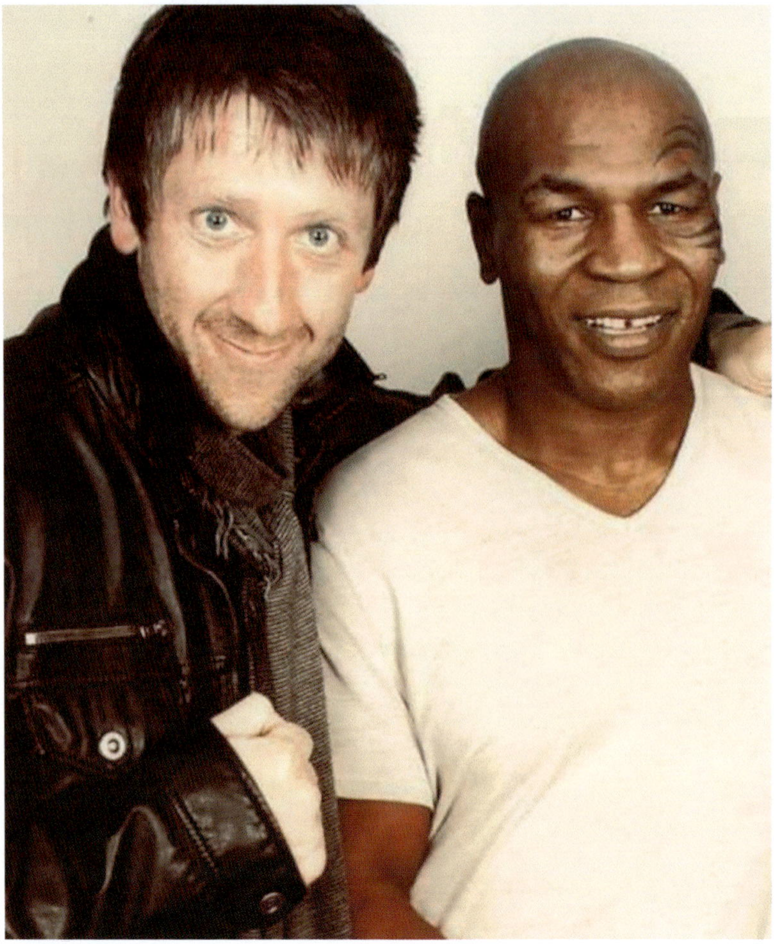

SHIHAN JACK MORALES

Shihan Jack Morales a native New Yorker from the Bronx. He's been in the martial arts for over 50 years in the art of Goju Ryu under the late Gm Aaron Banks (2011). He's rank is Shichidan Black Belt and a Brown Belt in Kyokushin under the late Shuseki Shihan William Oliver (2003), also holds rank in ju jitsu under Master William Estela (1986). He a 3x former World muay Thai Champion, 2x Men of the year, Archangel of the year with the New York City Guardian Angels Safety Patrol. Martial Arts is his life and serving the community is an honour. He thanks his family and Instructors for his many achievements and sacrifices.
HUMBLE BOW

TYLER FORD

Tyler Ford nicked named "The Champ" Is 15 years old and lives in Swansea, South Wales. Tyler started training in Martial Arts at the age of 3 years old. Tyler has a very impressive record on the national and international tournament circuit, by his 5th birthday was fighting for Team Wales in overseas events. Tyler racked up a total of 236 gold medals, winning major event tournaments both here in the UK and abroad, including, 9x World Kickboxing champion, multiple times Welsh, British and European champion. Kwon grand champion. Lordswood Combat series grand champion, Tyler then travelled to Germany to compete in the WAKO German Open where he took both gold medals for Wales. After this success he then travelled to Amsterdam to compete in the Wako Yokoso Dutch open kickboxing championships, with Tyler again proving victorious bringing home yet again both gold medals for Wales. Tyler then received an invite to compete in the World Martial Arts Games in Switzerland , representing Team Wales at the age of just 10 years old entering all 3 divisions. Tyler was yet again untouchable scoring 10-0 scores against the best from around the globe. Tyler came home a World Games triple gold medallist, after beating Russia in the finals. Tyler also won gold medals in BJJ, Judo, Combat Jui jitsu, Karate, and a British title in MMA. After winning the gold Medal at the WKA British championships in Kickboxing, and the Boxing category. Tyler went onto join his local amateur Boxing club with a future dream to become a professional Boxer. Tyler's most recent success was taking the Gold medal at the William Wallace Box Cup in Stirling Scotland, beating the all-Ireland Boxing champion and World Silver medallist from Belfast. Tyler was inducted in the Martial Arts Hall of Fame, and the Hall of Honours in Italy at a very young age. Tyler was also invited to The Palace of Westminster in London where he was presented with the BCA honours medal for his service to Martial Arts for his country. Tyler then went onto win the Saint David's award in Wales, and most recently crowned, The Child of

Britain 2022. Tyler has trained with some of the best in the World such as, Benny the Jet, Bill Superfoot Wallace, Silvio Simac, Bob Sykes and many more household names. Tyler now trains under former Team GB and Olympic 3-star AIBA Boxing coach Nigel Davies. Nigel has trained the best that Great Britain has to offer including, Anthony Joshua, Tyson Fury, Nicola Adams, Billy Jo Saunders, Luke Campbell, Tony Jeffries, Anthony Ogogo to name just a few. Tyler has also starred in many a film such as Rise of the Foot soldier, and tv soaps such as Keeping Faith, Casualty and many more, working alongside Rebel Wilson on, The Almond and the seahorse. Tyler would also like to thank a few good people who have really helped him in life, namely Bob Sykes, Silvio Simac, Ross O'Hennessy, Rick Manning, Keith Baites, Leigh Davies, Samuel Kwok and Mark Sears.

GARY WASNIEWSKI

Grandmaster Gary Wasniewski has been honoured worldwide for his abilities and dedication to the martial arts worldwide. Gary has been training in martial arts since 1966. Gary started training in Wado-Ryu Karate with Amateur Karate Association under Meiji Suzuki and has received his Dan grades with Meiji Suzuki and Tom Hibbert Chairman AKA/ English Karate Federation.

Gary was international squad fighter for Amateur Karate Association 1979-1985.

GM Gary Wasniewski holds rank 10th Dan WHFSC, and Amateur Karate Association 10th Dan T.Hibbert EKF Chairman 2001 and many other governing bodies.

Gary has trained Full Contact Karate with Steve Morris in Cambridge Circus, London 1978-79 and been a member Professional Karate Association 1979-1982.

He is regarded as a Martial Arts legend and has received many awards and ranks worldwide. Grandmaster Gary Wasniewski has been called and received the World Record Kicker Championship Belt from the WKL-World Kickboxing League USA.

Gary has appeared on the front covers of over 29 martial arts magazines worldwide, he has received awards from all the Major Halls of Fame around the world.

Gary was also featured in the famous Black Belt Magazine USA 2006 centre fold article and photos "Lightning Legs"

Gary also produces and has founded the world's elite events "London International Hall of Fame" and "World Martial Arts Championships London" both events support Cancer Research.

Gary's favourite sayings is "It's not the belt or the grade, it's the man within the belt" and "Talk is cheap, Action is everything!

69 years later, he still trains, teaches, travels and spars every day.

Gary is also a successful Movie Actor/Director/Producer, Action, Drama, Supernatural and Sc-Fi movies.

His movie career started in 2006 meeting Leo Fong in Los Angeles.

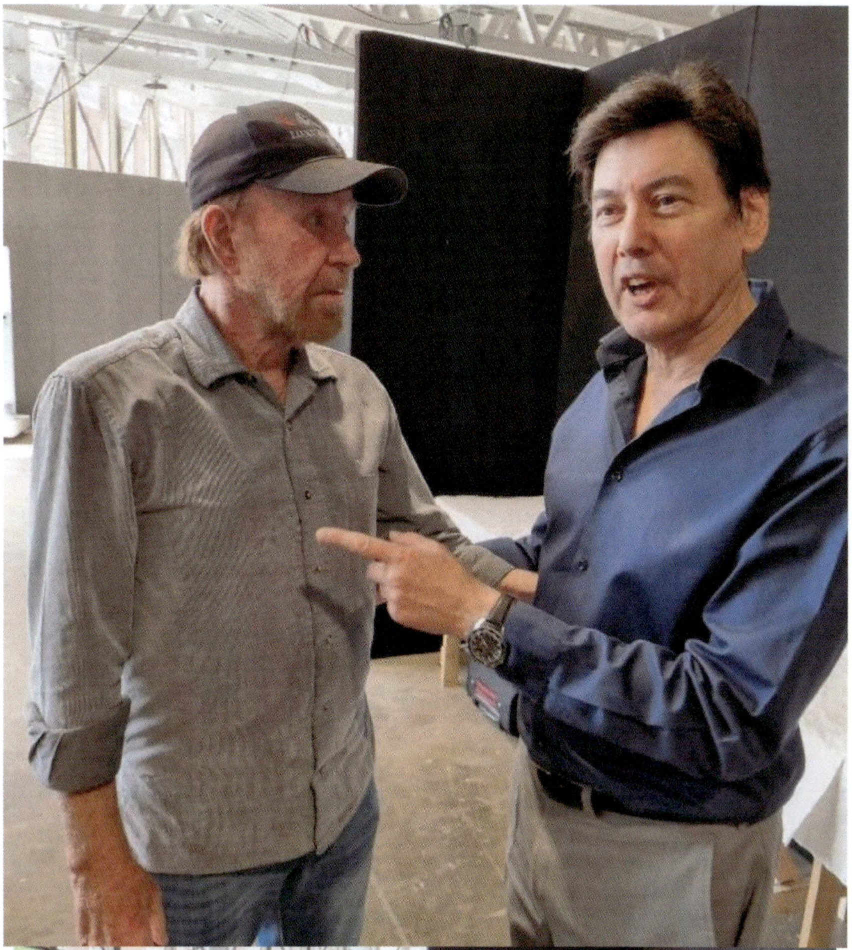
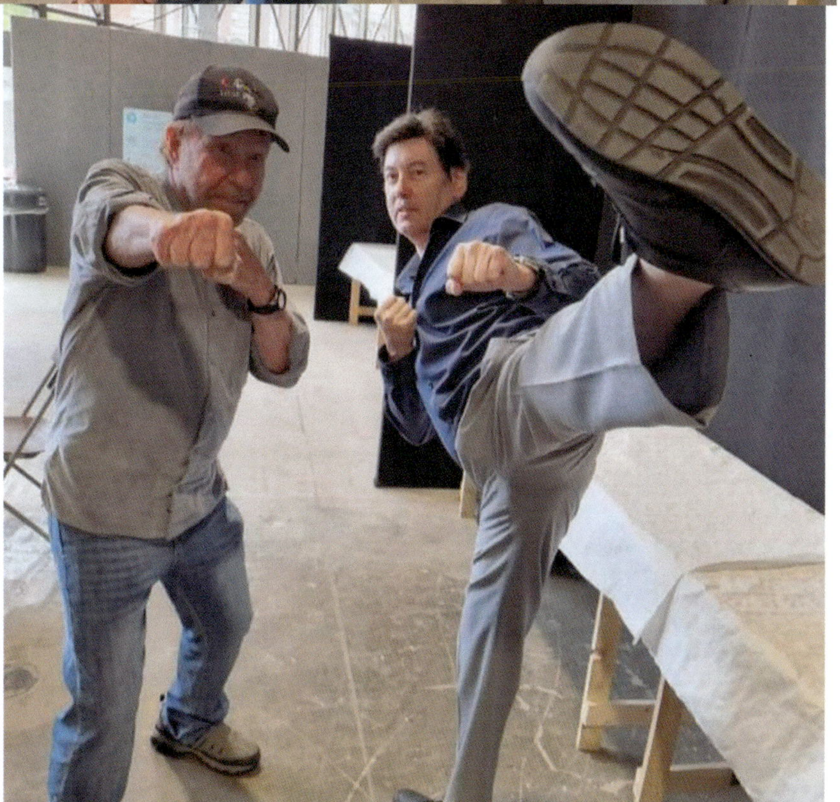

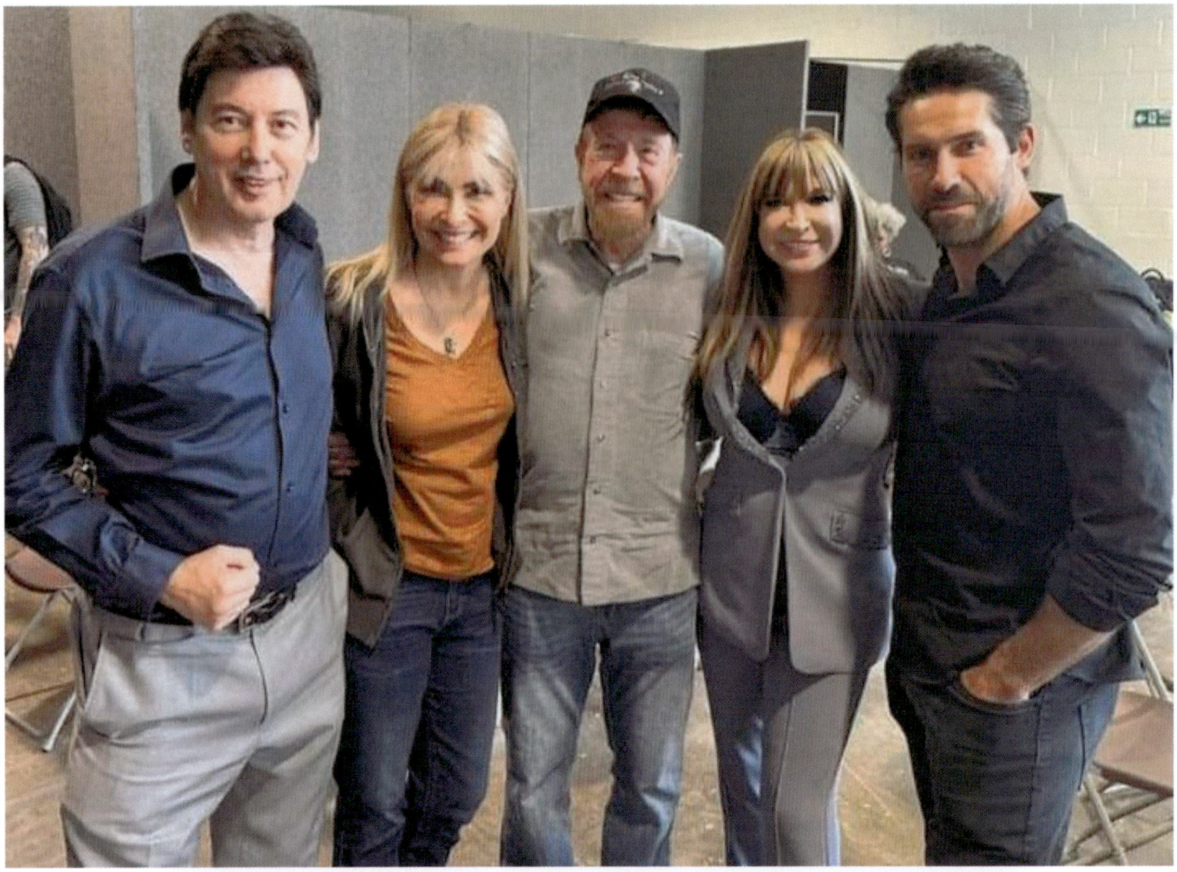

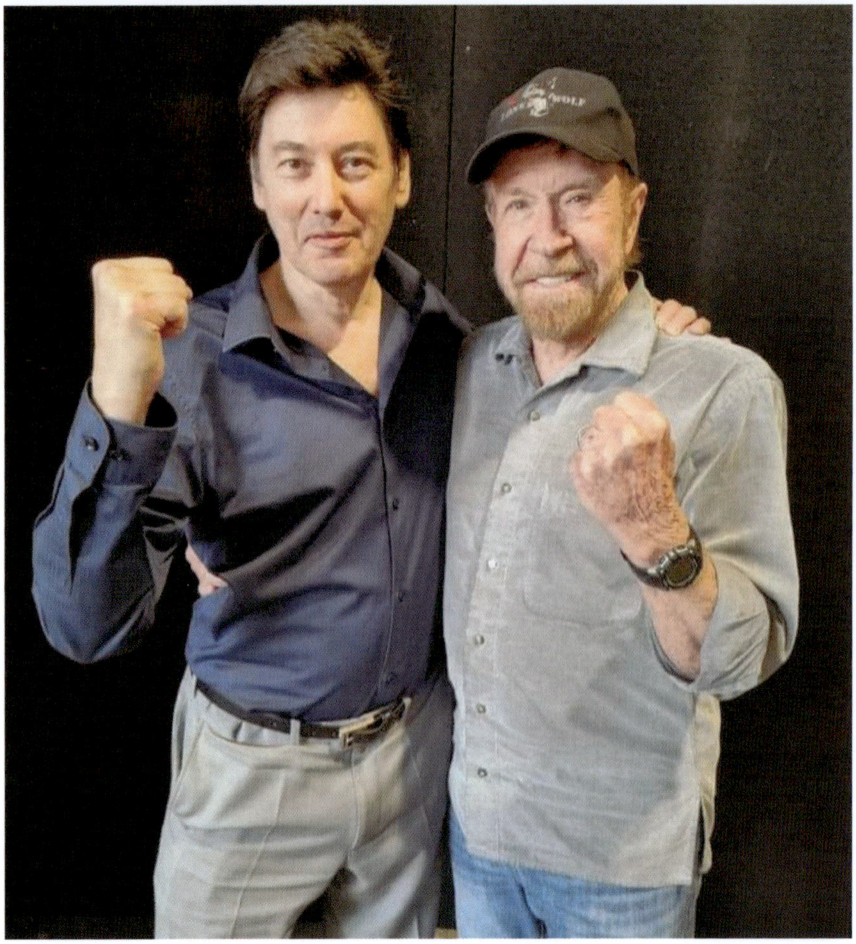

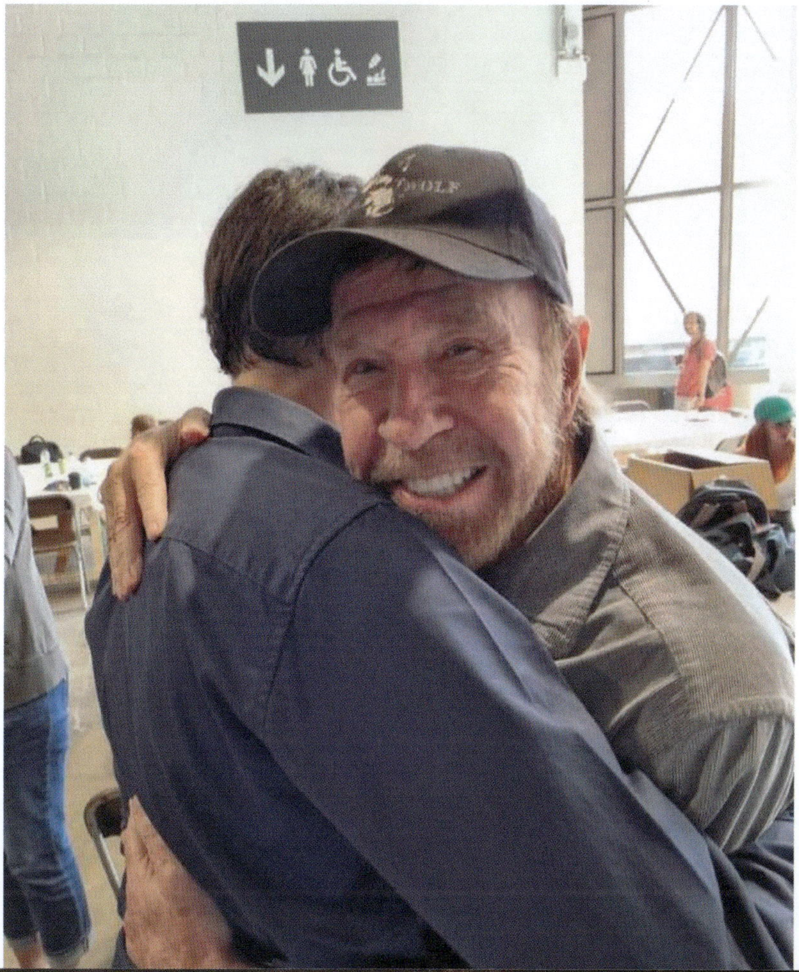
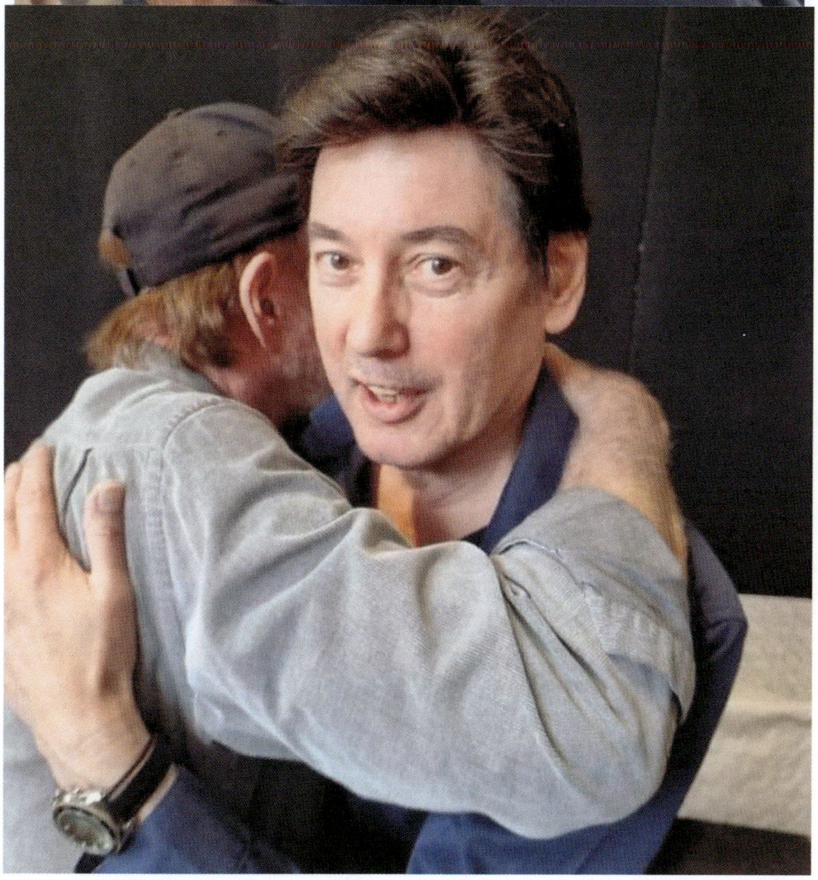

LONDON INTERNATIONAL HALL OF FAME
INTERNATIONAL MARTIAL ARTS
HALL OF FAME LONDON
LET IT BE KNOWN THAT ON THIS DATE
24TH JUNE, 2023
Gm Chuck Norris
HAS BEEN INDUCTED INTO THE
18TH ANNIVERSARY LONDON HALL OF FAME
Lifetime Award
FOR CONTRIBUTIONS TO MARTIAL ARTS WORLDWIDE

Gary,
All the best
from your friend,
Chuck Norris

TRADITIONAL
KARATE
Paul Mitchell
The Way I See It!
Master Eiichi Miyazato
10th Dan
Free
POSTER
Gary Wasniewski
PLUS

TRADITIONAL
KARATE
DAVE HAZARD
THE WAY OF THE WARRIOR
JOHN RICHARDS
FROM DOJO TO HOMBU
DEFEATING FEAR
THE OFFICIAL E.K.G.B. COLUMN
TICKY DONOVAN
TALKS FRANKLY ABOUT THE EUROPEAN CHAMPIONSHIPS
YAWARA
A LETHAL WEAPON
GARY WASNIEWSKI
KICKING'S A HABIT
THE HISTORY OF THE RYUKYU KOBUDO

TYGA
MARTIAL ARTS
INTERNATIONAL

KEVIN SANDERS

PROFESSIONAL BOXING PROMOTER, MANAGER AND TRAINER

Working with fighters in professional boxing has been my passion for 30 years. I was the youngest person ever to hold the BBBocC trainer, manager and promoters licences consecutively. I learnt my trade in the UK and in Las Vegas and was fortunate to train under the great Eddie Futch and Thell Torrence. I currently continue to train professional fighters.

Summary of my career

- 33 world championship fights with 27 wins
- Won every title from English title to world championship at various weight levels
- Youngest person to hold trainer, manager and promoter licences at the same time at the age of 25
- Learnt techniques of training with the late Eddie Futch in Las Vegas
- Dealt with world class promoters, for example Frank Warren and Don King – contract negotiation, television and purse bids
- Local fight promotions to gain experience for my stable of fighters and local, up-and coming fighters

Highlights of my career

- Lloyd Honeyghan undisputed welter-weight champion of the world
- Nigel Benn – super-middleweight champion of the world
- Mike McCallum – middle, super-middle and light heavyweight champion
- Frank Bruno vs Mike Tyson

- Matt Skelton – British, Commonwealth, European and Heavy-weight champion of the world
- Robert McCracken – British, commonwealth and world title contender and now is the director of the GB boxing squad
- Advisor to Jamie McDonnell former IBF and current WBA Bantam-weight champion of the world

Other fighters include

- Pat Mullings – IBO world champion, British and commonwealth champion
- Matthew Barney – world champion
- Kevin Leushing – British and Commonwealth champion
- Neil Linford – British, commonwealth and world title contender
- Henry Castle
- Shaun Cummings – WBA inter-continental champion
- Gary De Roux – British champion

My promotional experience centred on my stable of fighters to ensure they had a good grounding in boxing professionally. I also organised boxing at testimonial events in London including at the Savoy Hotel.

- Awards
- Herald and Post Sports Personality of the Month – April 2001
- Evening Telegraph Service to Sport – 2000 (finalist)
- Evening Telegraph Service to Sport – 2001 (winner)

- Evening Telegraph Sports Personality of the Year – 2004 (winner)
- WBC Services to Boxing – 2010 (WBC = World Boxing Council)
- Civic award for Sport – 2018 – Peterborough City Council

CELEBRITY DINNERS

My career in professional boxing gave me the contacts to diversify into celebrity dinner events where I was

fortunate to be able to promote some the boxing greats and put many professional fighters on the circuit.

Previous guests from the world of boxing:

Amir Khan, Anthony Joshua, Barry McGuigan, Bill Schwer,

Carl Froch, Chris Eubank, David Haye, Earnie Shavers,

Evander Holyfield, Frank Bruno, Henry Cooper, Joe Calzaghe,

Joe Frazier, Joe Bugner, John Conteh, Larry Holmes,

Marvelous Marvin Hagler, Michael Watson, Micky Cantwell, Mike McCallum, Nigel Benn, Richie Woodhall, Ricky Hatton, Roberto Duran, Steve Collins, Sugar Ray Leonard, Thomas Hearns, Tyson Fury.

Previous guests from the world of football and rugby:

John Barnes, Micky Skinner, Victor Ubogo

1966 World Cup Team The Hard Men of Football

At these events, I have also raised money for local charities and ran gymnasiums for the youth of Peterborough.

KEVIN SANDERS BOIXING AND FITNESS ACADEMY

To transfer the skills and discipline from professional boxing to help young people, I have established a boxing academy. Since 2015, I have worked in partnership with Peterborough City Council and education organisations that support young people who are not in mainstream education. This has proved a great success to the young people themselves and the local community. This is based on my gym In Alfric Square in Peterborough.

Dave Pierre - a local Peterborough fighter who won Southern Area light-welterweight championship. He was the first champion I had

Pat Mullings - he was from harrow and ne trained in Peterborough. He went on to win the IBO world champion, British and commonwealth bantam weight championships

Gary De Roux - another Peterborough fighter who won the Southern Area featherweight title and became British champion

Matt Skelton - a former K1 world champion who came to train in Peterborough. He became the British, Commonwealth, European and WBU champion of the world

For Lloyd Honeyghan, I brought him back from the Mark Breland loss at Wembley to regain his commonwealth title and fought for the eliminator for the light-middleweight title in Atlantic City against Vinny Pazienza where Lloyd got stopped in 9 rounds.

I am now retired from professional boxing and spend part of the year in Spain. When I am back in the UK, I'm back in the gym doing 1-2-1 boxing training.

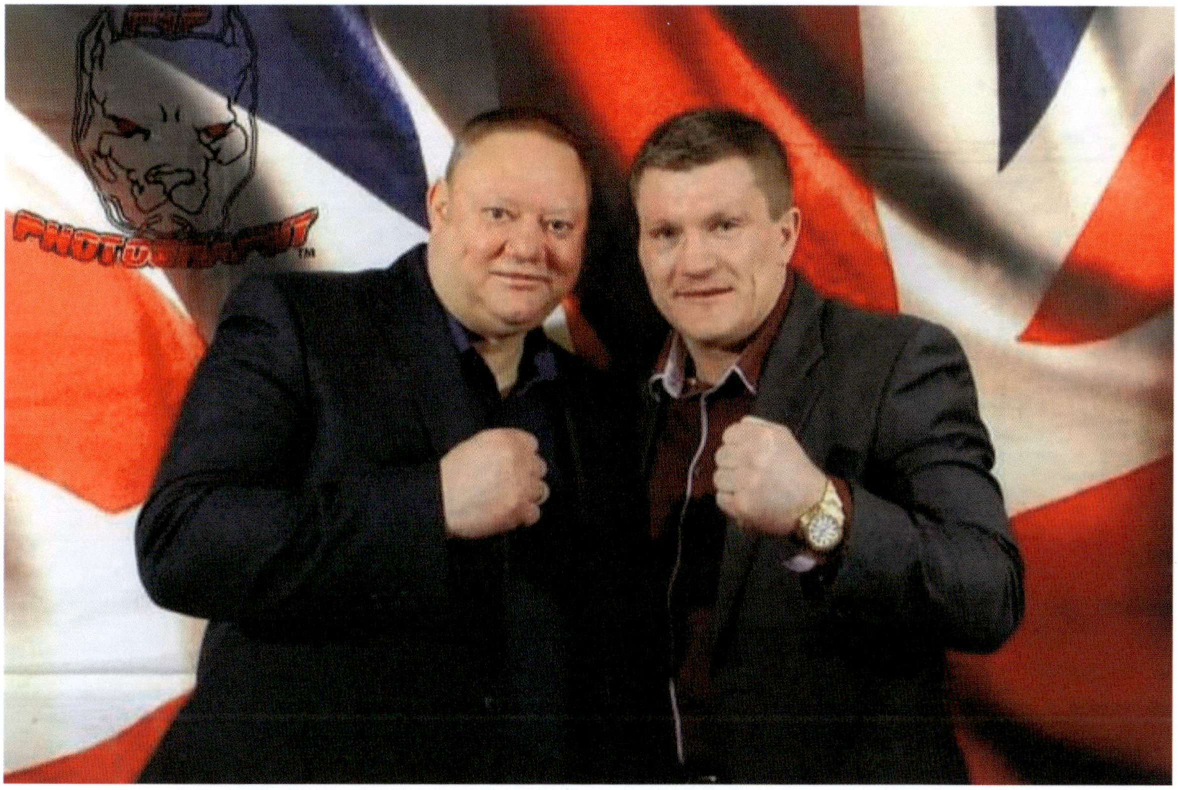

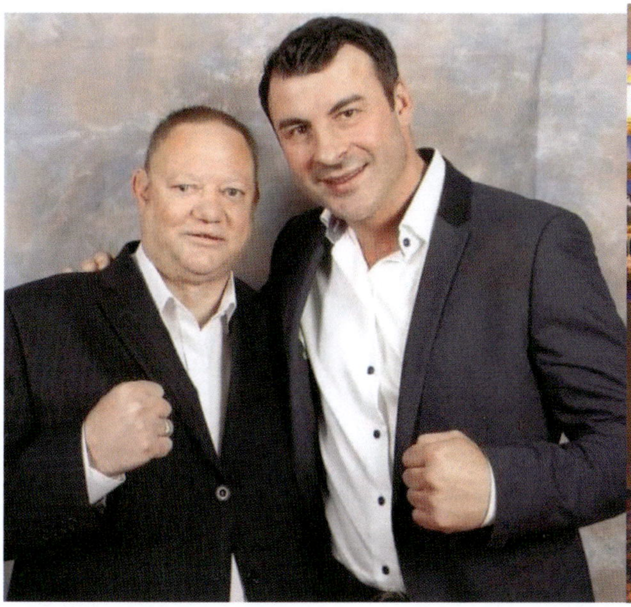

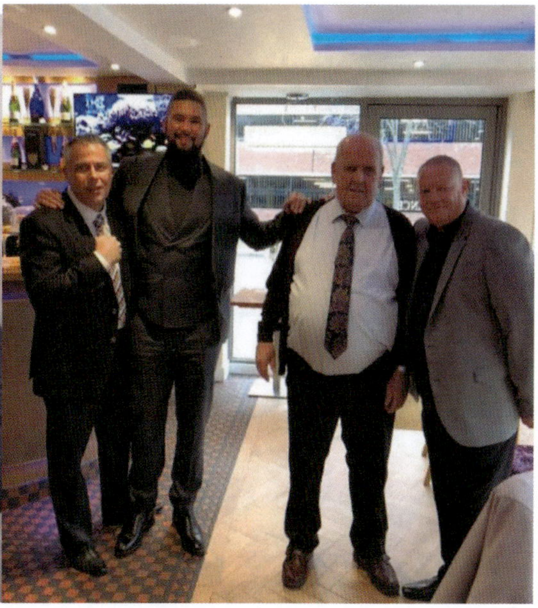

MARK VALLINT

I began my Fitness and martial arts journey at a very young age it has been and will continue to be a massive and important part of my life. I began the journey learning Wado Ryu karate, a few years later I then began to learn Aikido before starting my journey in Taekwondo going on to becoming an instructor, I have attended and done multiple seminars, competitions including national and world level competitions and have been inducted into multiple national and international Hall of Fame. I also hold a world record for a 250kg Wall sit with Record Breakers and Record Holders Republic. I'm also a recognised Level 2 Gym Instructor & Level 3 Personal Trainer.

Some of the professional seminars and instructor courses I have attended over the years include: BTC Instructor course, AMA Coaching Diploma, SDUK Self Defence Instructor, KEWAP Instructor and level 2 Forms Judge.

Since these early years I have gone on to become a proud member of TYGA Martial Arts International under my Grandmaster, Grandmaster Gary Wasniewski. I have been with Grandmaster Gary Wasniewski TYGA Martial Arts International for the last 10 years and will continue my martial arts journey with Grandmaster Gary Wasniewski for many more years. Grandmaster Gary Wasniewski has given me opportunities to compete in prestigious world championships and has inducted me into his prestigious International Hall Of Fame. Grandmaster Gary Wasniewski graded me for my 3rd and 4th DAN grades and made me an instructor for TYGA Yorkshire. It is a privilege and honour to be a part of TYGA Martial Arts International Grandmaster Gary Wasniewski

The Fitness and Martial Arts journey will continue for many more years

2022 World Record 250KG Wall Sit – Registered with Record Holders Republic & Record Breakers

London International Hall Of Fame
2015 Spirit Award

2016 Dedication Award
2017 Instructor Award
2018 Instructor Award
2019 Spirit Award
2020 Excellence Award
2021 Excellence Award
2022 Platinum Award
2023 Supreme Fitness Award

UK Martial Arts Show Hall Of Fame Inducted
 2016
 2017
 2018
 2019
 2023

Martial Arts Illustrated Hall Of Fame
2015 Gold Award
2016 Student Award

2021 inducted into The Black belt Hall Of Fame
2018 Inducted into The Martial UK Digital Magazine

2021 Spartan Hall Of Fame – Silver Category Award

Action Martial Arts Magazine Hall Of Honour
2022 Elite Modern Warrior Award
2023 Respect and Honour Award

Haider Academy Of Martial Arts Hall Of Fame
2019 Martial Arts Spirit Award

2022 Martial Artist Of the Year Award
2022 World Martial Arts Heroes Award

2021 Flame International London UK 2021 Award for Dedication & Passion in Martial Arts

2021 Inducted inti The India International Martial Arts Hall Of Fame

North American International Martial Arts Hall Of Fame
2019 / 2020 Sensei Of The Year
20202 / 2021 Martial Artist Of The Year
2022 Creative Fitness Martial Artist Of The Year Award
     Competitor Of The Year Award

Legends Martial Arts Hall Of Fame
2017 silver Lifetime Achievement Award

I would like to thank everyone who has supported and been a part of my fitness and martial arts journey and those who continue to support and be a part of the journey.

Special Thanks :
John Stephenson Author
Grandmaster Gary Wasniewski TYGA Martial Arts International.
Mathew Wooley personal Trainer .

Man's Health
magazine
martial artist
7th
dan
bareknuckle
MENTAL
HEALTH
MEN WHO
TALK
HEAL
STAY FIT
NOT STILL
STYLE FASHION

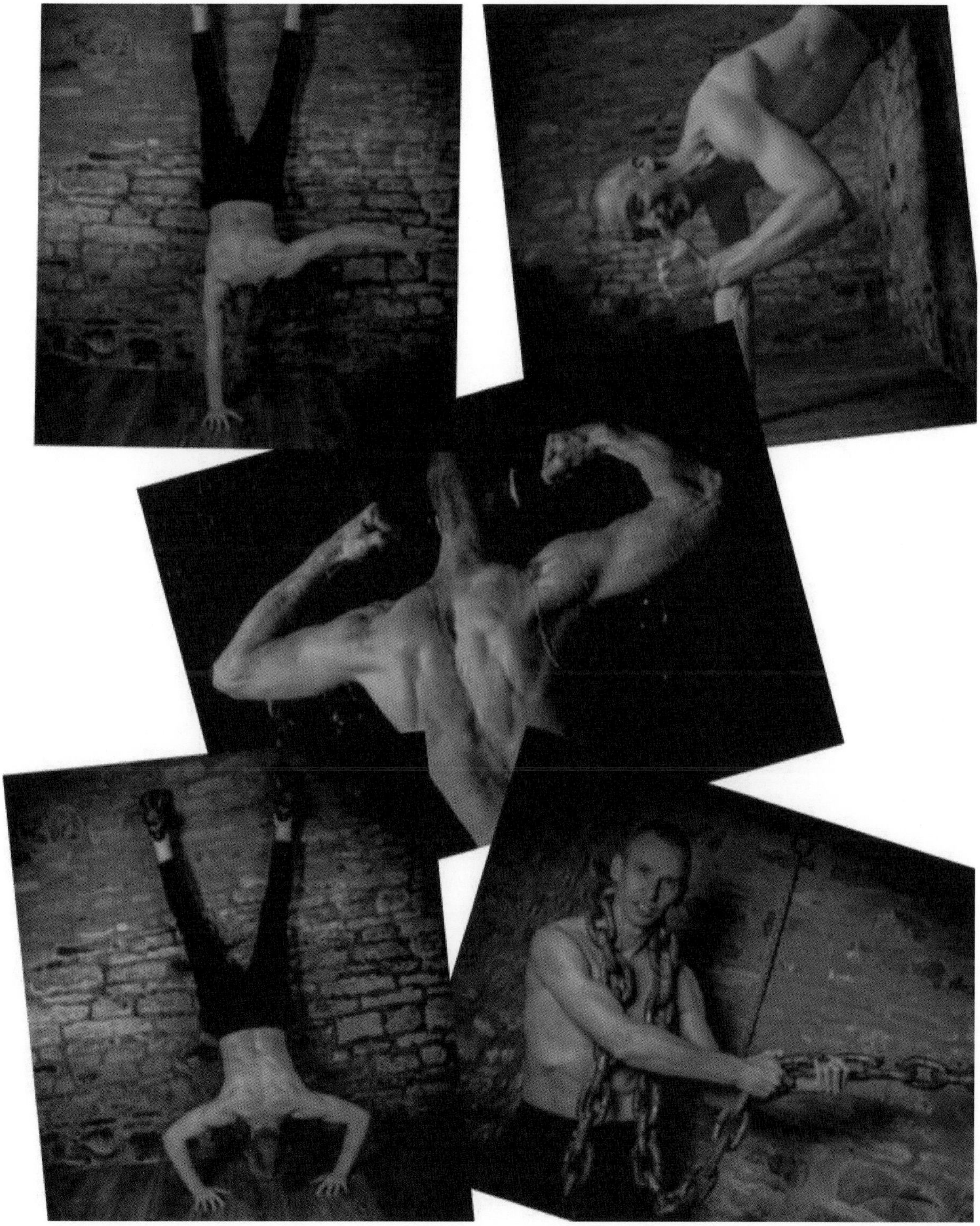

IAN BISHOP

Right I have to start at the root of why, my great Grandfather George Bishop was a bare-knuckle champion and South China seas boxing champion first World War Royal navy. He actually beat the old boxing Booths, My Grandfather William Harold Bishop was a great Boxer world war 2, then my father Brian Bishop who was a judo man, extremely powerful and wild like my great Grandfather, so 1973 my dad started teaching me how to Box, and wrestle. I was 5 years old, Then I started at the Cwm and District ABC Boxing club in Beddau in 1975 age 7years old, I had my first contest in the welfare Hall Beddau in 1977 and continued Boxing competitively until 1980, I studied judo for a year in Cardiff but soured under the not good instructor there, I then found my true calling in 1982 after I'd discovered Bruce Lee, to say I was inspired is a huge understatement. Bruce Lee was the reason and continues to be the reason for everything I've achieved in Martial Arts. So I started Lau Gar Kung Fu, main instructor was the legendary Frank Lynch, my instructor under him was Martin Harding, I trained continuously through the 1980s 7 days a week 5 hours a day, I was Welsh free fight full Contact Kung Fu champion age just 17, I also trained with the top Knock down Karate champions in John snellings famous gym back in the mid-1980s when I was 15 16 17, they taught me a lot, I also trained in muaythai speed and power training for a long time coinciding with my lau Gar, I started cross fit training in 1988, went back to boxing that year also to compete at senior level at light Heavyweight at the time, but I was never serious about boxing, I think it was more to prove something to myself, even so I was in the top 5 light Heavyweight Boxers in the early 1990s also sparring with former light middle and welterweight British Professional champion Pat Thomas many many times, and beating up and coming professional boxer Jimmy farrel in one round during a heavy sparring session, I went back to kung fu after my senior stint which lasted till 1992, I competed in cross fit competitions from 1988 till 2004 won gym fitness test 3 years running against all comers from 2002, 2003 and 4, then I started teaching old lau gar friends to improve there fighting down at the old squash courts in Barry, did this for a long time, also trained a lot with my old friend Clinton Brown Birmingham A team lau Gar, then I started teaching a friend Frank perrin, who was a very intelligent guy, and that's when everything started to click into place and the development of my Transporter Street MMA fighting Concept began, oh by the way I look took up sprinting for 3 years eventually competing in the Veterans British indoor Championships, at 35, although you had to be 40 to be a vet, there was a special category for our event, anyway, teaching Frank, I began to really find myself, and developed by pure hard training a way to punch faster and harder than anyone else, well most definitely faster and more fluid anyway, So I'm a Master Martial artist and founder of Transporter Street MMA fighting Concept which has gone down in the Martial arts hall of fame as a new world Martial art, not bad for 1 man who made it happen alone more or less, through 1000s of setbacks etc, so In short, Transporter Street MMA fighting Concept is all that I have learned and studied then stripped away until my truth has been revealed, it leans heavily on Bruce Lee's principles of body Mechanics and philosophy, but as Bruce Lee stated, all type of knowledge ultimately means self-knowledge, in other words I understand all the principles and am able to adapt and apply to my own self, so unlike most that go into a set style and become part of that style, and part of like a hive mentality, I'm very much an individual who has a very strong foundation, but I'm flexible in my approach to actual fighting as it is with no rules, I'm not a point fighter or cage fighter etc although I've been a judge at these events, and trained many professional cage guys and Boxers etc. my concept is about honesty expressing myself as Bruce Lee stated. The 8 official World Records I have been purely a by product of the shear streamlined effect of my art, I have 14 or 15 Black belt hall of fame awards around that, have done many seminars, and continue to teach privately it's what I was built to do. I've tried to make it as brief as I possibly could. Grand Master ian Bishop, martial arts Expert and chief instructor and founder of Transporter Street MMA fighting Concept. Official 8 Time World Record Holder For fastest Puncher of all time, former Amateur Boxer, schoolboy and senior Light Heavyweight. Trained in Lau Gar kung fu under Frank Lynch. Also trained in Muaythai, kick boxing, judo, Welsh champion full contact Free fight Kung fu, knock down Karate and fitness under John snelling, plus, cross fit champion.15 times UK, London international, Worldwide winners and WMF Black belt hall of fame award winner.

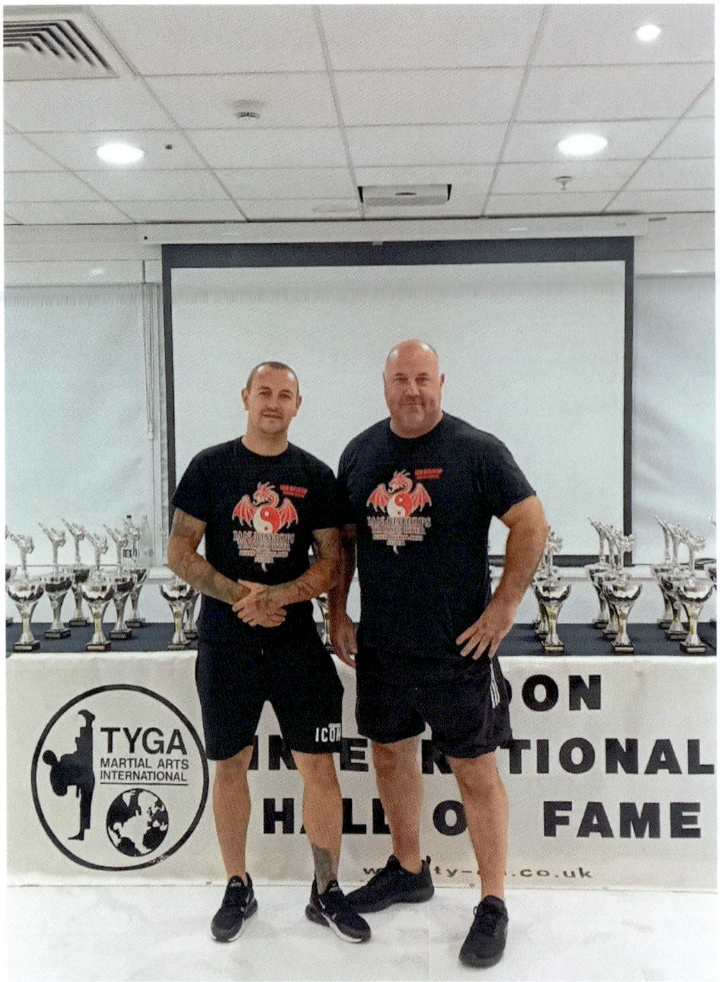
TYGA
MARTIAL ARTS
INTERNATIONAL
FAME

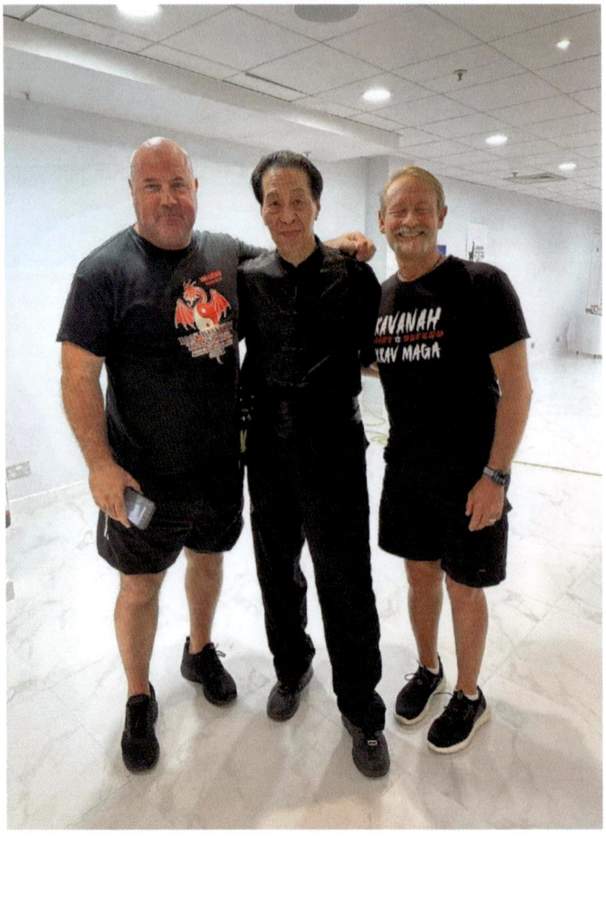

LONDON
TERNATIONAL
HALL OF FAME
www.ty-ga.co.uk
CER RESEARCH UK

KAVANAH
KRAV MAG

JAY EGGLESTON
(BAM BAM)

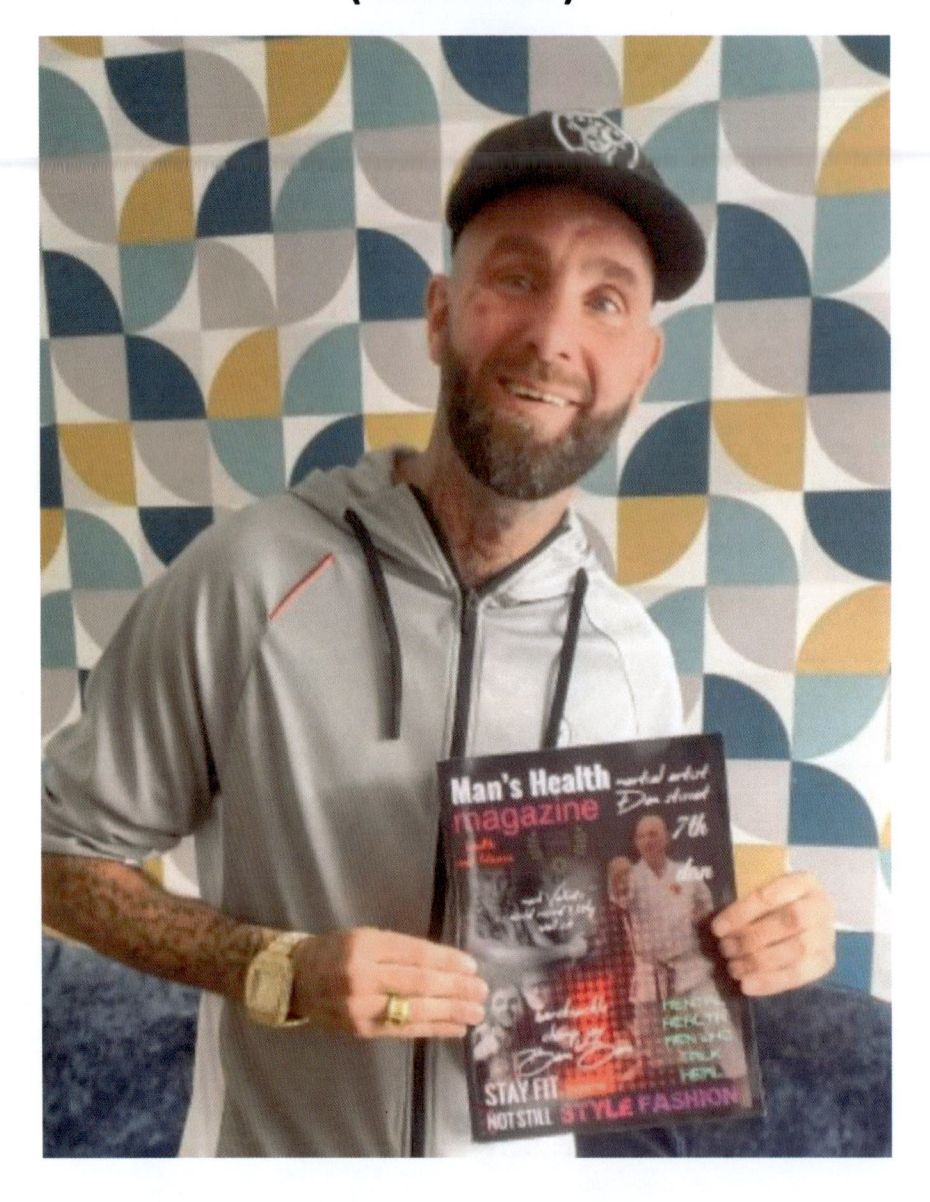

I Started out with fighting on streets of Sheffield as a kid I was always fighting then I joined Paul Powers gym had many fights in k1 kickboxing also arranged my own fights in boxing also learned mma ground game and grappling off Dan Gibbon and Paul Cole and fought in mma on machine mma also British fight league and almighty fighting championships threw many fights in k1 kickboxing I received a message of Luke akin 2 times bareknuckle champ who told me Shaun smith wanted me to try out for bareknuckle I then met Shaun smith and Amanda smith who was very welcoming I then fought many fights for them in bareknuckle on ubkb I then went on to fight for bare fist association who then became bkfc uk I also fought on bad to bone and bkbtm threw my career I won 14 wins and 4 losses not bad for bareknuckle I became a bareknuckle champion I also became a champion in boxing winning the Yorkshire area title threw my career I got to meet my idols and many amazing ppl.

I owe all this to my coach David Needham who pushed me to become the best that I could be an now I get to coach at Sheffield mma wolfpack juniors with Andy Marlow.

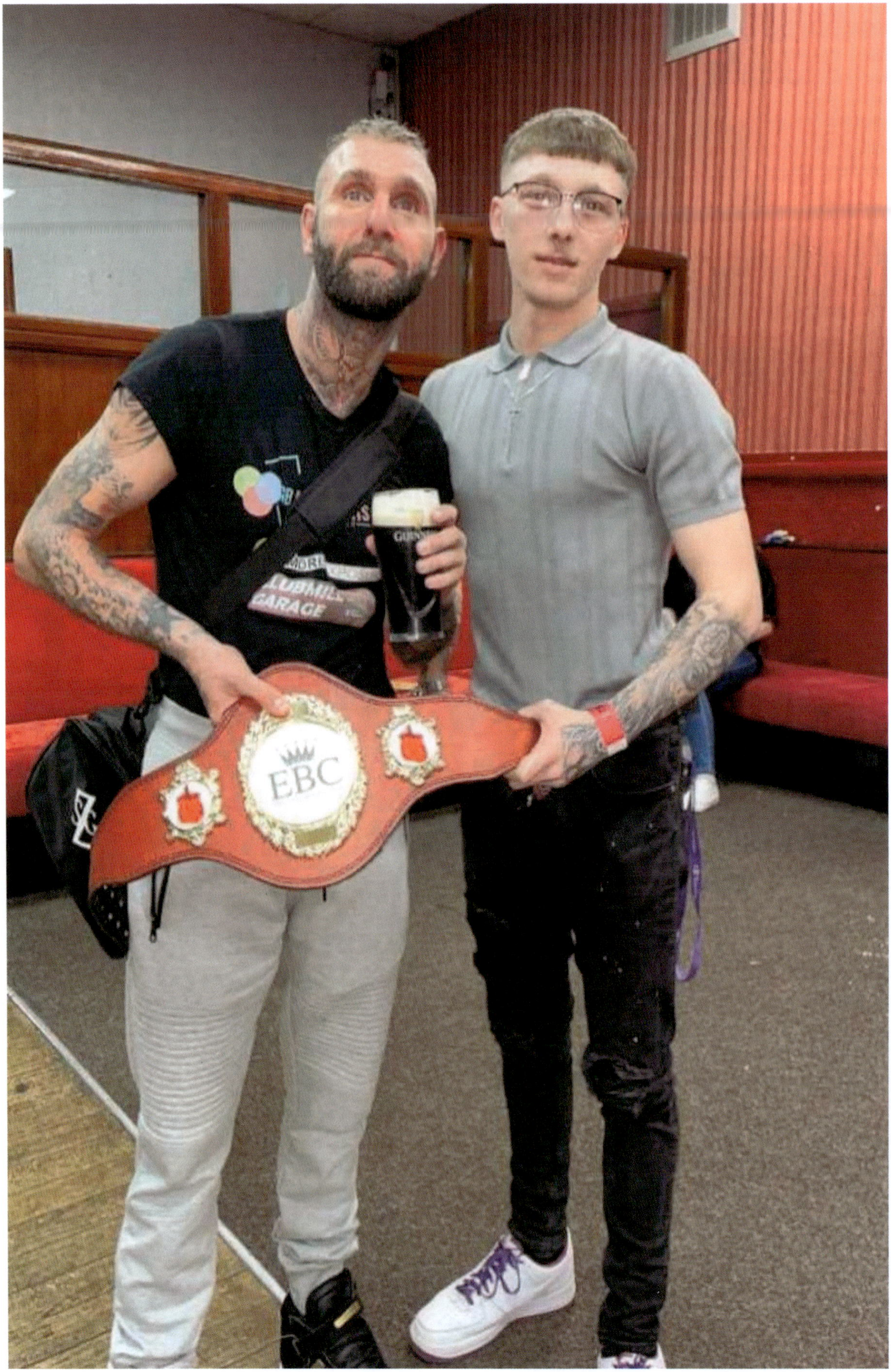
EBC

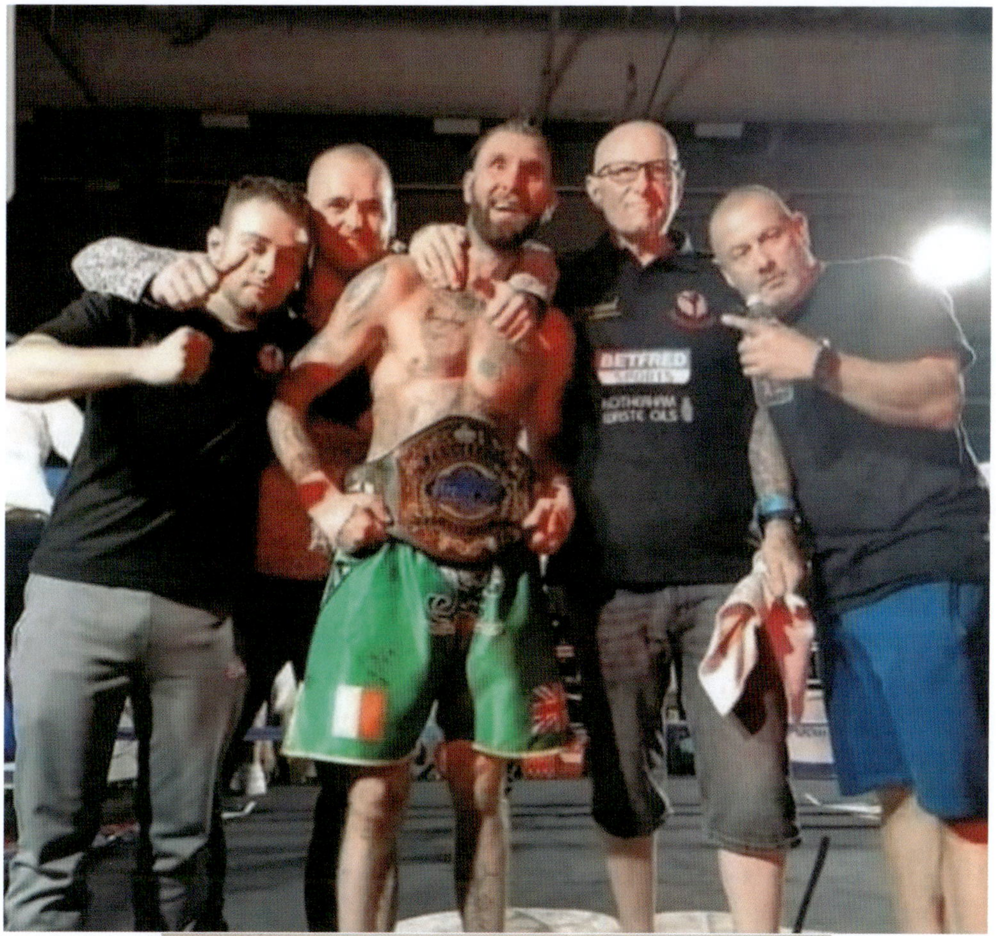
BETFRED

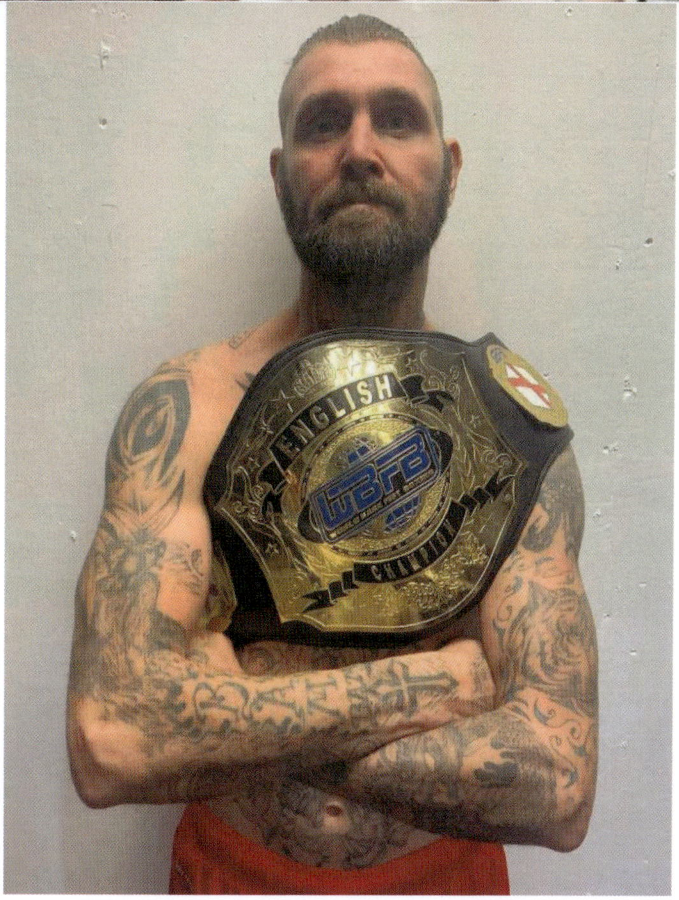
ENGLISH

VINCE ANELLO

Lifting LEGEND

- VINCE ANELLO -
- FIRST TO DEADLIFT 800 POUNDS (821) AT A BODYWEIGHT UNDER 200 POUNDS
- WON FIVE IPF WORLD CHAMPIONSHIPS
- BEST TRAINING LIFTS OF 880 DEADLIFT 500 RAW BENCH & 750 SQUAT IN WRAPS
- COMPETED IN BODYBUILDING THROUGHOUT HIS POWERLIFTING CAREER
- FAVORITE DEADLIFT ASSISTANCE MOVE WAS NEGATIVE DEADLIFTS

Vince Anello has been known as a powerlifting legend around the world for decades and is considered to be one of the greatest powerlifters in history. He was the first ever to deadlift over 800 lbs at a bodyweight under 200 lbs! Vince was inducted into the Strength Hall of Fame in York, Pennsylvania in 1998, and the AAU World's Strength Sports Hall of Fame in 2015. He holds 5 world championship titles in addition to 20 world records in deadlifting, and was included in the Top 100 Strongest Coaches To Learn From In 2016.

Vince is a proponent of physical activity for all age groups. He taught physical education classes in the Cleveland area for years. He is also an avid greyhound lover and has rescued six retired racing greyhounds to date.

Although training with a powerlifting legend may sound intimidating, Vince is anything but that! He really gets to know his clients and their specific needs. His many years of experience in the physical health field have moulded his approach to physical fitness.

VINCE TODAY

Although Vince spends a lot of time training his clients at Anello Body Fitness, he also likes to spend time with his wife, Sue, and their five rescued greyhounds.

Vince has been training people since 1968, and still takes every opportunity to share his knowledge with those around him. what you can learn from a real American Strength Legend!

DAVE BUCKLES

I began training in March 1993 TyGa Karate under Grandmaster Gary Wasniewski 10th Dan (then Shihan Wasniewski 7th Dan) in London, England.
I trained at sessions 3 - 4 times per week and attended numerous sparring and kata courses as well as the annual outdoor course that was held at the beginning of February each year in Wales.
I have competed annually at the TYGA Martial Arts Championships both in Kata and Kumite.

I have also had the honour of travelling with GM Wasniewski and assisting him when he was delivering a seminar at the Eastern USA Martial Arts Hall of Fame in Pittsburgh in 2003.

30 years later and at the age of 51, I continue to train regularly under GM Wasniewski and TYGA Karate and TYGA Martial Arts International.

Grades and Awards:

1995: Promoted to 1st Dan
1997: Promoted to 2nd Dan
1999: Promoted to 3rd Dan
2002: Promoted to 4th Dan
2007: Promoted to 5th Dan
2015: Promoted to 6th Dan
2022: Promoted to 7th Dan

2004: Inducted into the 17th Annual Eastern USA International Black Belt Hall of Fame - National Instructor of the Year Award
2006: Inducted into the 1st London International Hall of Fame - Dedication to Martial Arts Award
2007: Inducted into the 2nd London International Hall of Fame - Master of the Year Award
2007: Inducted into the USA Action Martial Arts Hall of Fame - Exemplary Dedication to Martial Arts Award
2008: Inducted into the 3rd London International Hall of Fame - Martial Arts Spirit Award
2009: Inducted into the 4th London International Hall of Fame - Martial Arts Spirit Award

2010: Inducted into the 5th London International Hall of Fame - Martial Arts Excellence Award
2010: London International Hall of Fame - Martial Arts Team Award (TYGA Victoria)
2011: Inducted into the 6th London International Hall of Fame - Fighter of the Year Award
2012: Inducted into the 7th London International Hall of Fame - Excellence Award
2013: Inducted into the 8th London International Hall of Fame - Silver Award
2014: Inducted into the 9th London International Hall of Fame - Gold Award
2015: Inducted into the 10th London International Hall of Fame - Master Award
2016: Inducted into the 11th London International Hall of Fame - Platinum Award
2017: Inducted into the 12th London International Hall of Fame - Diamond Award
2018: Inducted into the 13th London International Hall of Fame - Master Award
2019: Inducted into the 14th London International Hall of Fame- Platinum Award
2020: Inducted into the 15th London International Hall of Fame - Excellence Award
2021: Inducted into the 16th London International Hall of Fame - Excellence Award
2022: Inducted into the 17th London International Hall of Fame - Diamond Award
2023: Inducted into the 18th London International Hall of Fame - Legendary Spirit Award

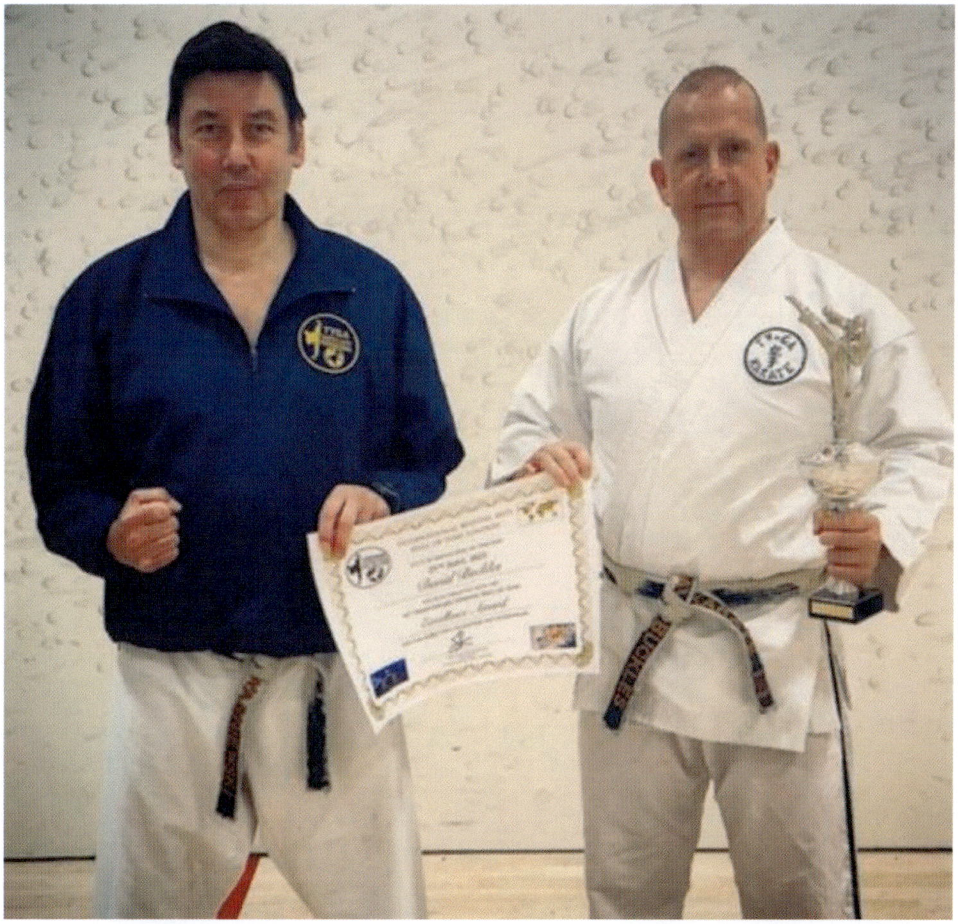

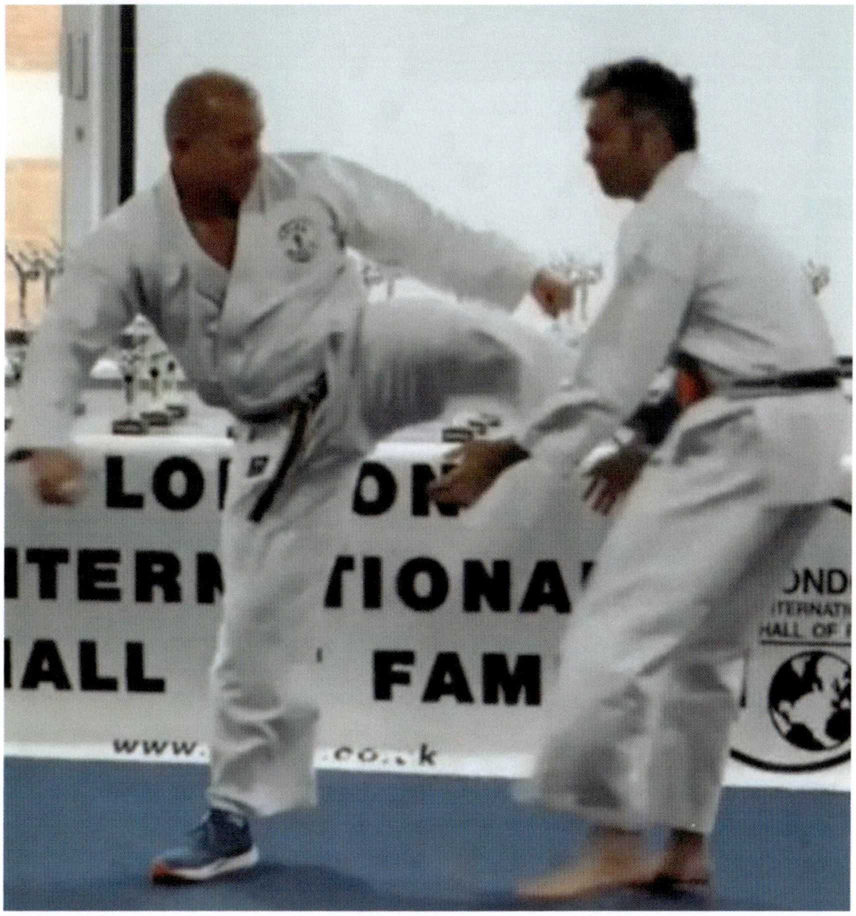
LO ON
ITERN TIONA
ALL FAM

NIGEL DAVIS

Thirty years ago I opened Cwmavonhornets ABC after previously being a coach at Croeserw ABC. At Cwmavonhornets I produced over a hundred national champions. I then went on to become National coach of the year and worked with the Welsh team as a staff coach gaining my advanced coaching certificate. Whilst working with Wales I was asked to help with the Podium squad at GB and they must have liked what they saw because I was then offered a permanent position and became a high performance coach for GB gaining my 3 star AIBA coaching certificate. I was at GB for two Olympic cycles qualifying eight boxers and winning three Olympic medals one gold and two bronze at the Beijing games and qualifying ten boxers for London winning three gold , one Silver and one bronze medal. I worked with the likes of Anthony Joshua, Frazer Clarke, Tyson Fury, Joe Joyce, Tony Bellow, Tony Jeffries, Luke Campbell, Billy Joe Saunders, Fred Evans, Callum and Stephen Smith, Gamal and Khalid Yafai, George Groves, Charlie Edwards, James Degale, Andrew Selby and Lee Selby whilst with Wales to name but a few. I was then asked by the CEO of GB to take on the role of head coach for the ladies team for the London Olympics and trained Savannah Marshall, Nicola Adams, Natasha Jonas, Chantelle Cameron and many more.

I left GB after the London Games thinking I would spend more time at home but then the Netherlands made me an offer I couldn't refuse. I became head national coach for Holland setting up their Olympic programme and in the two years I spent there we took 23 medals in tournaments throughout Europe. Once the program was set up I came home but it wasn't long before I was approached by Sweden and asked if I could help with their Olympic program. For the next two years I was Head national coach/

performance director for Sweden and agaim we took many medals throughout Europe.

In more recent years I have taken back the running of Cwmavon Hornets and have many prospective champions in the making. We entered three box cups last season and took five Gold medals.

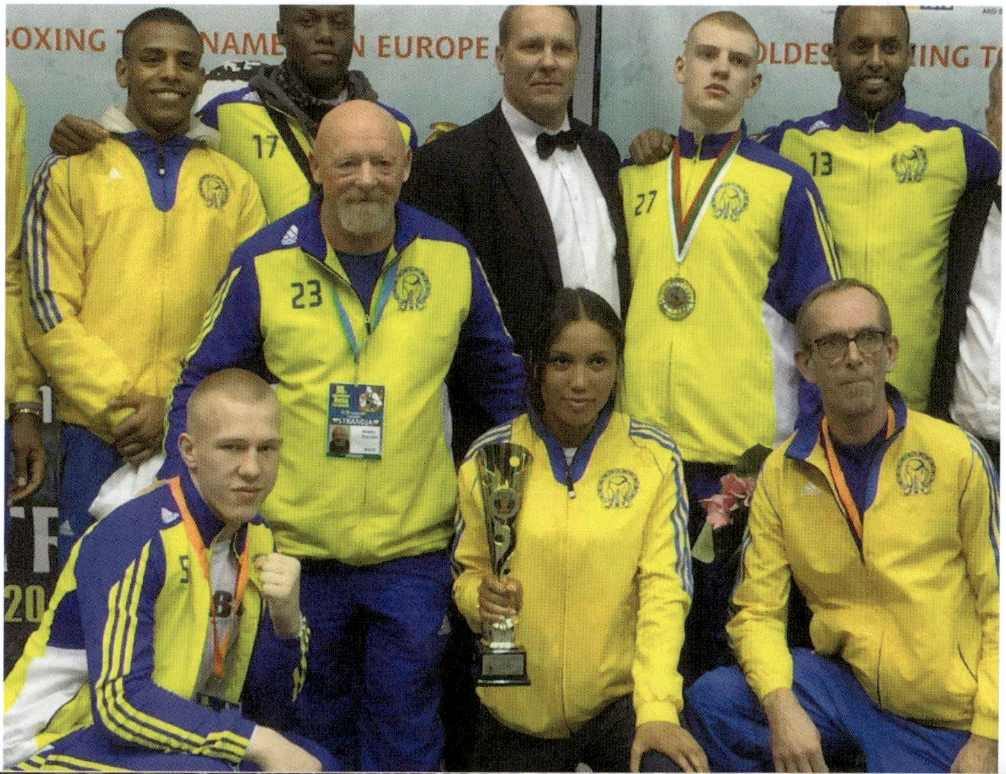

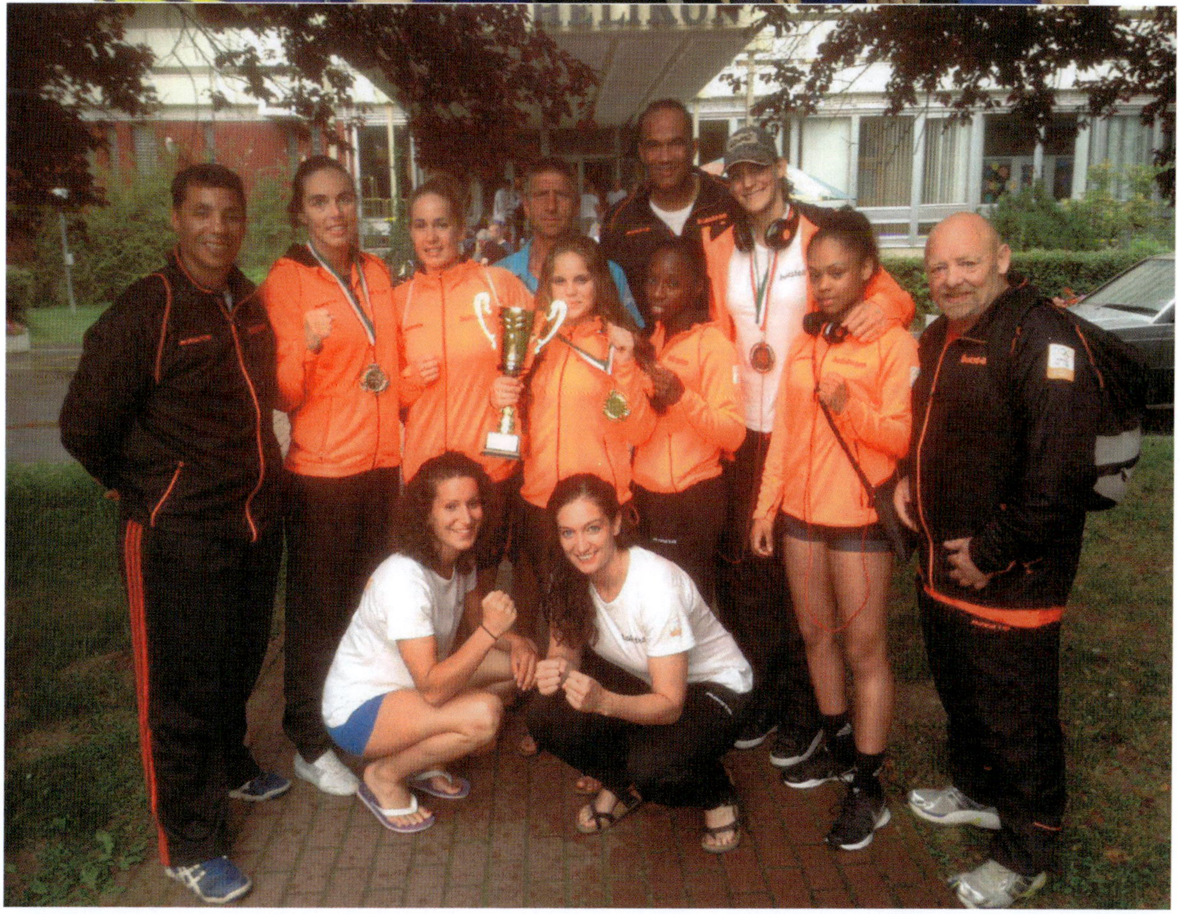

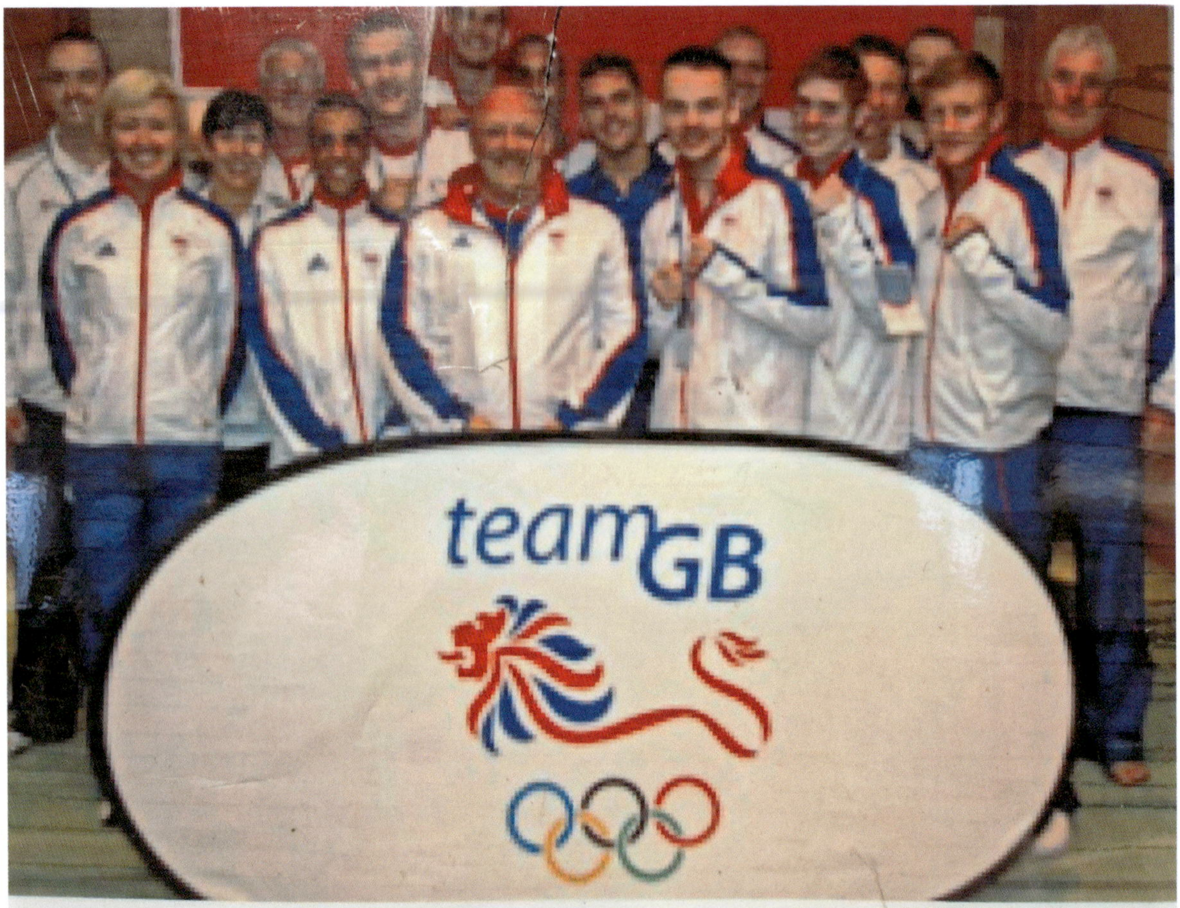
teamGB

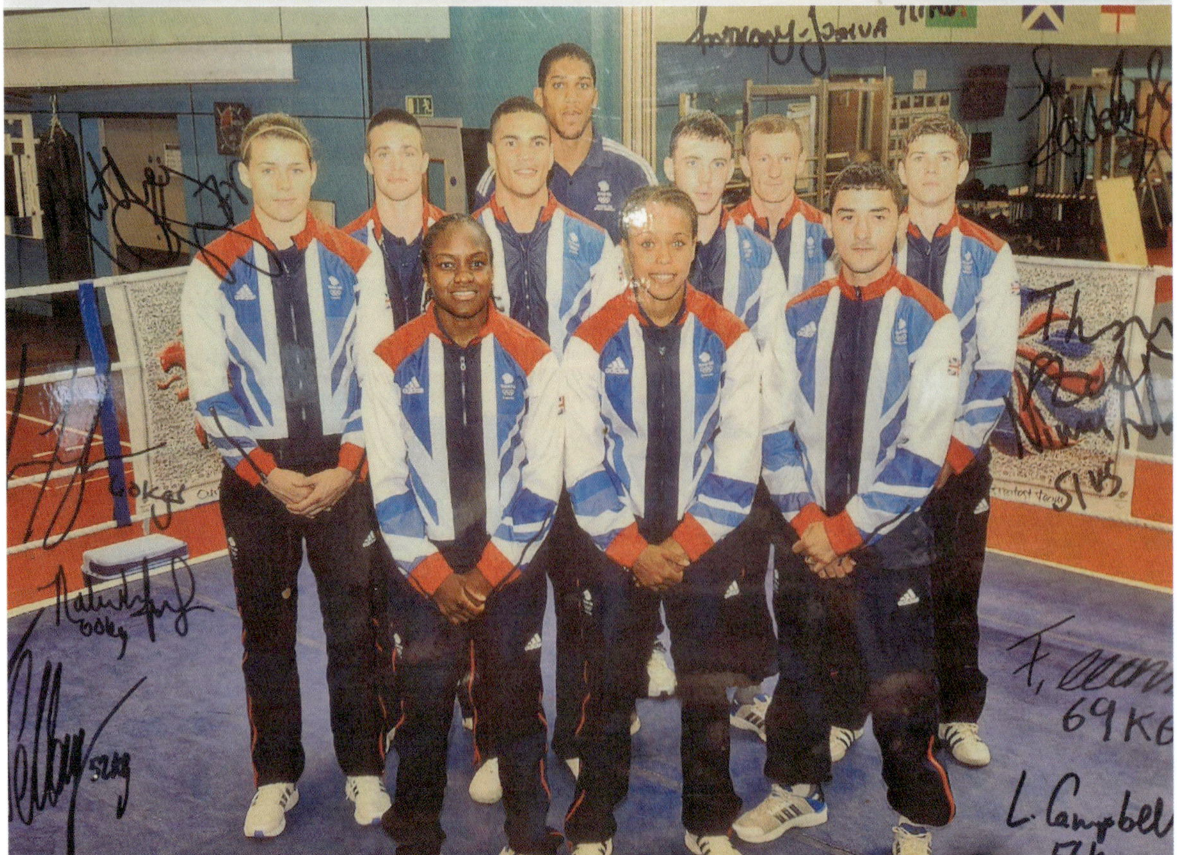
60kg
69KG
52kg
L. Campbell
56kg

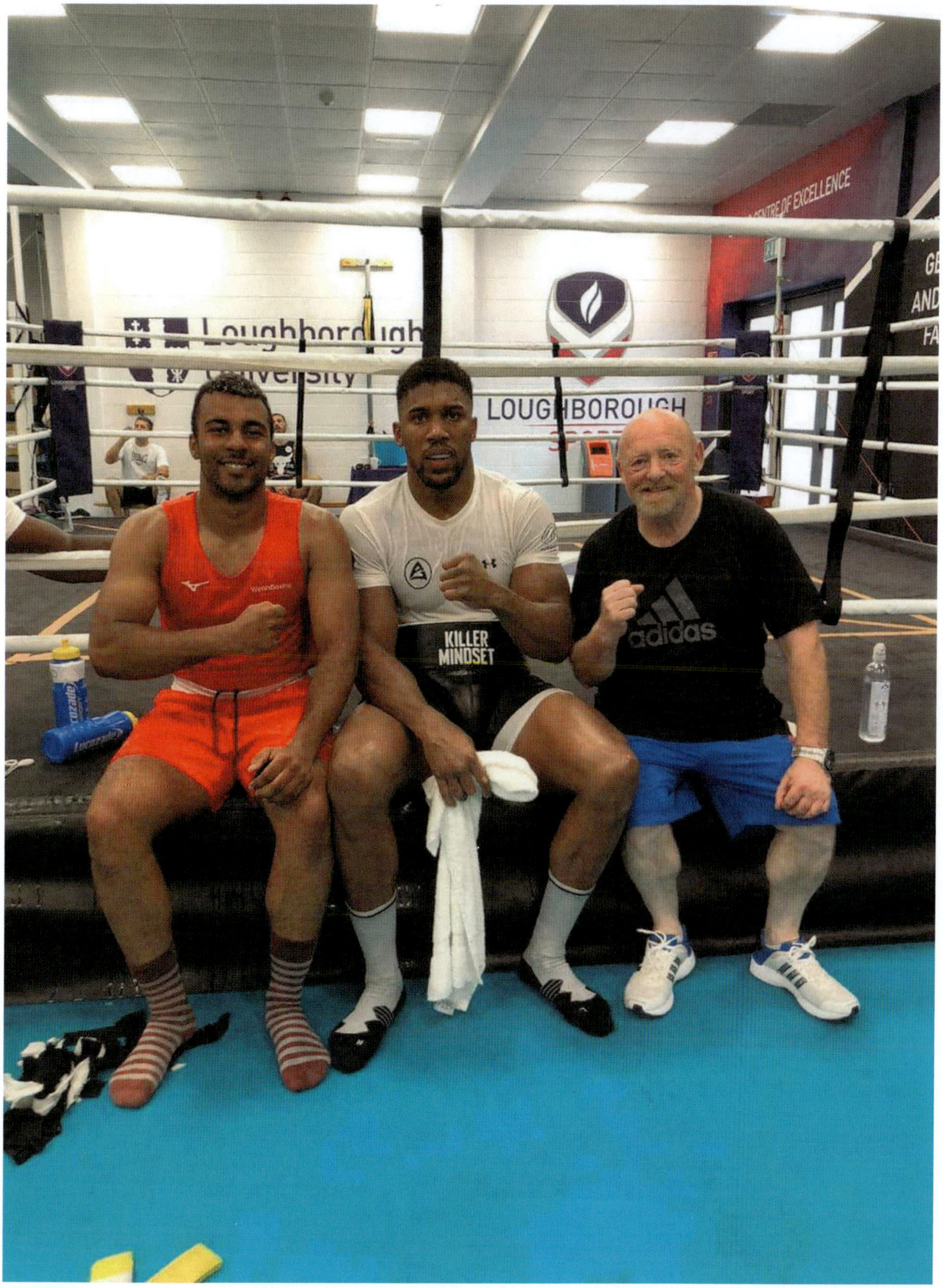
LOUGHBOROUGH
KILLER
MINDSET
adidas

JOHN STEPHENSON

My life was quiet difficult some years ago after the loss of my late mother, in my early year's I was quiet care free and very materialistic and money orientated however that was all about to change in 2008 after the passing of my mam life well and truly humbled me I reached for the bottle to try an numb the pain however life had other ideas, I fell into a cycle of excessive drinking and depression I became a loner and very withdrawn my world had fell apart I remember clear as day going to my mums house to clear her belonging's I sat and looked around and thought to myself is this it my mums lifelong belongings. I sat there in deep thought reminiscing of all the good times trying to wrap my head around the reality of I'm never going to see my mam again' I then had the dreaded task of clearing all mums stuff out and going through her personal belonging's this was very heart breaking for me So my next task was to start clearing the house out I rang a house clearance service he said he would come and give me a price for the whole house contents, he arrived the next day looked around and offered 200 for everything he was clearly trying to take advantage of my situation I felt like chinning him on the spot I guess that's the nature of the selfish I refused, he then left and it was then I decided to donate everything to charity in my mums name. so I spent many years drinking myself into oblivion my life had become unmanageable I lost my wife due to my addiction I was no good to my self let alone my family cutting a long story short I remember sat in my room and looking in the mirror and I didn't like the person who was looking back at me I remember braking down and sobbing uncontrollably I had to strip back my whole way of life and look deep within myself, I didn't want to live like this anymore I was a shell of my former self, I went to rehab and got sober I wanted to be a better person I come to realise everything we have in life is borrowed and what's important is enjoying each day as tomorrow is never promised I then stripped back my selfish nature and began to help others, countless charity work feeding the homeless, animal charities, raising money for DVD players for the children's ward at our local hospital. Cancer charities the list goes on. I wanted to see people smile because for me id spent so long in the darkness of grief and addiction. it's very important for me to teach my young children to be kind in an ever growing selfish world that my legacy I want to leave behind for my children, I'm also a firm believer you can achieve anything in life if you truly want to the only limitations we have are the limitations we put on ourselves I look at my life today and I'm very grateful that life humbled me as it showed me a new path and outlook on life I'm no longer selfish and have a good understanding of the real meaning of life I'm very grateful to some of the sacrifices my mum made for me like paying for all my martial arts training as a kid and making sure I was fed and clothed and doing her best with very little

through my sobriety I have set myself different goals I tried bareknuckle boxing the focus of the training was always the rush for me to set a goal and achieve it to the best of my ability however it doesn't matter how much I changed my life I still live with a mindset that tries to kill me It's called addiction, I have to keep on top of this daily as my addiction sits at the bottom of my bed with 12 ounce gloves on waiting for me to slip up, I become to realise that I have an addictive personality, this can be a great thing but like everything in life there's a down side if my mindset is positive I flourish, if its negative things can go down hill very fast for me anyway enough of my rambling I started martial arts as a teenager and became a blackbelt at 19 years old and I never did anything further after that until I hit my 40s I spent a year doing a bit of jujitsu as a developed an interest in ground work the beautiful thing about martial arts is there is a never-ending array of skills one can learn and adapt to ones skill set, I then fancied some boxing training for fitness and spent around 8 mth doing so I've achieved many things in my life and feel blessed I sat one day and thought to myself id like to give something back to martial arts and this is what I came up with, doing books on martial artists that have made this art form away of life and adopted the principles into everyday life, I'm not a professional author by any means but I'm doing it to the best of my ability to give back, and to bring recognition to many people I believe if you have the ability to do something then share that with other's I'm sure my mum will be looking down on me now smiling, one can only hope. So there's a little insight into my life and where I am today.

I have one last achievement id like to accomplish that's a republican world record of some sort I'm now back in training and have full confidence in myself.

I guess what I'm trying to say no matter how bad life gets there's always hope if you dig deep.

Thankyou oss.

Central YMCA Qualifications

Certificate in Assistant Fitness
Circuit Training
Level One

John Stephenson

Exercise and Fitness
Unit Certificate
Level One

John Stephenson

B.W.L.A. Award

John Stephenson

B.W.L.A. Leaders Award

Sports Leaders

John Stephenson

BST Level 1 Award in Community Sports Leadership
National Accreditation Number

Approved Assessment Centre: Ashwell Leisure Centre

Tutor/Assessor: Stan Boles

Date: 29 November 2004

Linda Plowright
Chief Executive

Unit Certificate

John Stephenson

Loughborough College

Karen Green
Peter Harwood, Chair of OCNSEM
Date: 28/01/2005

Achievements

26/07/2005 Exercise and health level 2

Nutrition and weight management level 2

Stress and stress management level 2

NOVENBER 29TH 2004
BTS LEVEL 2

16/ 12/ 2004 B.W.L.A AWARD

07/O3/2005 EXCECISE AND FITNES KNOWLEDGE

LEVEL 1

07/ 03/2005 FITNESS INTRUCTING

CIRCUIT TRAINING.

14/3/1995 ACHIEVED MY BLACK BELT.

B.A.W.A. 7/01/ 1997 ACOMPLISHED A DEEP KNEE BEND 100KG

BENCH PRESS OF 100KG

TWO HAND DEAD LIFT 130KG TOTAL 330 KG AT THE BODY WIEGHT OF 75KG.

MAY 7TH 2023 INDUCTED INTO THE UK MARTIAL ARTS HALL OF FAME

JUNE 24TH WAS INDUCTED INTO THE INTERNATIONAL LONDON MARTIAL ARTS HALL OF FAME BY GRANDMASTER GARY WASNIEWSKI.

8TH JUNE SPARTAN HALL OF WARRIORS GOLD CATEGORY

29TH APRIL ACTION MARTIAL ARTS MAGAZINE HALL OF HONORS.

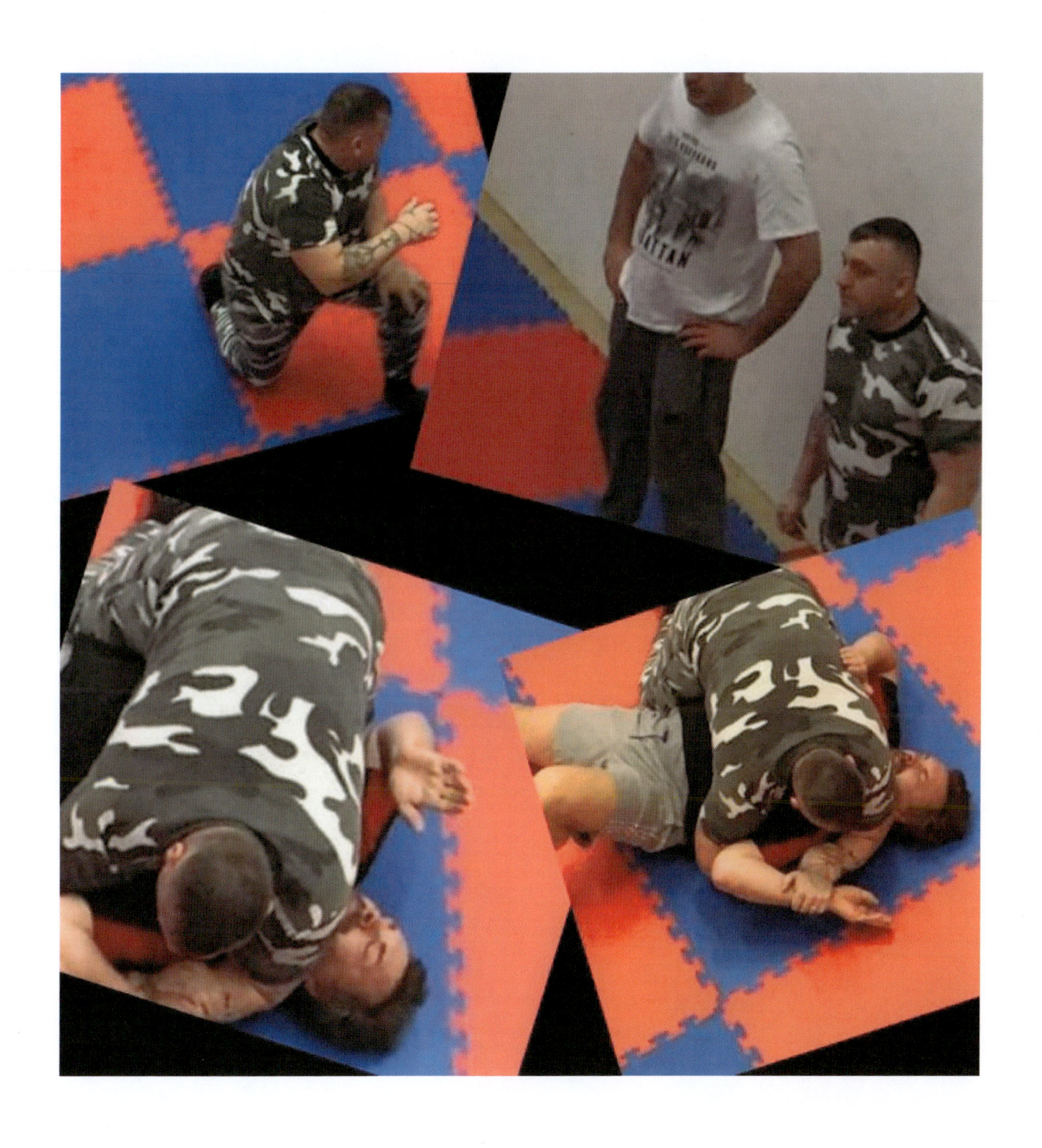

ABIT OF GROUND WORK TRAINING

AFEW BKB FIGHTS I HAD AS A WARMUP FOR A BIGGER EVENT BUT UNFORTUNATELY NEVER HAPPENED DUE TO A BIG SHOW THAT WAS CANCELED AS THE PROMOTER WAS VERY POORLY.

SOME CLOSE QUARTERS TRAINING FOR HAYBALES

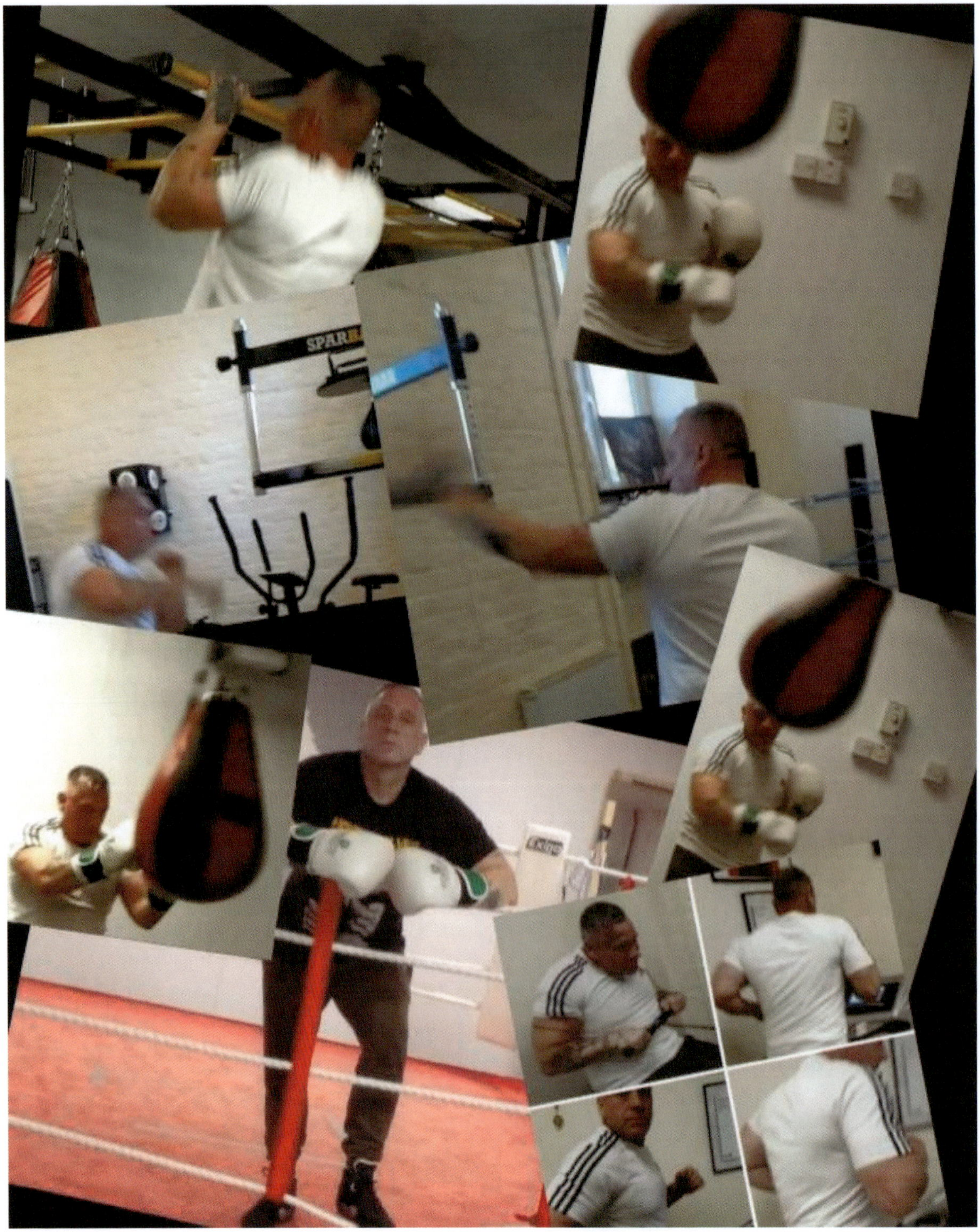

BARE KNUCKLE
TEAM
STEPHENSON
BARE KNUCKLE
TEAM
STEPHENSON
TEAM
STEPHENSON
THE LONE
TEAM
LONE
BARE KNUCKLE
TEAM

TEAM STEPHENSON
BARE KNUCKLE
TEAM
STEPHENSON
TEAM STEPHENSON

BARE KNUCKLE
TEAM
STEPHENSON
Thankyou
for all of your
hard work!
From your sponsors
ES Stickers

BARE KNUCKLE
TEAM
STEPHENSON
Sponsored by
ES Stickers
STEPHENSON

BARE KNUCKLE
TEAM
STEPHENSON
BARE KNUCKLE
TEAM
STEPHENSON

BARE KNUCKLE
TEAM STEPHENSON

TEAM STEPHENSON

THE LONE WOLF
TEAM STEPHENSON

BARE KNUCKLE
TEAM STEPHENSON

SOME CUPS WITH LONE WLF LOGO AND PICS OF ME

BAREKNUCKLE
TEAM
STEPHENSON
BARE KNUCKLE
THE LONE WOLF
BAREKNUCKLE
TEAM
STEPHENSON

SOME OF MY MERCH DONE FROM MY SPONSOR

T SHIRTS

HATS

SOME SIGNED PICTURES I WAS GIVING

SOME ART WORK DONE FOR ME BY MY FRIEND PETE

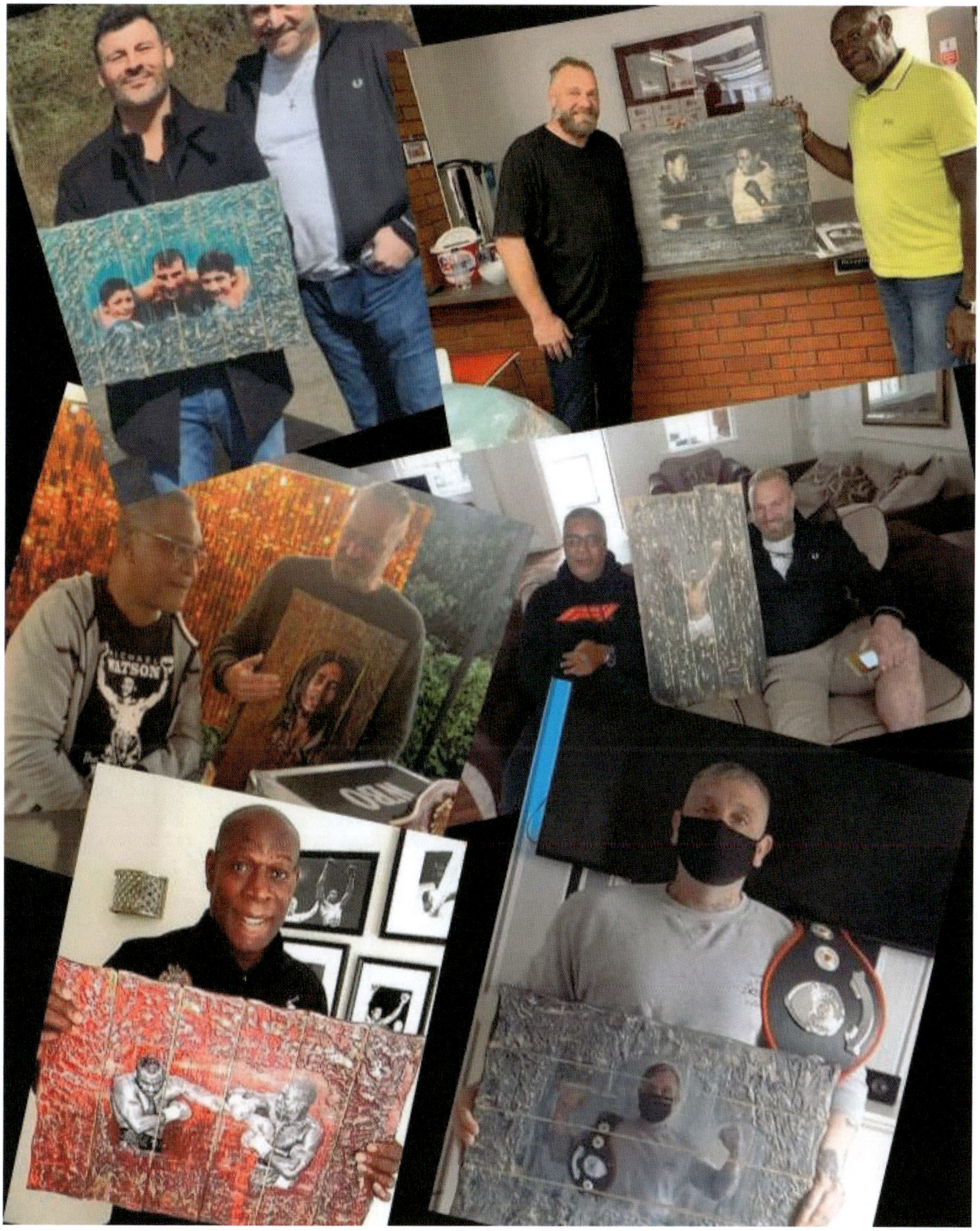
WATSON

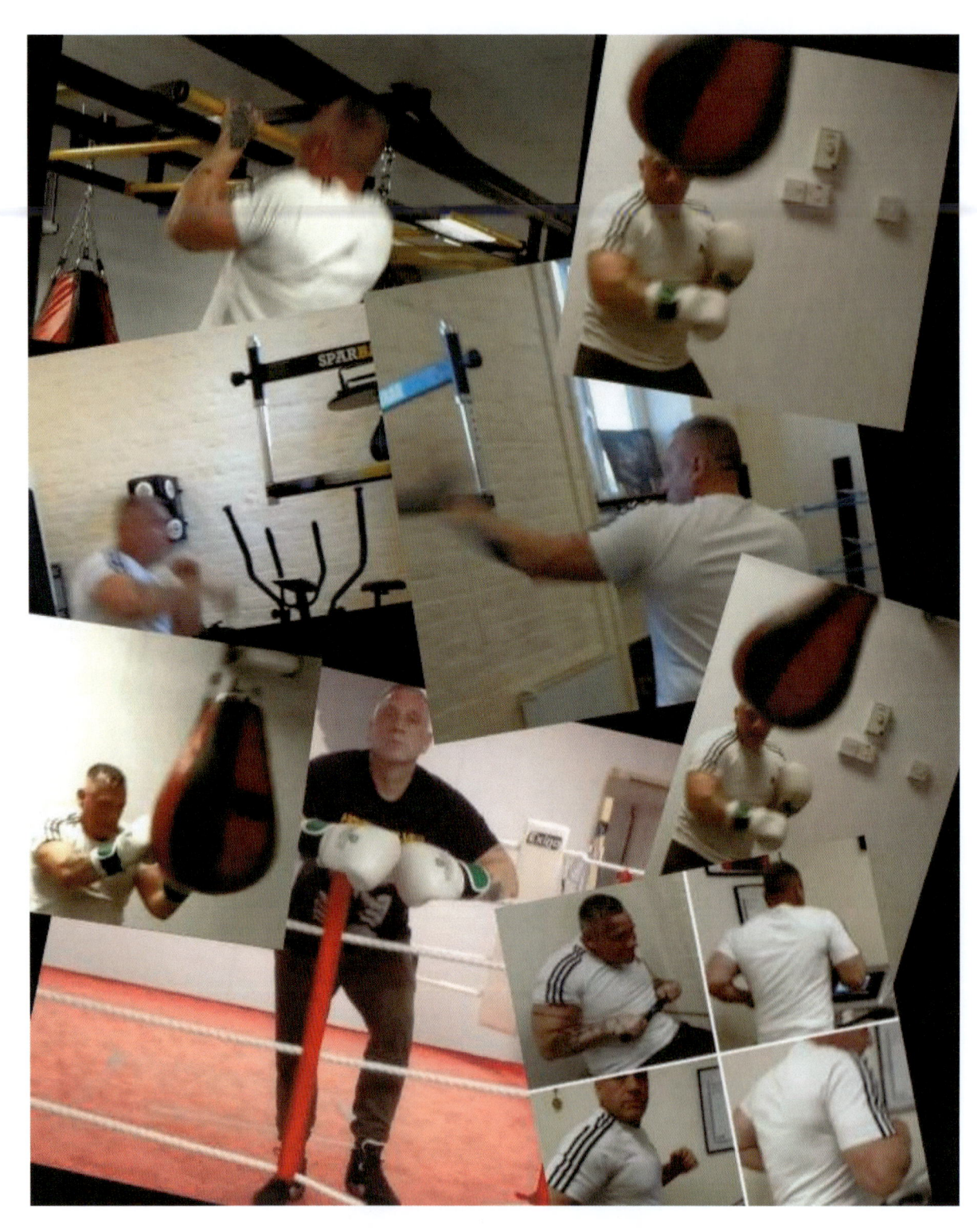

SOME TRAINING PICS

I WAS GONNA FIGHT ON RAGEMANIA BUT THE SHOW WAS PULLED AFTER ANDY TOPLIFF BECAME POORLY......AND I HEARD ON FACEBOOK NOT SO LONG BACK ANDY HAD PASSED AWAY REST IN PEACE ANDY. DEEPEST OF BOWS.

DAN HODGSON

I started martial arts when I was 5 years old. My dad got me into martial arts, something to give me discipline and structure. I joined a local karate club and fell in love with it. I practiced daily. My dad bought videos of old sensei's demonstrating kata and I would be idolising every move. Any martial arts film I watched; I was trying to recreate the moves! My parents definitely didn't like me trying to do somersaults in the living room! Due to moving around a lot as a kid, I constantly found myself starting over again a lot.

Straight back to white belt. Either because the style was different or because my instructor thought it would be better to start again. This didn't bother me, I just wanted to continue my training.

When I left for college, they didn't have a karate club nearby but, they did have a tae-kwon do club at the college. Just like karate, I loved every moment of being there, more jumping spinning kicks! I spent 3 years learning tae-kwon do and whilst I didn't get a black belt from there, I definitely learnt a lot and I found myself applying some of it to my karate.

Once I left college, I had to work shifts and I found it really difficult to constantly train. I ended up not being able to train for 7 years.

When COVID-19 hit the world, like many of us, we were in lockdown. This gave me a lot of time to think. I spoke to my wife; I told her that I miss karate and I hated not having it in my life. There was a hole where karate should be. My wife encouraged me to get back into karate and when the lockdown lifted, that's exactly what I did.

I found Hampshire Academy of Shotokan Karate. This club was unlike any other martial arts school I have ever attended. I have been pushed further than any other club I have been to. From that, I have reached higher personal levels than I could have imagined. When my Renshi told me I was going to participate in a world championship, I was blown away. I wasn't even nervous about losing, I was just so excited to be competing, something I have never done before. I won 2 bronze medals in kata and kumite, I couldn't have been happier with those results, it showed me where my skill level is and how I could further progress.

Since 2022, I have been made a sensei at my club, I have been inducted into the UKMAS Hall of Fame awards and I have been nominated again for the black belt hall of fame awards in November 2023. Karate for me is more than just a sport, it's a way of life. A journey that never ends.

ACADEMY OF SHOTOKAN
CERTIFICATE OF ACHIEVEMENT
松濤館
空手道
D. HODGSON

AUTHORS NOTE

I WOULD LIKE TO THANK ALL WHO TOOK PART IN THIS BOOK AND WOULD LIKE TO DEDICATE THIS BOOK IN MEMORY OF MY BELOVERD MOTHER FLY HIGH UNTIL WE MEET AGAIN.

ALSO TO MY BEAUTIFUL DAUGHTER STORM.

Printed in Great Britain
by Amazon